Human Resources Management Issues, Challenges and Trends: "Now and Around the Corner"

A Volume in:
Contemporary Human Resources Management:
Issues, Challenges and Opportunities

Series Editor:
Ronald R. Sims

Contemporary Human Resources Management: Issues, Challenges and Opportunities

Series Editor:

Ronald R. Sims
College of William and Mary

Human Resources Management Issues, Challenges and Trends: "Now and Around the Corner"

Edited by:

Ronald R. Sims
Sheri K. Bias

INFORMATION AGE PUBLISHING, INC.
Charlotte, NC • www.infoagepub.com

Library of Congress Cataloging-in-Publication Data

The CIP data for this book can be found on the LIbrary of Congress website (loc.gov).

Paperback: 9781641135351
Hardcover: 9781641135368
eBook: 9781641135375

Printed in the United States of America

CONTENTS

ACKNOWLEDGEMENTS

We are indebted to George F. Johnson at Information Age Publishing, Inc. who continues to provide the collective outlet for our ideas. A most deserved thank you and acknowledgement goes to our group of contributors. Without their collective professional and personal efforts, based upon their own human resources management (HRM) experiences as practitioners, academics and researchers to share their views on the challenges, opportunities and issues this book would not exist. We believe that when reading through the content of their chapters you will agree that they have made a significant contribution to our understanding of HRM today and around the corner. We are indebted to them all as colleagues and friends.

SIMS ACKNOWLEDGMENT

A very, very special thanks goes to my colleague, friend and co-editor, Sheri K. Bias and Herrington Bryce who continues to serve as my colleague, mentor and valued friend. The administrative support of the Raymond A. Mason School of Business at William and Mary is also acknowledged.

Thanks and appreciation goes to my family who have supported me throughout my work over the years.

Human Resources Management Issues, Challenges and Trends:
"Now and Around the Corner", pages vii–viii.
Copyright © 2019 by Information Age Publishing
All rights of reproduction in any form reserved.

BIAS ACKNOWLEDGEMENT

I am so very grateful for the contributions of my colleagues in preparation of this text and the support of Information Age Publishing in bringing this to fruition. A special thanks to Ron Sims who has been an amazing mentor, friend, colleague, and co-editor on this project. I hope the readers of this work find it interesting and informative.

As always, a special appreciation goes to Jim and Justin for their constant support of my endeavors.

CHAPTER 1

AN INTRODUCTION TO HUMAN RESOURCES

Management Issues, Challenges and Trends "Now and Around the Corner"

Ronald R. Sims and Sheri K. Bias

INTRODUCTION

These continue to be uncertain times which are dominated by a rapidly transforming business landscape. The uncertain times and rapidly transforming business landscape mean that all organizations must deal with issues like tighter labor markets, economic uncertainty and globalization. These and other issues will continue to shape the workplace, the human resource management (HRM) challenges and the HRM profession now and around the corner.

It is absolutely clear that HRM plays a key role in determining the survival and effectiveness of contemporary organizations. Thus, the effective management of an organization's human resources is a major source of competitive advantage and may even be the single most important determinant of an organization's per-

Human Resources Management Issues, Challenges and Trends:
"Now and Around the Corner", pages 1–29.
Copyright © 2019 by Information Age Publishing
All rights of reproduction in any form reserved.

formance and success long-term. An organization's HRM practices help support a company's business strategy and provide services the customer values.

Anyone who is familiar with the major organizations in their area has probably observed first-hand how dramatically the environment for contemporary organizations has continued to change in recent years. These changes have had a significant impact on organizational efforts to be successful. In practically every instance organizations have tried to more clearly identify and then focus on factors that impact their success and create a sustainable competitive advantage. One factor that continues to receive more attention than any other is the people who work for organizations. What organizations are realizing is that their likelihood of sustained success is most dependent on learning to get the maximum out of their employees. Such a realization has had a significant impact on the practice of HRM. What's more, forecasters predict that the role of employees, managers, and HRM personnel regardless of the sector (i.e., private, public, or not-for-profit) are likely to see more changes in the decades ahead (see Gibson, Ziskin, & Boudreau, 2014; May, n.d.; Noe, Hollenbeck, Gerhart, & Wright, 2019, p. 2017). Thus, individuals entering the world of work today (and tomorrow) require an understanding of the issues, challenges and opportunities that will continue to impact an organization's ability get the most out of their human resources as they strive for both a competitive advantage and success.

Organizations are increasingly realizing that their success is dependent on their ability to attract, develop, and retain talented employees. More than two decades ago, former Secretary of Labor Robert Reich emphasized this point when he suggested that in the future, the organization's ability to attract, develop, and retain a talented workforce will be a critical factor in developing a high-performance organization. Long-term, sustained organization success in today's changing and challenging world of work involves senior leadership's commitment to designing and implementing HRM programs and policies geared to developing both high-performing employees and organizations. This means that senior leadership anticipates the future need for employees and develops specific plans to obtain, develop, and retain the type of employees who meet the needs of a high-performing organization. Only by anticipating and working towards the development and retention of the "right type" of employees, can any organization expect to be successful in the global, dynamic and competitive environment.

An important element of any organization's success in the days, weeks, months, and years to come is a strategy where every employee is treated as a valuable resource. To do this means that organizations and its HRM professionals must be sensitive and responsive to the relevant issues, challenges and opportunities.

The objective of this book is to explore and provide an updated look at some of the challenges, trends and issues HRM professionals will need to focus on now and around the corner. Like other departments in the broader organization HRM professionals will need to increasingly demonstrate how they add value and contribute to the organization's success. While the trends, challenges and issues impacting organizations and HRM professionals will continue to change over the years the bottom-line of organization success is the clear reality that employees are their best assets and the need for effective HRM.

It is our hope that you the readers of this book will better understand the ongoing transformation of HRM given the issues, challenges and opportunities offered by the contributors. This means the book will discuss the ever-evolving role of HRM professionals to include discussion of how the profession must continue to become more adaptive, resilient, quick to change direction and customer-centered in its efforts to help meet the human resource needs of contemporary organizations and their employees. It is also our hope that the book will contribute to the ongoing dialogue and insights offered by HRM experts on what HRM professionals and their organizations can do in the face of such challenges, trends and issues in their efforts to win the talent wars.

This opening chapter first defines HRM and its role in helping organizations succeed. Next, the chapter takes a brief look at the interlinked activities typically taking place within organizations. Then, the chapter describes the history and contemporary growth of HRM. We conclude the chapter with a discussion of the contemporary challenges confronting organizations and HRM in the years to come.

Before taking a closer look at several of the challenges, trends and issues that will impact HRM professionals in the near and far term it's important to take a brief look at what we mean by HRM and the responsibilities of HRM.

WHAT IS HRM?

What makes one organization successful whereas another fails to make use of the same opportunities? For our purposes, the key to continued survival and organizational success lies not in the rational, quantitative approaches, but increasingly to a focus on things like people, employee involvement and commitment. Organization success for organizations of today and tomorrow is being increasingly seen as dependent on effective HRM. Effective HRM positively affects performance in organizations, both large and small.

HRM is the term increasingly used to refer to the philosophy, policies, procedures, and practices related to the management of an organization's employees (Quttainah, 2005; Sims, 2002) or that influences employees' behavior, attitudes, and performance (Noe, et al., 2019). Many organizations refer to HRM as involving "people practices." HRM is particularly concerned with all the activities that contribute to successfully attracting, developing, motivating, and maintaining a high-performing workforce that results in organizational success.

In the process of HRM, there is an increasing emphasis on the personal needs of the organization and its members. How effectively employees contribute to organization goals depend to a larger extent upon the ability of its HRM professionals. The challenge is to create an organizational environment in which each employee can grow and develop to their fullest extent. Such an environment increases the likelihood of a successful organization, and this is what HRM is all about, helping make organizations successful.

HRM efforts are planned, systematic approaches to increasing organizational success. They involve HRM programs aimed at developing HRM strategies for the total organization with an eye towards clarifying an organization's current and potential problems and develop solutions to them. It is oriented toward action, the individual, the global marketplace, and the future. Today it would be difficult to envision any organization achieving success without efficient HRM programs and activities.

The purpose of HRM programs is to increase organizational success and also to develop the potential of all members. HRM also emphasizes that HRM planning needs to be closely related to the organization's strategic goals and plans. Finally, there are a series of planned HRM practices that will ultimately influence the success of an organization. The strategy underlying these practices needs to be considered to maximize their influence on organization performance. These HRM practices are briefly discussed in the next section.

The importance of recruiting, selection, training and developing, rewarding, and compensating employees is recognized by employees at all levels or parts of today's organizations. Clearly, HRM and other functions must work together to achieve organizational success and compete locally and internationally. In order for an organization to be successful (i.e., prosper, earn a profit or meet society's or customer's needs), reasonable goals in each of these components much be achieved.

HUMAN RESOURCES MANAGEMENT FUNCTIONS

Fortunately, contemporary leaders and their organizations are increasingly looking at HRM practices as a means to contribute to profitability, quality, and other organizational goals through enhancing and supporting organizational operations. This means HRM professionals and their department or function be integrated with the organization, and able to help leaders throughout the organization in attracting, building, engaging and retaining talented employees. In addition, HRM professionals must also build their own talent and skills so they can help the organization meet current and future competitive challenges.

HRM professionals can perform many different roles and responsibilities depending on the size of the organization, the characteristics of the workforce, the industry and the value system of organization leadership. HRM professionals may take full responsibility for human resource activities in some organizations, whereas in others it may share the roles and responsibilities with managers of other functions in the organization such as operations information technology, or finance. In some organizations HRM professionals advise top-level leadership; in others the HRM department may make decisions regarding staffing, training, and compensation after senior leadership has decided relevant organization issues.

Within each functional area of HRM, many activities must be accomplished so that the organization's human resources can make an optimal contribution to the organization's success. These activities are briefly discussed in this section.

Strategic Management of Human Resources

The amount of time that the HRM function devotes to being a strategic business partner, change agent, and employee advocate has increased substantially in organizations over the past decade and a half (see Bersin, 2015; Ruona & Gibson, 2004). Astute senior leaders know that HRM professionals can help them improve, to comply with the law and help the bottom line by streamlining employment costs, for example, by redesigning work to foster innovation, by forecasting labor trends, by recruiting and motivating employees, and by measuring their effectiveness. HRM professionals also help their organizations with business strategies, as well as mergers, acquisitions, and ways to enter new and global markets. According to Art Mazor "If you look at the evolution going back to when we called HR 'personnel,' it's come a long way as a function" (p. 6) (Snell & Morris, 2019). New HRM tools and technologies are allowing the HRM function to look outside the tactical, administrative reporting and data gathering to bring insights to drive business strategy and results (Lindzon, 2015).

HRM needs to be closely integrated with managerial planning and decision making (i.e., international human resources, forecasting, planning, mergers and acquisitions). As noted earlier, increasingly senior leaders in organizations recognize that the time to consider the organization's HRM strengths or limitations is when strategic organizational decisions are being formulated, not after critical policies have been decided. A closer integration between top management's goals and HRM practices helps to elicit and reward the types of behavior necessary for achieving an organization's strategy. For example, if an organization is planning to become known for its high-quality products HRM staff should design appraisal and reward systems that emphasize quality in order to support this competitive strategy.

Strategic management of human resources includes HRM planning. The HRM planning process involves forecasting HRM needs and developing programs to ensure that the right numbers and types of individuals are available at the right time and place. Such information enables an organization to plan its recruitment, selection, and training strategies. For example, let's say an organization's HRM plan estimates that 12 data analysts will be needed during the next year. The organization typically hires recent data analyst graduates to fill such positions. Because these majors are in high demand, the organization decides to begin its recruiting early in the school year, before other organizations can "snatch away" the best candidates.

Recruiting and Selecting (Staffing) Talent

Once HRM needs are determined, the next step is recruiting talent (i.e., interviewing, recruiting, screening and selecting the most qualified candidates, filling some positions through transfer or promotion, and temporary employment coordination). Recruitment is a form of business contest and it is fiercely competitive. Just as organizations strategize to develop, manufacture, and market the best product or service, so they must also vie to identify, attract, and hire the most qualified people. Recruitment is a business, and it is big business (Cahuc, Carcillo, & Zilberberg, 2014; Ehrenberg & Smith, 2016).

Regardless of the size of an organization, or what sector or industry it is in, recruitment and selection of people with strategically relevant abilities is more important than ever. And, recruiting and staffing is a far more complex activity than in previous times when HRM professionals could rely on recommendations from current employees or a "help wanted" sign in front of the business. The increased complexity of positions to be filled and equal employment opportunity (EEO), require more sophisticated procedures to identify and select prospective employees. Consider, for instance, the impact antidiscrimination laws have had over the years on organizations hiring practices. Prior to the passage of these laws, many organizations hired people in somewhat arbitrary ways. Applicants were often hired because they had an organization handshake or because they graduated from the employer's alma mater. Today, such practices could result in charges of discrimination. For instance, a woman denied a job because she is pregnant may end up suing the organization for sex discrimination.

To protect themselves from such charges, employers must conduct their selection practices "by the book." This means they should carefully determine needed job qualifications and choose selection methods that accurately measure those qualifications.

In order to plan for future selection efforts and training programs and to ensure that performance appraisal and compensation systems are rationally based on job demands HRM professionals must complete careful descriptions and analysis and design of current and future work and jobs. The development and use of job analysis information continues to be a critical part of strategic HRM planning and as the foundation for all other HRM functions.

Organizations may recruit candidates internally (i.e., recruit current employees seeking to advance or change jobs) or externally. While the aim of recruitment is to identify a suitable pool of applicants quickly, cost efficiently, and legally, selection or staffing involves assessing and choosing job candidates. Internal recruitment often relies on succession plans, job posting, employee referrals, or temporary worker pools (Polyhart & Kim, 2014). Many external recruitment sources are also available (Cascio, 2019).

To be effective, selection processes must be technically sound (i.e., accurate) and legal. But more importantly, in staffing an organization or department it is important for HRM professionals and other decision makers to consider its developmental stage-start-up, high growth, mature, or aging-in order to align staffing decisions with organizational strategy. It is also important to communicate an organization's culture, because research shows that applicants will consider this information to choose among jobs if it is available to them (see Kristol-Brown & Guay, 2011; Polyhart, Schmitt & Tippins, 2017).

Training and Development (Human Resource Development)

Like years gone by today's employees look at the chance to develop and move up as important in where they will seek employment. In order to facilitate employee progression and performance best practice or benchmark training and development organizations choose to spend substantial sums to train and develop their employees on operational knowhow but also superior job expertise; knowledge about competitive, industry, and technological trends; and the ability to continually learn and utilize new information. By focusing on these characteristics HRM professionals and their organizations are in a better position to adapt and innovate to compete far more effectively in today's fast-paced global business world. The reality is, that because training and talent development plays a critical role in nurturing, strengthening, and expanding the capabilities of an organization in this way, it is critical to achieving strategic objectives.

Training and development or what is often referred to as human resource development (HRD) (i.e., orientation / onboarding, performance management skills training, and productivity enhancement) are planned learning experiences that teach employees how to perform their current and future jobs. Training tends to be more narrowly focused and oriented to short-term performance concerns or present jobs, whereas development tends to be oriented more toward broadening an individual's skills for future responsibilities or jobs.

Procedures for determining training and development needs then constructing, delivering, and evaluating HRM development programs to meet these needs are the cornerstones of HRD and most often the responsibility of HRM professionals. However, in order to ensure that their organizations get the most out of their training investments, today HRM professionals must pay attention to training and development trends like the following (Cascio, 2014, 2017; Noe, 2017):

- A growing demand for personal and professional development. Among young adults the most important feature they look for in a new job is opportunity for continuous learning (Hirsch, 2016).
- The effects of digital technology on work. Technology, especially information and communication technology, continues to change the manner in which organizations create and capture value, how and where we work, and how we interact and communicate. Technologies such as cloud and mobile computing, big data and machine learning, sensors and intelligent manufacturing, for example, continue to transform the very foundations of

global business and organizations that derive it while enabling employees to decide where they work, when they work, and in some cases even how they accomplish work (see Cascio & Montealegre, 2016; Friedman, 2016).

- Structural changes in labor markets. Today's organizations increasingly employ workers from a variety of labor markers which include, for example, temporary-help services, online job boards, and social media sites which means that 1) HRM professionals and their organizations can no longer assume that everyone who works at a given organization is an employee of that organization and 2) and these employees who work for themselves may on any given day make up as much as 24 percent of the American workforce as nonstandard workers (Pofeldt, 2015).
- Training as an important part of an organization's brand. In general, the public and especially potential talent are attracted to good-name brands and repelled by bad-name brands. Organizations that provide superior opportunities for learning and growth have a distinct advantage when competing for talented employees (Kane & Sherr, 2011).

HRM professionals must ensure that their organization's HRD efforts provide an atmosphere that will support the investment in talent while being cognizant of the ever-evolving trends in training and development.

Performance Management

Through the performance management process, HRM professionals must see that their organizations measure the adequacy of their employees' job performance and communicate these evaluations to them. An effective performance management process provides an organization to 1) ensure that employee's activities and outputs are congruent with the organization's goals and 2) with the opportunity to achieve a competitive advantage through their employees by managing the behavior and results of all its employees. Performance management is a critical link in the HRM process as it assesses how well employees are performing and determine appropriate rewards or remedial actions to motivate employees to continue appropriate behaviors and correct inappropriate ones.

The HRM professional's role in performance management is one of working with other managers and employees at all levels in the organization to establish the appraisal process, the performance dimensions to be measured, the procedures to ensure accuracy, and requirements for discussion of appraisal results with employees. This also means that HRM professionals help instill a culture of understanding in the organization that sees effective performance management as a process and not an event. The emphasis on performance management as a process highlights the importance of providing feedback and the formal performance evaluation but notes that they are not the only important parts of an effective performance management process that contributes to the organization's competitive advantage (Dahling & O'Malley, 2011; Goler, Gale & Grant, 2016; Mone, Eisinger, Guggenheim, Prie, & Stine, 2011).

Today's HRM professionals and other organizational managers and leaders must effectively use performance management and specifically performance appraisals as a tool for making HRM-related decisions, such as promotions, demotions, discharges, and pay raises. Performance appraisal continues to not be one of the pleasant activities for managers, yet it is important that it be undertaken in a timely manner and be done as accurately as possible.

There is every indication that measuring and managing performance will continue to be a challenging endeavor and one of the keys to organizational success and gaining and maintaining competitive advantage. HRM professionals must never let the organization lose sight of the importance of a performance management system in serving strategic, administrative, and development purposes for the organization. That is, for example, performance is critical for today's organizations to execute their talent management strategy, that is, to identify employees' strengths and weaknesses, drive employee engagement, link employees to appropriate training and development activity, and reward good performance with pay and other incentives (Noe & Links, 2014). In the end, acquiring, training & developing and retaining top-notch employees is more likely to occur when HRM professionals and their organizations look at the performance management system as a tool for motivating and fostering the growth of employees so they can contribute the maximum value to the organization.

Career Development

Organizations are becoming more active in developing career development programs as part of their HRD efforts. Many organizations are designing career programs in an attempt to increase overall organizational performance, employee productivity, and attract, develop, and retain the most qualified employees in this increasingly competitive and global environment.

HRM professionals and proactive organizations see career development as a strategic imperative, and therefore, as an ongoing process designed to maximize the talents of their employees and retain them. In the years to come, HRM professionals and other organizational members must regularly work to understand their organizations' strategies in conjunction with their organizational charts, job analysis and work design information, and external factors such as the labor market and the competition, and their efforts to recruit and train and develop proactively and continually.

In addition to being concerned about their own interests, organizations are increasingly concerned about the long-term interests of their employees. However, with pressures to improve efficiency and overall effectiveness organizations have also expected individuals to accept more responsibility for managing their own careers. This means that individuals must do everything they can to grow and realize their full potential in order to improve their value either to their current or future employers. Individuals have begun to view careers as "boundaryless" and protean (see Briscoe, Hall, & De Muth, 2005; Gerli, Bonesso, & Pizzi, 2015; Gubler, Arnold & Coombs, 2014) including several employers and possibly different occupations.

A common factor in the occurrence of various definitions of a boundaryless career is "one of independence from, rather than dependence on, traditional organizational career arrangements" (p. 6) (Arthur & Rousseau, 1996). A protean career is based on self-direction with the goal of psychological success in one's work. Employees take major responsibility for managing their careers and their careers change frequently due to both changes in the person's interests, abilities, and values and changes in the work (Noe et al., 2019).

The important takeaway from the boundaryless or protean career for HRM professionals is that they and their organizations must understand is that today's careers will often change. A career may include movement across several employers (job hopping) or even different occupations. The reality is that employees will be unlikely to stay at one organization for their entire or even a significant part of their career. This means that organizations and employees should add value to each other (Hoffman, Casnocha, & Yeh, 2016; Lublin, 2016). In the end, HRM professionals and their organizations will need to focus their energies on creating an employee development planning or career management system that views career management as a partnership between employees and their organization and is based on a positive relationship through which employees are committed to the organization but can take personal control for managing their own careers to benefit themselves and the organization.

Compensation

Compensation is a key strategic area for any organization as it impacts the organization's ability to attract and retain talent and ensure optimal levels of performance from employees in meeting the organization's strategic objectives. HRM professionals must also understand that compensation is a key economic issue as compensation programs continue to assume an increasingly large share of an organization's operating expenses. A critical balancing act must occur to ensure that compensation attracts, motivates, and retains talent; at the same time, compensation should allow the organization to maintain a cost structure that enables it to compete effectively and efficiently (Mello, 2019).

A logical result of the performance management process is determining which employees most deserve rewards. Compensation entails pay and benefits (i.e., wage and salary administration, job descriptions, executive compensation, incentive pay, insurance, vacation-leave administration, retirement plans, profit sharing, stock plans). Allocating rewards is a complex and specialized activity. Rewards include both direct compensation and (salary and hourly wages) and indirect compensation (benefits) that organizations offer to employees. The aim of compensation practices is to help organizations establish and maintain a competent and loyal workforce at an affordable cost.

Compensation is affected by forces as diverse as labor market factors, collective bargaining, and senior leadership's philosophy regarding pay and benefits (Newman, Gerhart, & Milkovich, 2017). Like other HRM activities, compensation practices are also affected by government legislation, for example, like legal requirements of equal pay for equal work, minimum wage and overtime provisions, and required benefits such as Social Security. In addition to the level of pay, a successful compensation system is based on fairness. Employees bring a variety of perspectives to bear in deciding whether they are satisfied with the compensation they receive, thus making management of compensation a particularly challenging HRM activity.

In working with organizational leaders HRM professionals should ensure that compensation systems are designed to mesh with the strategic objectives of the organization. They also need to integrate the realities of prevailing pay levels in the labor market with an organization's profitability and ability to pay. Further, in fulfilling their role in organizations, HRM professionals will need to remember that compensation, as part of an organization's total reward system, will continue to evolve strategically relative to the changing needs of organizations and employees in a number of ways (see Mathis, Jackson, Valentine, & Meglich, 2017; Mello, 2019). First, greater emphasis is being placed on employee performance and contribution, rather than seniority, in compensation decisions. Second, employers are taking a more holistic approach to compensation in offering enhanced and flexible benefits to meet individual employee needs and preferences. Third, greater emphasis is being placed on more immediate and intermittent rewards, rather than waiting for the annual performance review to announce compensation decisions. Fourth, organizational rewards are becoming more directly linked to the organization's mission, strategy, and goals. Fifth, compensation decisions and rewards are becoming more individualized, rather than applied equally, "across the board," to all employees.

Strategic compensation as suggested in the five ways listed above will help organizations to better compensate employees in ways that enhance motivation and growth, while at the same time aligning their efforts with the objectives of today's organization. Strategic compensation will also continue to help redefine the role and perceived contribution of compensation. No longer a "cost of doing business," when used strategically, compensation can help serve as a tool to secure organization success and competitive advantage.

In the end, like other HRM practices the effectiveness of a compensation system can be assessed by using a compensation scorecard. The scorecard collects and displays where all departments and functions sit in terms of their relative compensation. It increases transparency of compensation systems, the accountability of managers and leaders, and helps organizations align their compensation decisions with organizational objectives (see Snapka & Copikova, 2011).

Employee Safety, Health and Security

An important source of workplace change has been the desire to promote a safer and more healthful work environment. Legal, social, and political pressures on organizations ensure the health and safety of their employees continue to have a great impact on HRM practices. Part of the impact and concern is a result of the Occupational Safety and Health Act of 1970. A second source of change is societal concern about exposure to hazardous substances or stress in the workplace. Organizations try to respond to pressures and concerns by instituting accident prevention programs and programs designed to ensure the health and mental well-being of their employees. Organizations continue to take responsibility for helping employees deal with problems caused by stress or substance abuse through wellness and employee assistance programs as part of safety, health and security program or risk management efforts (see Pate-Cornell & Cox, 2014).

HRM professionals play an important role in ensuring employee health and safety, as they know the workplace, the employees and their job demands. While HRM professionals are not expected to know the technical aspects of workplace health and safety, today they must know when and how to use existing resources to respond to employee concerns. In many organizations, health and safety (and sometimes security) responsibilities are within HRM function or department. In order to meet these responsibilities, HRM professionals must:

- Understand the health and safety responsibilities of employers, managers, supervisors and employees within the organization;
- Implement HRM policies to ensure that everyone in the workplace is aware of his/her responsibilities;
- Establish effective ways of meeting health and safety responsibilities; and
- Ensure that employees fulfill their health and safety responsibilities as outlined in the organizational policies and programs.

Health, safety and security are closely related terms because they affect each other in practice and are often taken into consideration together by HRM professionals and other organizational members when creating policies in an organization. Health refers to a general state of physical, mental, and emotional well-being. A healthy person is free from illness, injury, or mental and emotional problems that impair normal human activity. In most organizations, heath management efforts strive to maintain that overall well-being. Safety refers to a condition in which people's physical well-being is protected. The main purpose of effective safety programs in organizations is to prevent work-related injuries and accidents by identifying and communicating hazards, reinforcing safe practices, and promoting safety internationally (see Bryan, 1990; Maurer, 2014). Thus, safety awareness programs attempt to instill symbolic and substantive changes in the organization's emphasis on safety.

Today and in the years to come, HRM professionals need to integrate workplace health, safety and security in HRM practices throughout the organization which include:

- Preventing work related injuries and illnesses;
- Fostering a workplace safety culture in which employees and their supervisors work together to ensure workplace safety;
- Establishing administrative procedures that encourage employees to report unsafe conditions and unsafe practices to their supervisors without fear of being disciplined;
- Developing appropriate hiring, training and performance appraisal practices;
- Recruiting and retaining the best employees who care about their own well-being and the well-being of co-workers.
- Ensuring that the health and safety policies and procedures conform with the applicable occupational health and safety legislation and accepted best practices in similar organizations;
- Establishing procedures for enforcing company safety rules;
- Helping reduce costs associated with losses due to absenteeism injuries, workers' compensation, disability, and health care;
- Maintaining records of injuries, illnesses and workers' compensation;
- Coordinating first aid training and the provision of first aid to employees;
- Providing advice to employees and the employer in matters of occupational health and safety.

Table 1.1 provides an overview of some health, safety and security responsibilities related to HRM.

Labor Relations and Collective Bargaining

More than ever before, the relationship between managers and their employees must be handled effectively if both the employees and the organizations are to prosper together. And, the relationship is even more important when one considers the increasing number of organizations that are drawing on and contributing to a global economy (Budd, 2018; Lansbury & Wailes, 2016). As these organizations have gone global, the number of employees abroad has increased. With more employees abroad, HRM professionals and departments have had to tackle new global challenges. Additionally, as the ebb and flow of pressures to downsize and outsource and calls for more efficiency and effectiveness continue in public, private and not-for-profit organizations, there is the possibility of increased tension between organizations and their employees. HRM professionals are increasingly called on to help their organizations tackle these and other challenges by proactively identifying and implementing HRM policies and practices which effec-

TABLE 1.1.   Health, Safety and Security Responsibilities Related to HRM

Examples of HRM Activities	Relevance to Workplace Health, Safety and Security
Compliance with various regulations regarding HRM practices	Health, safety and security of employees with special needs
Coordinating, safety and security activities	Supervision of health and safety personnel, coordination of health, safety and security committee activities
Managing employee benefits and compensation	Modified work assignment
Maintaining employee records	Special needs of: • Pregnant and nursing employees • Employees with illness or injury • Employees with disabilities (i.e., physical or mental issues)
Ensuring that employees are aware of new and existing HRM policies	Orientation / onboarding, training and ongoing communication with: • New employees • Transferred employees • Promoted employees • Entire workforce • Volunteers and students/interns
Career development, training, and organizational development	Training needs arising out of changing work practices, equipment and relocation
Promoting leadership in management and supervision	Health, safety and security environmental responsibility of employees at all levels
Promoting safety culture	Recognizing safe behavior

tively address the new global challenges and opportunities along with improving (or protecting) wages and benefits and working conditions.

Labor relations are considered the study of the relationships existing in the workplace between employers and workers or between workers, the organizations that represent employers, and workers, the government, and other types of institutions in society as a whole (Dunlop, 1958). In addition, the field of labor relations includes the study of HRM, collective bargaining, labor laws, and social insurance systems (Napathorn & Chanprateep, 2011). It is important for HRM professionals to understand all of the subfields of labor relations as it provides them with insights into the real world of work and how to solve the problems existing within such a world such as workplace disputes between employers and labor unions, strikes, and lockouts, to promote fairness, efficiency, and a satisfying relationship between the two parties as well as to foster win-win solutions for the labor-management problems in the workplace (see Kaufman, 2006).

It is also important for HRM professionals to continue to recognize that labor relations are often country specific (Caulfield, 2004). That is to say, labor relations are considered a system and tend to be different between countries. Thus, under-standing the labor relations system as well as the collective bargaining situation in each country helps HRM professionals understand the nature of the economy, industry, production methods, technological and socio-cultural dimension, as well as the background and development of such a country (Kuruvilla, 1994). On the other hand, understanding the external developments, economic expansion, and other stimuli and changes affecting each country also helps HRM professionals understand the labor relations system in a specific country as well. Therefore, la-bor relations and collective bargaining must continue to be of paramount interest to HRM professionals.

As evident in the paragraph above, labor relations continue to be a key strate-gic for HRM professionals and their organization because the nature of the rela-tionship between the employer and employees can have a significant impact on morale, motivation, and productivity. Employees who feel that the terms and con-ditions of their employment are less than advantageous will not be as committed to perform and to remain with an organization. Consequently, how organizations manage the day-to-day aspects of the employment relationship can be a key vari-able affecting their ability to achieve strategic objectives locally and globally (see Katz, Kochan, & Colvin, 2015; O'Brien & Kessler, 2014).

Today's and tomorrow's HRM professionals and other organizational mem-bers will need to continue to pay attention to labor-management relations and collective barging issues and help to implement organization, national and inter-national polices, and workplace policies to solve problems and foster a positive relationship between employees and organizations, especially because employees are one of the most important mechanisms that will drive organization success. Additionally, HRM professionals will need to regularly conduct such things as labor audits in every country where they operate as conducting such assessments will help identify any risks, issues, challenges, and opportunities they and their organizations will need to address in developing labor relations procedures, poli-cies and programs.

Global Human Resources Management

Simply put, global HRM is HRM that cuts across national boundaries. But as many organizations and their HRM professionals have found out from first-hand experience, it is not simple. Global HRM can be very complex. Globalization has created an array of employment scenarios based on such variables as citizenship, location, to whom the person reports, and the term of the assignment. Global, multinational or transnational corporations are growing in numbers and complex-ity. An example of this complexity is an organization building a manufacturing plant in Spain to produce engine parts designed by another organization in Japan for motorcycles to be sold in Europe and the United States (Sims, 2007).

The international aspects of HRM in the international arena require a global perspective. A perspective that recognizes the difference between domestic HRM and global HRM is one of complexity. This complexity affects all the major HRM processes as suggested in our discussion of management and employee relationships and recognizes the importance of organizations ceasing to only be local but to also be global. Today, even those organizations who consider themselves immune to transactions across geographical boundaries are connected to the wider network globally. They are in one way or the other dependent upon organizations that may even not have heard about. Thus, HRM professionals must recognize that there is an interdependence between organizations in various areas and functions.

In looking to the future, HRM professionals and the function of global HRM is that the organization carries a local appeal in the host country despite maintaining an international feel. To exemplify, any global / multinational / international company would not like to be called as local, however the same wants a domestic touch in the host country and there lies the challenge.

HRM professionals may therefore, enumerate the objectives of global HRM as follows:

1. Create a local appeal without compromising upon the global identity.
2. Generating awareness of cross-cultural sensitivities among managers globally and hiring of staff across geographic boundaries.
3. Training upon cultures and sensitivities of the host country.

In the end, all of the HRM activities briefly reviewed in this section are interlinked activities taking place within organizations. Additionally, external forces—legal, economic, technological, global, environmental, cultural/geographic, political, and social—have and will continue to significantly affect HRM activities and how they are designed, managed, and changed in the coming years. The next section of this introductory chapter takes a contemporary look at HRM issues, challenges, and opportunities.

CONTEMPORARY ISSUES, CHALLENGES AND TRENDS IMPACTING HRM

HRM is the term most often used to describe formal systems devised for the management of people within an organization. And, as our discussion to this point highlight, HRM is concerned with the development of both individuals and the organization in which they operate. HRM, then, is engaged not only in securing and developing the talents of individual workers, but also in implementing programs that enhance communication and cooperation between those individual workers in order to nurture organizational development. Essentially, the purpose of HRM is to maximize the productivity of an organization by optimizing the effectiveness of its employees. This mandate is unlikely to change in any fundamental way, despite the ever-increasing pace of change in the business world or any future laws or regulations. As Edward L. Gubman (1996) observed more than two decades ago in the *Journal of Business Strategy*, "the basic mission of human resources will always be to acquire, develop, and retain talent; align the workforce with the business; and be an excellent contributor to the business. Those three challenges will never change."

Until fairly recently, an organization's HRM professionals and department was often consigned to lower rungs of the corporate hierarchy, despite the fact that its mandate is to replenish and nourish what is often cited—legitimately—as an organization's greatest resource, its work force. But in recent years recognition of the importance of HRM to an organization's overall health has grown dramatically. And, perhaps one of the main reasons for this increased recognition is HRM's role in helping the organization achieve its goals of obtaining and maintaining while also navigating the never-ending changes of the world of work.

So, what are some of the main issues, challenges and trends facing HRM professionals now and around the corner? The issues, challenges and trends confronting HRM professionals and their organizations center around the continuing need to build an HRM mindset more ingrained in the fabric of the organization and creating much better integration of their operations and, for example, talent management functions. Emerging trends and challenges in areas like new developments in technology, increased competition for talent, demographic changes and demands for data-driven HRM practices (for example, cybersecurity threats or responses to data breaches) will need to be successfully addressed by HRM professionals and their organizations. There will be much more pressure on HRM professionals to show that their organization do indeed put employees first and have a strong employer brand.

Attracting the top talent while not new remains a continual issue, challenge and trend for HRM professionals. But what is new are the ways organizations will have to address attracting talent to include, for example, the increasing need to focus on millennials and how they go about making decisions on joining organizations. Must HRM professionals spend more time on ensuring their organizations create cultures or work environments that spend less time on how much millennials are paid or incentivized to work but base them on enhanced quality of work life, service opportunities and attractiveness on issues like the reputation of the organization in terms of their role in society and what they are doing to support their employees both in and outside the organization? Consider, for example, that a recent Korn Ferry study (2017) found that 73 percent of respondents said their No. 1 driver at work was doing a job that had meaning and purpose, while only 3 percent said pay was the top driver. For millennials and the next generation of employees the pay check is no longer king when it comes to sourcing, retaining and motivating talent. Today's employees—irrespective of their generation—want to work for organizations they believe in, from both a vision and development perspective. HRM professionals must continue to recognize and that organization culture, ability to grow and upskill and location of work will be key motivators above salary for candidates choosing their next employer.

HRM professionals must make sure their organizations focus on and invest in their employer brand to help prospective (and current) employees understand the organization culture and motivations within the workplace. Through this investment, HRM professionals and others in the organizations can enhance their employer reputation or brand in a customized, dynamic way that moves the needle to attract, engage and retain employees as an employer of choice.

An increased emphasis on the benefits of and investment in technology or automation by many organizations creates opportunities to decrease cost and improve the customer experience, and by doing this they are able to reduce the number of employees they need. And this in turn forces HRM professionals and other organizational leaders to have to make decisions on how best to continue to achieve cost savings to be more competitive. For example, reducing the number of employees presents the challenges or issues of needing to determine whether or not to hire new people (just-in-time hiring) as the need arises, invest in up-skilling their employees whose jobs will be eliminated with new technology or automation and commit to preparing them for a new and different, but needed job in the organization. In short, HRM professionals must work with others in the organization to increase organizational efficiency and productivity while also being excessively sensitive to the way they treat their employees and the reputation and scrutiny they will face from current and potential employees. Meister (2016) has referred to the need for the "Consumerization of HR," referring to how companies create a social, mobile, and consumer-style experience for employees which also requires HRM professionals and their departments to transform themselves and have a new mindset, plus a set of consumer-focused and technological skills to creating new HR solutions (Meister, 2017).

Related to the technology or automation issue for HRM professionals and their organization is the trend of the increasing emergence of the Freelancer or Gig economy or "Me Inc." as some reports estimate, for example, that by 2020 as much as 40% of the American workforce will be contingent workers or independent contractors (Korn Ferry, 2016; Meister, 2017; Phillips, 2017; Schrader, 2015). The reality is that employees can no longer be easily parsed into full-time and part-time, exempt and non-exempt. As a result, HRM professionals will need to grapple with how to recruit, orient and socialize gig and other workers, while staying in compliance with evolving laws and regulations (Waters & Alonso, 2017). HRM professionals will need to continue to develop and use tools like talent networks, crowdsourcing and internal social networks to support a virtual workforce.

When considering today and what is around the competitive landscape corner, HRM professionals must be able to tie their talent investments to the organization objectives. And this means HRM professionals must be proficient in understanding the impact and importance of the big data and analytics trend on their efforts to recruit, develop, and retain talent for the organization. New trends in workforce analytics call for metrics that go beyond, for example, cost-per-hire and time-to-fill metrics. But instead focus on meta-metrics like return on workforce investment and assessing opportunity costs associated with workforce processes. Such sophistication of people analytics provides the organization with a holistic view of people productivity using a combination of operational and talent data (Vorhauser-Smith, 2017). Several writers (see Waters & Alonso, 2017; Meister, 2017) also suggest the importance of HRM professionals blending in marketing tools like net promoter scores to enhance the information gathered about an organization's effectiveness when promulgating brand and consumer value propositions.

The rise of and need to be attentive to millennials in the workforce creates the opportunity and challenge of HRM professionals needing to help their organizations create a culture of continuous, regular or ongoing feedback. HRM professionals and organizations that are committed to developing a stronger workforce which positively impacts their overall organization goals must develop and adopt tools that enable employees to receive regular feedback from multiple sources, such as peers, customers or multiple managers or leaders. The growing millennial workforce expect more engagement and feedback and HRM professionals and organizations that fail to recognize such expectations and trend will clearly lose out in the talent war and not be able to build a strong employer brand as mentioned earlier.

Numerous HRM professionals and organizations have already focused their attention on reinventing traditional performance management practices and clearly made it easier for those in management or leadership positions to capture and provide ongoing feedback to their individual and team direct reports. Tools continue to become smarter and, for example, embed activity streams, pulse surveys and other techniques for feedback. As with other HRM technological innovations, tools like performance management apps are helping to make regular feedback a formalized process that can be provided and captured from any mobile device (see Vorhauser-Smith, 2017). This and similar technology trends will continue to create issues, challenges and opportunities for HRM professionals and their organizations as the look to transform or complement their traditional performance review efforts with ongoing, just-in-time or everyday feedback.

Along the same vein as alluded to earlier is the rise of digital HRM. A plethora of new HRM technology continues to transform the profession as we know it today and forcing HRM professionals, their department and organizations to undergo a degree of digital transformation. The emergence of machine learning and artificial intelligence which mimics human decision-making processes whereby algorithms can learn from and make predictions based on patterns of behavior, will relentlessly foster smarter recruiting and talent management practices. Whether helping HRM professionals to tailor the employee experience or analyzing the traits of star performers in order to guide future recruiting decisions, the rise of digital HRM practices will continue to change the profession as we know it today and increasingly make the profession data-driven.

It should be clear by now that technology will continue to drive HRM innovations and a further focus on data-driven decision-making with the ability to correlate people data to business performance, and in some cases predict business performance, as well as plan future workforce needs. Today and tomorrow, what will matter most is how quickly and easily HRM can access a multitude of people data and explore it alongside other types of data to improve organization outcomes.

While technology has made today's employees' lives exponentially easier, it has also opened the door to a number of threats of hacking and data theft. Cybersecurity breaches are costly and destructive for organizations. Today, news of data breaches seemed to make headlines almost daily. It is clear that no type of organization is exempt, including HRM. For example, in 2016, more than 700,000 candidates on the books of one international recruitment organization had their details hacked in one of the biggest security breaches in the recruiting industry (see English, 2016). While information security is not a new challenge for HRM professionals, as the use of technology continues to gather and store an exponential amount of data on both candidates and companies alike, HRM professionals must continue to realize that data security is not simply a 'nice to have' - it's a necessity. Now and around the corner, holistic security and data privacy will be a business priority within the HRM profession and industry. Why?

Given the reality that many cybersecurity problems emerge due to the actions of an organization's own employees, HRM professionals, alongside others like information technology professionals, will need to play a crucial role in the fight against cyber-crime at the office (Global HR Research, 2016). This is especially true because the data that HRM professionals work with is often the most vulnerable to attack. The Society for Human Resource Management noted that HR records contain highly sensitive and private information like: social security numbers, dates of birth, bank detail and home addresses, to name just a few. As a result, HRM professionals now and tomorrow must not only have a comprehensive understanding of how to protect data within their own department, but also the organization as a whole.

Finally, there is every indication that federal and state laws and regulations will continue to change and have an increasing impact on HRM professionals and their organizations. Stephen Miller, Lisa Nagele-Piazza and Allen Smith (2017) in a recent article titled "Top 7 Workplace Legal Trends for 2017" noted that employment attorneys predict uncertainty at the federal level and an uptick in state laws. As one should surmise the HRM legal and regulatory environment will continue to change and is quite likely the area that changes more than any other in HRM. HRM professionals will need to continue to examine, analyze and discuss the challenges, issues and opportunities related to HRM legal and regulatory issues and the implications for employees and their organizations.

Contemporary Expectations of HRM

It should be evident in our discussion that gone are the days when HRM professionals received direction from the senior leadership team as to their priorities and needs. HRM is now expected to sit at the senior leadership table and recommend processes, approaches, and organization or business solutions that improve the ability of the organization's people to effectively contribute.

The new role of HRM involves strategic direction and HRM metrics and measurements to demonstrate how they add value throughout the organization (Heathfield, 2017). HRM professionals must continue to find ways to demonstrate and communicate their value by keeping those at all levels of the organization aware of how people contribute to the organization's success and by keeping it safe from lawsuits and the resulting workplace chaos one finds in an increasingly global work environment. HRM professionals must perform a balancing act to serve all of an organization's stakeholders: customers, senior leaders, owners, government' officials, other members of the community, managers, employees, and stockholders.

It is difficult to underestimate the importance of an effective, modern and proactive HRM function and its professionals within today's organization. An employee who retired from HRM ten or twenty years ago would not recognize the competence and capability of the best HRM organizations today. It is our belief that HRM professionals will continue to move their HRM function further and further into the role of a valued strategic partner. HRM professionals and functions that do will best serve their organizations today and tomorrow.

SUMMARY

Effective HRM is clearly an important component to todays and tomorrows organizational success. And the HRM function and professionals is an organization's most critical source of information about employment practices, employee behavior, labor relations, and the effective management of all aspects of human resources. HRM is made up of an identifiable set of activities that affect and influence the people who work in an organization. These activities include strategic HRM planning, work design and job analysis, recruitment, selection or staffing, career management, training and development, designing performance safety, health and security, management and compensation systems, and labor relations.

The ongoing challenge and opportunity for HRM professionals is to integrate programs involving human resources with strategic organizational objectives. Today's organizations continue to be under tremendous competitive pressure in their host countries and worldwide. As a result, HRM professionals must find ways to develop effective local and global programs that meet this challenge.

Issues, challenges, problems and opportunities for HRM today and tomorrow center on changing workforce demographics and diversity, competing in a global environment, technological changes, eliminating the employee skills gap, developing human capital-lifelong learning and organizational learning, and achieving societal goals through organizations. HRM must work as a strategic partner with others in the organization to make their organizations better, faster, and more competitive.

In conclusion, in an environment where competitive pressures will continue to grow, and new techniques and concepts will constantly be developed, no function can stand apart from change. The world of management and human performance will also continue to evolve and as it does the expectations of HRM professionals and their function will constantly grow. The requirement for HRM to be a strategic partner and results focused carries a significant message for HRM professionals of today and tomorrow—learn how to respond or be left behind. The trend will continue to expect a more results oriented HRM function and professional presence that satisfies the following needs:

1. The need to understand and contribute to business strategy
2. The need to produce business results
3. The need to add value and demonstrate HRM Professionalism
4. The need to be able to turn strategy into reality

We believe HRM will continue to meet these and other expectations as it has for the past 100 some years.

THIS BOOK AND THE CHAPTERS THAT FOLLOW

The objective of this book is to explore and provide an updated look at some of the various challenges, problems, trends and issues HRM professionals will need to focus on now and around the corner. Like other departments in the broader organization HRM professionals will need to increasingly demonstrate how they add value and contribute to the organization's success. While the trends, challenges and issues impacting organizations and HRM professionals will continue to change over the years the bottom-line of organization success is the clear reality that employees are their best assets and the need for effective HRM.

It is our belief that this book will provide an updated, current and future look at the transformation of HRM. This means the contributors to this book will discuss some of the ever-evolving roles of HRM professionals to include discussion of how the profession continues to become more adaptive, resilient, quick to change direction and customer-centered in its efforts to meet the needs of contemporary organizations and their employees.

The Chapters that Follow

Here is the information you will encounter as you read the chapters that follow this introductory piece.

In Chapter 2, "Globalization and Human Resource Management," Ronald R. Sims notes that the environment in which today's organizations find themselves continues to be more globalized as the world is becoming a "global village." Overall, this chapter discusses a number of the HRM challenges, issues and opportunities HRM professionals and their organizations will need to address in today's and tomorrow's global world of work. The chapter first takes a look at today's global organization and some HRM issues. Next, the discussion turns to the globalization of business and factors affecting HRM in global markets before focusing on an analysis of levels of global or international and HRM operations. Finally, the chapter discusses globalization and implications and impacts on HRM in the future.

In Chapter 3, "Organizational Drift: Why Organizations Drift off Keel and What Human Resource Professionals can do about it," Jim Eicher and William J. Mea identify the symptoms of what they call *Organizational Drift* and provides human resource professionals with a guide for recognizing and correcting the issue. The chapter first provides assessment questions and a framework for organizational drift. The second section describes the signs of organizational drift. It describes *"the tells"* for each component of the organizational drift framework and how the tell is a symptom of organization dysfunction that may adversely affect organization performance. The third section explains why well-intended organizational changes fail to yield good results. Finally, the last section of the chapter provides guidelines to avoid organizational drift and offers guidance on how to create organizational alignment in a way that can mitigate the underlying causes of organizational drift.

In Chapter 4, "Watering the Organizational Landscape: Meeting Employee Needs through HRM Flexibility," Alexandra E. MacDougall, Zhanna Bagdasarov, and M. Ronald Buckley discuss the changing organizational landscape and the corresponding implications for contemporary human resource management. Specifically, the chapter begins with a brief description of how socio-demographic and technological changes are influencing employee expectations. In light of this discussion, and in line with the new career model, the chapter makes the case for flexible work arrangements that grant employees agency in deciding how, when, and where their work tasks are completed. Finally, the chapter provides a detailed review of four key types of flexible work arrangements that may be capitalized on by human resource professionals.

In Chapter 5, "Equal Rights for Women—Not Yet," William Woska takes a look at the history and failure of the proposed 28th Amendment to the Constitution. The chapter addresses equal rights issues impacting women with examples of what Woska sees as glaring examples which led to the proposed amendment. Next, the chapter discusses the continuing interest and approach that may be used by Congress to again activate the proposed amendment. The chapter concludes with a discussion of the implications of the proposed amendment for organizations and their HRM efforts.

In Chapter 6, "Wearables in the Workplace: An Analysis of Ethical Issues," James S. Bowman and Jonathan West argue that Smartwear may impact daily life like personal computers did near the end of the last century. Their analysis weighs the ethical prospects and problems confronted by human resources managers in the utilization of wearables. To investigate this topic, classical philosophical and modern behavioral approaches to ethics are used. West and Bowman's inquiry begins with the importance of the issue, followed by its evolution and current status. After describing the method of analysis, the chapter examines arguments for and against the efficacy of body-worn computer devices. The conclusion of the chapter discusses accountability standards, model legislation provisions, and regulatory criteria for wearables in the workplace.

In Chapter 7, "A Consideration of Social Media Movements on Gender-Related HR Policy," Angela N. Spranger and Brenna Gonsalves offer an analysis of how current gender-related social media phenomena such as the #MeToo, #TimesUp, and other movements are encouraging changes in business through Human Resource (HR) policy. The chapter analyzes current literature addressing the impact of social media on policies regarding harassment, bullying, and discrimination in the workplace. Further, the authors address the implicit leadership theories (ILTs) in the workplace that influence perceptions of women and women's leadership ability leading in some cases to stereotypes and even discrimination. The chapter also discusses how current trends in the literature help create an understanding of how these movements are encouraging changes in business through policy and training.

In Chapter 8, "Attracting and Retaining Millennials: Is Servant Leadership the Answer?," Shannon O. Jackson, Pamela Chandler Lee, and Jonathan Shoemaker first discuss the millennial generation and their presence in the workplace. Next, the chapter provides a review of leadership research and discusses the relevance of leadership for creating an organizational culture which respects, attracts, and engages millennial workers. The authors' analysis emphasizes the principles of servant leadership and its relevance for the millennial generation. The chapter concludes with recommendations on specific strategies for attracting and retaining this expanding sector of the employee population.

In Chapter 9, "Millennial Workers and the Employee Engagement Phenomenon: Has the Wave Crested?," Angela N. Spranger and Sierra Chen discuss employee engagement and note that in the early years of employee engagement research, practitioner-driven definitions and studies established the framework for the scholarly dialogue to follow. However, in later years, multiple worthy scholarly definitions and analyses of the employee engagement construct have emerged. Spranger and Chen note that since 1990 several instruments and varied studies have dissected the concept, and in both scholarly and practitioner circles some have asked if the employee engagement wave has crested. The chapter asks the question as to whether or not the concept of employee engagement has been exhausted or not? The authors situate their consideration of employee engagement in the framework of individual psychological motivation, review the literature on employee engagement, and connect Kahn's definition of engagement with specific relevance to millennial employees. The chapter concludes by asserting that no, the employee engagement wave has not crested, and proposes new research on the millennial worker's desire to feel seen, safe, and valued.

In Chapter 10, "The Unconscious Bias; Managing Diversity and Inclusion in the Workplace," Ronda Mariani highlights the importance of diversity and inclusion in today's workforce. Mariani notes that globalization and the reduction of borders has forced business to not only understand these concepts; diversity and inclusion but to also embrace the true meaning of what it entails to have a workplace that truly has an understanding of its multicultural foundation. Additionally, she asks and offers responses to the questions of whether or not organizations are really addressing the idea of what it means to have a diverse work environment that promotes inclusion? In offering a response to this question the chapter first discusses the role of bias, the many forms of bias, and how bias effects building diversity and inhibits the proper management of inclusion within the workplace. Mariani suggests that bias is something that all individuals have. And given this reality, questions whether if the end result is to create organizational diversity, what roles and responsibilities then does human resources play in achieving organizations that are well equipped to engage in building human capital that promotes this organizational diversity? An important takeaway from this chapter is that hiring diverse individuals is only the first step, but achieving inclusion without bias is a matter of tactics, training, and a fundamental change in organizational culture.

In Chapter 11, "Solving the "Quarterback Problem": Using Psychological Assessment to Improve Selection Decisions in Professional Sports," Kenneth Yusko, Juliet Aiken, Harold Goldstein, Charles Scherbaum, and Elliott Larson first describe key current challenges in psychological assessment in sports. Next, the chapter reviews the psychological attributes and characteristics that can and should be measured in a professional sports context. Then, the chapter discusses how these attributes and characteristics can be measured (e.g., standardized testing, interviews, player observations and scouting "intel," etc.). The authors then review how these results may be leveraged for different purposes (e.g., selection, training). Finally, the chapter discusses how some of the lessons learned in sports analytics can be generalized to better understand strategic human resources decision making more broadly.

In Chapter 12, "Human Resources Certification: Trends and Acceptance in Industry," J. Adam Shoemaker, Sheri Bias, Sean Gibbons, Henry Adu, and Nicole Hawkins note the importance of certification as a component of demonstrating professionalism in many industries. The chapter focuses on the authors' research on the various human resources certifications offered by credentialing bodies in the human resources industry, namely HRCI and SHRM. The chapter describes in detail the researcher approach (i.e., using Linked-In to analyze hundreds of human resources-related job postings in 6 large metropolitan areas of the U.S. to determine what certifications employers requested as either minimum or preferred requirements). The results of the research are discussed and based upon the results the authors suggest that the human resource management industry has work to do to help employers to see why professional certification is an important indication of professional ability.

REFERENCES

Arthur, M. B., & Rousseau, D. M. (1996). *The boundaryless career: A new employment principle for a new organizational era.* New York, NY: Oxford University Press.

Bersin, J. (2015, January/February). What's in store for HR in 2015, *HR Magazine*, 32–51.

Briscoe, J. P., Hall, D. T., & DeMuth, R. L. F. (2005). Protean and boundaryless career: An empirical exploration. *Journal of Vocational Behavior, 69*(1), 30–47.

Budd, J. W. (2018). *Labor relations* (5th ed.). New York, NY: McGraw-Hill.

Bryan, L. (1990). An ounce of prevention for workplace accidents, *Training and Development Journal*, 44, 101–102.

Cahuc, P., Carcillo, S., & Zilberberg, A. (2014). *Labor economics.* Cambridge, MA: MIT Press.

Cascio, W. F . (2014). Investing in HRD in uncertain times now and in the future. *Advances in Developing Human Resources, 16*(1), 108–122.

Cascio, W. F. (2017, November). Training trends: Macro, micro, and policy issues. *Human Resource Management Review*. Retrieved from https://www.researchgate.net/publi-cation/321055303_Training_trends_Macro_micro_and_policy_issues

Cascio, W. F. (2019). *Managing human resources: Productivity, quality of work life, prof-its*. (11th ed.). New York, NY: McGraw-Hill Education.

Cascio, W. F., & Montealegre, R. (2016). How technology is changing work and organiza-tions. *Annual Review of Organizational Psychology and Organizational Behavior, 3*, 349–375.

Caulfield, N. (2004). Labor relations in Mexico: Historical legacies and some recent trends. *Labor History, 45*(4), 445–467.

Dahling, J., & O'Malley, A. O. (2011). Supportive feedback environments can mend broke performance management systems, *Industrial and Organizational Psychology, 4*(2), 201–203.

Dunlop, J. T. (1958). *Industrial relations system.* New York, NY: Henry Holt.

Ehrenberg, R. G., & Smith, R. S. (2016). *Modern labor economics* (12th ed.). New York, NY: Routledge.

English, S. (2016, November 11). Recruiter page falls victim to huge cyber attack. *Evening Standard*. Retrieved from https://www.standard.co.uk/business/recruiter-page-falls-victim-to-huge-cyber-attack-a3393326.html

Friedman, T. (2016). *Thank you for being late: An optimist's guide to thriving in the age of accelerations.* New York, NY: Farrar, Straus & Giroux.

Gerli, F., Bonesso, S., & Pizzi, C. (2015). Boundaryless career and career success: The im-pact of emotional and social competencies. *Frontiers in Psychology, 6*(1304), 1–17. Retrieved from https://www.ncbi.nlm.nih.gov/pmc/articles/PMC4554953/

Gibson, C., Ziskin, I., & Boudreau, J. (2014, January). What is the future of HR? *Work-force, 30–33*, 48.

Global HR Research. (2016, February 24). *The role of HR in mitigating cyber security threats.* Retrieved from http://www.ghrr.com/the-role-of-hr-in-mitigating-cybersecurity-threats/ http://www.ghrr.com/the-role-of-hr-in-mitigating-cyber-security-threats/

Goler, L., Gale, G., & Grant, A. (2016, November). Let's not kill performance evaluation, *Harvard Business Review*, 90–94.

Gubler, M., Arnold, J., & Combs, C. (2014). Reassessing the protean career concept: Empirical findings, conceptual comments, and measurement. *Journal of Organizational Behavior*, *35*(S1), 23–40.

Gubman, E. L. (1996, November/December). The gauntlet is down. *Journal of Business Strategy*, *17*(6), 33–35.

Heathfield, S. M. (2017, November 11). *What is human resource management?* Retrieved from https://www.thebalancecareers.com/what-is-human-resource-management-1918143

Hirsch, A. S. (2016, January 26). *What emerging adults want in a job: 9 requirements.* Retrieved from https://www.shrm.org/resourcesandtools/hr-topics/employee-relations/pages/emerging-adults.aspx

Hoffman, R., Casnocha, B., & Yeh, C. (2013, June). Tours of duty: The new employer-employee compact, *Harvard Business Review*, 48–58.

Kane, Y. I., & Sherr, I. (2011, June 15). Retail secrets from Apple. *The Wall Street Journal*, A11–A12.

Katz, H. C., Kochan, T. A., & Colvin, A. (2015). *Labor relations in a globalizing world*. Retrieved from https://digitalcommons.ilr.cornell.edu/cgi/viewcontent.cgi?article=1104&context=books

Kaufman, B. E. (2006). Industrial relations and labor institutionalism: A century of boom and bust. *Labor History, 47*(3), 295–318.

Korn Ferry. (2016, December 13). *Korn Ferry futurestep makes 2017 talent trend predictions.* Retrieved from https://www.kornferry.com/press/korn-ferry-futurestep-makes-2017-talent-trend-predictions/

Kristol-Brown, A., & Guay, R. P. (2011). Person-environment fit. In S. Zedeck (Ed.). *APA handbook of industrial and organizational psychology* (Vol. 3, pp. 3–50). Washington, DC: American Psychological Association.

Kuruvilla, S. (1994). *National industrialization strategies and firm level IR/HR practices: Case studies in Malaysia and Philippines* (CAHRS Working Paper #94-070). Ithaca, NY: Cornell University.

Lansbury, R. D., & Wailes, N. (2016). Employment relations in Australia. In G. J. Bamber, R. D. Lansbury, N. Wailes, & C .F. Wright (Eds.), *International and comparative employment relations: Globalization and change*. (pp. 117–137). London, UK: Sage.

Levitz, J. (2010, April 60. UPS thinks outside the box on driver training. *The Wall Street Journal*, B1–B2.

Lindzon, J. (2015, May 20). Welcome to a new era of human resources, *Fast Company*. Retrieved from https://www.fastcompany.com/3045829/welcome-to-the-new-era-of-human-resources

Lublin, J. (2016, July 2016). Job hopping is losing its stigma. *The Wall Street Journal*, B8.

Mathis, R. L., Jackson, J. H., Valentine, S. R., & Meglich, P. A. (2017). *Human resource management* (15th ed.). Boston, MA: Cengage.

Maurer, R. (2014, June 1). How to make your safety training talks effective. *SHRM Online*, Retrieved from https://www.shrm.org/resourcesandtools/hr-topics/risk-management/pages/safety-toolbox-training-talks.aspx

May, K. E. (n.d.). *Work in the 21st century: The changing role of human resources*. Retrieved from http://www.siop.org/tip/backissues/tipjan98/may.aspx

Meister, J. (2016, January 7). Consumerization of HR: 10 trends companies will follow in 2016. *Forbes*. Retrieved from https://www.forbes.com/sites/jeannemeister/2016/01/07/consumerization-of-hr-10-trends-innovative-companies-will-follow-in-2016/#12c0b1ec6b5a

Meister, J. (2017, January 5). The employee experience is the future of work: 10 HR trends for 2017. *Forbes*. Retrieved from https://www.forbes.com/sites/jeannemeister/2017/01/05/the-employee-experience-is-the-future-of-work-10-hr-trends-for-2017/#5e1bd66b20a6

Mello, J. A. (2019). *Strategic human resource management*. Boston, MA: Cengage.

Miller, S., Nagele-Piazza, L., & Smith, A. (2017, January 3). *Top 7 workplace legal trends for 2017*. Retrieved from https://www.shrm.org/resourcesandtools/legal-and-compliance/employment-law/pages/workplace-legal-trends-for-2017.aspx

Mone, E., Eisinger, C., Guggenheim, K., Price, Price, B., & Stine, C. (2011). Performance management at the wheel: Diving employee engagement in organizations, *Journal of Business & Psychology, 26*(2), 205–212.

Napathorn, C., & Chanprateep, S. (2011). Recent labor relations and collective bargaining in Thailand. *Interdisciplinary Journal of Research in Business, 1*(6), 66–81.

Newman, J. M., Gerhart, B., & Milkovich, G. T. (2017). *Compensation* (12th ed.). New York, NY: McGraw-Hill.

Noe, R. A. (2017). *Employee training and development* (7th ed.). New York, NY: McGraw-Hill.

Noe, R. A., Hollenbeck, J. R., Gerhart, B., & Wright, P. M. (2019). *Human resource management: Gaining a competitive advantage* (11th ed.). New York, NY: McGraw-Hill.

Noe, R. A., & Links, L. (2014). *It's about people: How performance management helps middle market companies grow faster*. Columbus, OH: National Center for the Middle Market, Ohio State University Fisher College of Business, GE Capital.

O'Brien, P. J., & Kessler, J. H. (2014). *The global employer: The labor relations and collective agreements issue*. Retrieved from https://digitalcommons.ilr.cornell.edu/cgi/viewcontent.cgi?article=1090&context=lawfirms

Pate-Cornell, E., & Cox, L. (2014). Improving risk management: From lame excuses to principled practice. *Risk Analysis: An International Journal, 34*(7), 1228–1239.

Phillips, F. (2017, January 5). *Top five New Year's predictions for the gig economy*. Retrieved from https://www.jdsupra.com/legalnews/top-five-new-year-s-predictions-for-the-37360/

Pofeldt, E. (2015, May 25). *Shocker: 40% of workers now have "contingent" jobs, says U.S. government*. *Forbes*. Retrieved from https://www.forbes.com/sites/elainepofeldt/2015/05/25/shocker-40-of-workers-now-have-contingent-jobs-says-u-s-government/#2e0f545514be

Polyhart, R. E., & Kim, T. (2014). Strategic recruiting. In K. Y. T. Tu & D. M. Cable (Eds.), *The Oxford handbook of recruitment* (pp. 5–20). Oxford, UK: Oxford University Press.

Polyhart, R. E., Schmitt, N., & Tippins, N.T. (2017). Solving the supreme problem: 100 years of selection and recruitment at the *Journal of Applied Psychology*. *Journal of Applied Psychology, 102*(3), 291–304.

Quttainah, M. A. (2005). *Human resources management.* Retrieved from https://www.re-searchgate.net/publication/256064926_Human_Resources_Management

Ruona, W., & Gibson, S, (2004). The making of the twenty-first HR: An analysis of the convergence of HRM, HRD, and OD. *Human Resource Management, 43*, 49–66.

Schrader, B. (2015, October 15). Here's why the freelancer economy is on the rise. *Fast Company*. Retrieved from https://www.fastcompany.com/3049532/heres-why-the-freelancer-economy-is-on-the-rise

Sims, R. R. (2002). *Organizational success through effective human resources management*. Westport, CT: Quorum Books.

Sims, R. R. (2007). *Human resource management: Contemporary issues, challenges and opportunities*. Charlotte, NC: Information Age Publishing.

Snapka, P., & Copikova, A. (2011). Balanced scorecard and compensation. *International Conference on Business and Economics Research, 16*, 42–46. Retrieved from http://www.ipedr.com/vol16/8-ICBER2011-A00022.pdf

Snell, S. A., & Morris, S. S. (2019). *Managing human resources* (18th ed.). Boston, MA: Cengage.

Vorhauser-Smith, S. (2017, January 5). *The top five talent management predictions for 2017.* Retrieved from http://www.hcamag.com/hr-news/top-five-talent-management-predictions-for-2017-229074.aspx

Waters, S., & Alonso, A. (2017, January 5). *Five trends in talent*. The SHRMBlog. Retrieved from https://blog.shrm.org/blog/five-trends-in-talent

CHAPTER 2

GLOBALIZATION AND HUMAN RESOURCE MANAGEMENT

Ronald R. Sims

The environment in which today's organizations find themselves continues to be more globalized as the world is becoming a "global village." This globalization is driven in part by continued growth in multinational investment to include more and more companies entering into alliances with foreign companies, exporting their products overseas, and building plants in other countries. All of the human resource management (HRM) challenges, issues and opportunities discussed in previous chapters in this book are interrelated conceptually and operationally in the international context.

This chapter discusses a number of the HRM challenges, issues and opportunities HRM professionals and their organizations will need to address in today's and tomorrow's global world of work. The chapter first takes a look at today's global organization and some HRM issues. Next, the discussion turns to the globalization of business and factors affecting HRM in global markets before focusing on an analysis of levels of global or international and HRM operations. Finally, the chapter discusses globalization and implications and impacts on HRM in the future.

Human Resources Management Issues, Challenges and Trends:
"Now and Around the Corner", pages 31–52.

TODAY'S GLOBAL ORGANIZATION AND
HUMAN RESOURCE MANAGEMENT ISSUES

For the past decades, there have been profound changes in the international business scene. With geographic national borders being almost replaced by multinational firms, and a heightened level of labor mobility around the globe, the implication of HRM to design and develop firms' global business strategy, and to direct individuals (i.e. managers and professional staff alike) for working in different countries, is undoubtedly significant. Rosalie Tung (2016) has recently suggested that in the past three decades or so, globalization/regionalization, migration and reverse migration (also referred to as "brain circulation"), the ascendancy of emerging markets, the demand for people with a global mindset, and the worldwide war for talent have brought about fundamental changes to the nature, magnitude, and *raison d'etre* for HRM in a global context. And, that these changes require HRM professionals and their organizations to adopt new lenses to fully understand the dynamics that impact global or international human resource management policies and practices.

Organizations are attempting to gain competitive advantage, which can be provided by international expansion as these countries are new markets with large numbers of potential customers. For example, organizations that are producing below their capacity can use expansion to possibly increase sales and profits. Still other organizations are building production facilities in other countries as a means of capitalizing on those countries' lower labor costs for relatively unskilled jobs.

Importing and exporting goods and services is the easiest way to "go global." India has the world's second-largest population (1.2 billion people) and a growing middle class, so businesses are increasingly trying to expand their exports to that country (*U.S. News & World Report*, 2016). According to Snell and Morris (2019), Apple is one of those companies. Although the iPhone dominates the U.S. market, only 5 percent of smartphones in India are iPhone. Partnerships, mergers and takeovers are other ways companies are addressing globalization.

The reality is that most organizations now function in the global economy. For example, U.S. businesses are entering international markets at the same time that foreign companies are entering the U.S. market. Consider the reality that many American and foreign firms have partnered with Chinese firms to expand in China, which is the world's most populous country, with 1.3 billion people. In turn, cross-border mergers continue to increase (Noe, Hollenbeck, Gerhart & Wright, 2019; Shen, 2016) as Chinese and other foreign companies are merging with American firms (Sheng, 2016). Consider also that it has been suggested that globalization is the dominant driving force in the world economy, reshaping societies and politics as it changes lives (Cascio, 2019).

Globalization has also resulted in the blurring of national identities of products. Many may think of Budweiser as an American beer, but its maker (Anheuser-Busch) is owned by a Belgian company called InBev. Like many other companies, Anheuser-Busch InBev has been purchasing or partnering with factories and brands in other countries such as China and Mexico to expand its sales. Similarly, BMW is a German brand, but the automaker builds cars in the United States, China and elsewhere (Choi & Schreiner, 2014; Duprey, 2013; Snell & Morris, 2019).

Giant multinational corporations such as Nestlé, Unilever, and AstraZeneca, began to lose their national identities as they integrated and coordinated product design, manufacturing, sales, and services on a worldwide basis. Further, many other U.S. firms, for example, generate a substantial portion of their sales and profits from other countries; companies such as Coca-Cola, Exxon/Mobil, and Microsoft derive a significant portion of total sales and profits from outside the United States (Dewhurst, Harris & Heywood, 2012). In 1982 GE, for example, generated 20 percent of its sales outside the United States and 70 percent in 2017 (Mann & Spegele, 2017). Many foreign organizations have taken advantage of growth opportunities in the United States. For example, Toyota, based in Japan, has grown its market share and increased its number of jobs in the United States and elsewhere in North America. Also, Toyota, Honda, Nissan, and other Japanese automobile manufacturers, electronic firms, and suppliers have maintained operations in the United States (Mathis, Jackson, Valentine, & Meglich, 2017).

Higginbottom (2017) has recently argued that these are indeed "uncertain times" (i.e., for global (and local) organizations and HRM professionals). The last several years have played host to seismic political events such as Brexit and the election of Donald Trump as the U.S. president in 2016. The acronym VUCA which stands for volatility, uncertainty, complexity and ambiguity is a trendy management term that perfectly encapsulates the conditions that many multinationals are operating under.

Brexit, for example, which stemmed from a slim majority of U.K. voters deciding in a June 23, 2016 referendum, that they no longer wanted to be governed largely from a bureaucracy located in Brussels, Belgium, continues to pose a serious threat to the European Union. The EU and Britain are currently negotiating the terms of their separation which will have major implications for global businesses and many observers predict that, at least in the short term, this exit will have a negative impact on the British economy (see, Amadeo, 2018a; Partington, 2018; Romei, 2018).

Numerous free-trade agreements forged between nations over the past 60 years, like the General Agreement on Tariffs and Trade (GATT) in 1948 and the North American Free Trade Agreement (NAFTA) in 1994, helped quicken the pace of globalization. However, the election of Donald Trump as president of the U.S. in 2016 has created uncertainty for organizations making their location decisions in his efforts to renegotiate, for example, NAFTA which is the world's largest free trade agreement. In an effort to keep companies from moving production outside the United States, Trump announced a 35 percent tariff on steel and a 10 percent tariff on aluminum on Canada, Mexico and the EU. President Trump campaigned on renegotiating NAFTA and frequently berated companies seeking to build plants in Mexico, for example, particularly when it entails closing plants in the United States (see Amadeo, 2018b; Stoll & Colias, 2016).

While factors like Berxit and the election of Trump as the U.S. president are impacting globalization, perhaps none is more important that the rise of Internet technologies (Dreyfuss, 2017; Quora, 2017; Sato, 2014). The Internet, as it continues to develop, has certainly changed the ways that people live and work. Indeed, in some industries, such as music and e-commerce, it has completely revolutionized the rules of the game (Cascio, 2019).

The Internet gives everyone in the organization, at any level and in every functional areas, the ability to access a mind-boggling array of information-instantaneously from anywhere. Ideas can be zapped around the globe in the blink of an eye instead of seeping out over month or years. A global marketplace has been created by factors such as the following:

- Global telecommunications enhanced by fiber optics, satellites, and computer technology.
- E-commerce that makes organizations global from the moment their Web sites are up and running, as customers from around the world log on.
- Financial markets are now open 24 hours a day around the world (Lioudis, 2018).
- Cost pressures (that prod firms to move where labor and other resources are cheapest), coupled with a search for new markets (as firms and consumers around the world seek foreign goods and services).
- The integration of cultures and values through international travel, as well as the spread of goods such as music, food, and clothing. In combination, these have led to common consumer demands around the world (Tarique, Briscoe, & Schuler, 2016).
- The emergence of global standards and regulations for trade, commerce, finance, products, and services (Gunther, 2005).

The rapid increase in telecommunications and information technology enables work to be done more rapidly, efficiently, and effectively all over the world. Friedman (2016 has suggested that an expanding high-tech, information-based economy increasingly defines globalization and shapes the business cycles within it. That is, much of the flow of capital, labor, services, and goods among Asia, America and Europe are technology based. Without chips, screens, and software help from Asia, the U.S. economy would grind to a halt. Clearly, open borders continue to allow new ideas and technology to flow freely around the globe, accelerating productivity growth and allowing businesses to be more competitive than they have been in past decades.

Globalization and HRM

Due to globalization, companies have to balance a complicated set of issues related to different geographies, including different cultures, employment laws, and business practices, and the safety of employees and facilities abroad. HRM issues underlie each of these and other concerns. They include such things as dealing with employees today and tomorrow who, via the Internet and social media, are better informed about global job opportunities and are willing to pursue them, even if it means working for competing companies or foreign companies. Determining the knowledge and skill base of workers worldwide and figuring out how best to hire and train them (sometimes with materials that must be translated into a number of different languages) is also an issue for companies in the global environment.

There is every indication that the recent social and political changes have contributed to globalization and the movement toward international competition. Despite the reasons an organization may have for expanding operations globally, HRM is critical to the success of any global initiative. If one adopts the basic principle that HRM strategy must be derived from corporate strategy and that people do determine an organization's success or failure, then the HRM function needs to be a key strategic partner in any global operations. Still, in some instances HRM is often neglected in the planning and establishment of global endeavors. Despite such neglect, today's and tomorrow's HRM professionals must continue to develop their own and other organizational members competencies or skills in the ever-growing international context of the world of work. This means not only understanding the events and factors that continue to increase the global nature of business but also their role in helping to improve their organization's competitive advantage in global environments.

UNDERSTANDING THE GLOBAL ENVIRONMENT

It is important for HRM professionals to continue to recognize that because political, economic, social and technological conditions are constantly shifting around the world, how employees are managed in those changing environments will need to shift as well. HRM professionals can better understand the global environment by regularly conducting a political, economic, sociocultural, and technological (PEST) analysis which can act as an audit of a company's environmental influences to assist in determining the corporate strategy and accompanying HRM response(s) (see, for example, Post, 2017; Snell & Morris, 2019).

By conducting a PEST analysis HRM professionals and other organizational leaders are able to scan different contextual environments to understand the long-term trends and how they might impact a company. A PEST analysis can help HRM professionals to 1) spot business or human resource opportunities, and give them advanced warning of threats, 2) identify trends in the business environment so they can proactively adapt to these changes, 3) help to avoid implementing

HRM practices in a particular country where they may fail, and 4) put an end to old habits and assumptions about how people should be managed to help bring about innovative ideas for the entire organization.

Political Factors

Government regulations and legal issues affect a company's ability to be profitable and successful, and this factor looks at how that can happen. Issues that must be considered include tax guidelines, copyright and property law enforcement, political stability, trade regulations, social and environmental policy, employment laws and safety regulations. Companies should also consider their local and federal power structure and discuss how anticipated shifts in power could affect their business.

HRM professionals can assess the political factors by examining a country's labor laws, property rights, and patents. When Lincoln Electric, the Ohio-based welding company, for example, started operations in Brazil, they could not offer their yearly bonus program based on performance because any bonuses paid for two consecutive years became a legal entitlement (Siegel & Larson, 2009).

Property rights in many countries are poorly protected by governments. Whoever has the political power or authority can seize others' property with few or no repercussions. Civil unrest can also lead to the poor enforcement of property rights. Businesses have less incentive to invest in countries or locate factories in countries experiencing strife. Another issue that has implications for global companies relates to the intellectual property rights—rights related to patents, trademarks, and so forth.

Economic Factors

This factor examines the outside economic issues that can play a role in a company's success. Items for HRM professionals and other organizational members to consider include economic growth, exchange, inflation and interest rates, economic stability, anticipated shifts in commodity and resource costs, unemployment policies, credit availability, unemployment policies, and the business cycle followed in the country.

By looking at trends around market and trade cycles, specific industry changes, customer preferences, and country economic growth forecasts HRM professionals and other organizational members can best understand the economic issues that are bound to have an impact on the company. For example, in 1995, the World Trade Organization (WTO) was formalized as a cooperative forum for country leaders to come together and increase free trade across the world. As of December 2017, the WTO member countries represented over 164 member-nations and covered 97 percent of all international trade (Amadeo, 2018c). In addition, countries are continually negotiating free trade agreements with each other in hopes of increasing their economic activity.

Since China joined the WTO in 2001, its economy has grown dramatically, drastically altering its political and trading relationship with many nations. In a strange twist of fate, Xi Jinping, the leader of the communist world and China's president, has taken to defending free trade and globalization, whereas U.S. president Donald Trump, leader of the free world, has taken to attacking them as noted previously (Elliott & Wearden, 2017).

Sociocultural Factors

The sociocultural factor analyzes the demographic and cultural aspects of the company's market. These factors help companies examine consumer needs and determine what pushes them to make purchases. Among the items that should be examined are communications, religion, values and ideologies, education, social structure, demographics, population growth rates, age distribution, cultural limitations, lifestyle attitude, attitudes towards work and job market trends.

An understanding of sociocultural factors has important implications when it comes to a company's decision about when and how to do business in a country. For example, because of low labor costs and language similarities, many U.S. businesses have found India an attractive place to locate their facilities, particularly call centers.

By recognizing and accommodating different ideologies, religious beliefs, communication styles, education systems, and social structures, HRM professionals and other organizational members stand a better chance of understanding the culture of a host country—a country in which an international business operates. Even in countries that have close language or cultural links, HRM practices can be dramatically different. For example, employers might be expected to provide employees with meals while at work and transportation between home and work. In most of the Islamic Middle East, it is completely acceptable to ask coworkers very personal questions about their children, especially their sons, but never about their wives (Tulshyan, 2010; Vollmer, 2015).

Technological Factors

Technology issues affect how an organization delivers its product or service to the marketplace. Specific items that need to be scrutinized include, but are not limited to, government spending on the maturity of manufacturing equipment, information systems, technological research, technological advancements, the life cycle of current technology, the role of the Internet and how any changes to it may play out, and the impact of potential information technology changes. Even in less-developed countries where manufacturing is typically stronger due to low cost of labor and high cost of capital-intensive equipment, labor-saving technology is becoming more affordable and accessible. Take, for instance, a textile factor in Vietnam. It is more cost effective for the factory to purchase high-tech threading equipment to spin the cotton into thread than to hire hundreds of people to

TABLE 2.1.   Sample Pest Analysis

Political	Economic	Sociocultural	Technical
• New state tax policies for accounting • New employment laws for employee handbook maintenance • Political instability in a foreign partner country	• International economic growth • Changes in interest rates	• Shift in educational requirements and changing career attitudes • Population growth rate	• Automated processes in the industry • Rate of innovation • Changes in technology incentives

thread the cotton by hand, even when the average wage for such employees is less than $100 a month. Just like the other factors, companies should consider generational shifts and their related technological expectation to figure out how they will affect who will use their product and how it's delivered (Snell & Morris, 2019).

While advances in technology have pushed for more service-based jobs, information systems and technology platforms have also increased the rate at which these services can be traded across countries. Along with the creation of the WTO, 1995 also signifies the beginning of the Internet era mentioned early which is a major driver of the increase in globalization.

Table 2.1 provides an example of PEST analysis that can give HRM professionals and other organizational members a clear understanding of how this works:

Every country varies in terms of its political, economic, sociocultural and technological systems. These variations directly influence the types of HRM systems that must be developed to accommodate the particular situation. The extent to which these differences affect a company depends on how involved the company is in global markets.

Today, employees around the world continue to become empowered to compete without the need of a large company. For example, many websites such as guru.com have developed an online marketplace where individuals can offer various services and compete for business throughout the world. Consider the reality that one might be interested in developing a new website for their company. By going to the Internet one can select various individuals offering specific services. They may be from different parts of the world. In conclusion, these PEST factors shift the way companies are formed and how they and their HRM professionals go about managing their human resources in a global environment.

ANALYZING A COMPANY'S LEVEL OF INTERNATIONAL AND HRM OPERATIONS

Today's international business operations can take several different forms. A large percentage of these operations carry on their international business with only limited facilities and minimal representation in foreign countries. Others have extensive facilities and personnel in various countries of the world. Managing these resources effectively, and integrating their activities to achieve global advantage, is a challenge to a company's leaders and HRM professionals.

Often we hear companies referred to as "multinational" or "international." However, it is important for HRM professionals to understand the different levels of participation in international markets. This is especially important because as a company becomes more involved in international trade, different types of HRM challenges, problems, and opportunities arise.

Bartlett and Ghoshal (1991) identified the following four international organizational models:

- Decentralized federation in which each national unit is managed as a separate entity that seeks to optimize its performance in the local environment. (This is the traditional multinational corporation).
- Coordinated federation in which the center develops sophisticated management systems enabling it to maintain overall control, although scope is given to local management to adopt practices that recognize local market conditions.
- Centralized hub in which the focus is on the global market rather than on local markets. Such organizations are truly global rather than multinational.
- Transnational in which the corporation develops multi-dimensional strategic capacities directed towards competing globally but also allows local responsiveness to market requirements.

Adler (2008) offers another categorization of the four various levels of international participation from which a company may choose and includes the following levels of involvement or participation: domestic, international, transnational, multinational. The four basic types of organizations differ in the in degree to which international activities are separated to respond to the local regions and integrated to achieve global efficiencies.

Domestic. Most organizations begin by operating within a domestic marketplace. For example, a business that starts in the U.S. marketplace must recruit, hire, train, and compensate their employees who are usually drawn from the local labor market. The focus of the selection and training programs is often on the employees' technical competence to perform job-related duties and to some extent on interpersonal skills. In addition, because the company is usually involved in only one labor market, determining the market rate of pay for various jobs is relatively easy.

As the company grows it might choose to build additional facilities in different parts of the country to reduce the costs of transporting the products over large distances. In deciding where to locate these facilities, the company must consider the attractiveness of the local labor markets. Various parts of the country may have different cultures that make those areas more or less attractive according to the work ethics of the potential employees. Similarly, the potential employees in the different areas may vary greatly because of differences in educational systems.

Finally, local pay rates may differ. However, it is important to note that in most instances, companies functioning at the domestic level face an environment with very similar political, economic, sociocultural, and technological situations, although the variation might be observed across states and geographic areas.

International. As more competitors enter the domestic market, companies face the possibility of losing market share; thus they often seek other markets for their products. This usually means entering international markets, initially by exporting products but ultimately by building production facilities in other countries. The international corporation is essentially a domestic firm that builds on its existing capabilities to penetrate overseas markets. Companies such as Procter & Gamble, Honda and General Electric used this approach to gain access to Europe—they essentially adapted existing products for overseas markets without changing much else about their normal operations (Snell & Morris, 2019).

The decision to participate in international competition raises a host of HRM issues. All the problems regarding locating facilities are magnified. For example, HRM professionals must consider whether a particular location provides an environment where human resources can be successfully acquired and managed.

Global. The global corporation, on the other hand, can be viewed as a multinational frim that maintains control of its operations worldwide from the country in which it is headquartered. Japanese companies, such as NEC and Matsuhita, tend to treat the world market as a unified whole and try to combine their activities in each country to maximize their efficiencies on a global scale. These companies operate much like a domestic firm, except that they view the whole world as their marketplace.

Global organizations compete on state-of-the-art, top-quality products and services and do so with the lowest cost possible. Whereas MNCs attempt to develop identical products distributed worldwide, global companies increasingly emphasize flexibility and mass customization of products to meet the needs of particular clients. MNCs are usually driven to locate facilities in a country as a means of reaching that country's market or lowering production costs, and the company must deal with the differences across the countries. Global organizations, on the other hand, choose to locate a facility based on the ability to effectively, efficiently, and flexibly produce a product or service and attempt to create synergy through the cultural differences.

This creates the need for HRM systems that encourage flexible production (thus presenting a host of HRM issues). These companies proactively consider the sociocultural, political, economic, and technological systems to determine where production facilities can be located to provide a competitive advantage. Global companies have multiple headquarters spread across the globe, resulting in less hierarchically structured organizations that emphasize decentralized decision making. This results in the need for HRM systems that recruit, develop, retain, and use employees who are competent transnationally.

Transnational. Finally, a transnational corporation attempts to achieve the local responsiveness of a multinational corporation while also achieving the efficiencies of a global firm. To balance this "global/local" dilemma, a transnational uses a network structure that coordinates specialized facilities positioned around the world. More specifically, transnational corporations use geo-diversity to great advantage, placing their top executives and core corporate functions in different countries to gain a competitive edge through the availability of talent or capital, low costs, or proximity to their most important customers. Of course, it is all made possible by the Internet, as improved communication facilitates an integrated global network of operations.

By using this flexible structure, a transnational provides autonomy to independent country operations but brings these separate activities together into an integrated whole. For most companies, the transnational form represents an ideal, rather than a reality. McDonald's is an example of a transnational corporation, especially with culture-specific food items, like India's vegetarian McAloo Tikki, the McKebab in Israel, or a Hawaiian Deluxe Breakfast complete with span, rice, eggs, and hash browns. With over 31,000 restaurants across 119 countries serving 58 million people each day, it makes sense that McDonald's overseas revenue makes up nearly 65 percent of their total revenue, and that they cater McDonalds' core burger-fries-and-shakes menu to local tastes (Johnson, 2011).

The development of transnationals has led to a fundamental rethinking about the nature of a multinational company. Does it have a home country? What does headquarters mean? Is it possible to fragment corporate functions like HRM globally? To be sure, organizational structure directly affects all HRM functions from recruitment through retirement because to be effective, HRM must be integrated into the overall strategy of the organization. Indeed, from the perspective of strategic management, the fundamental problem is to keep the strategy, structure, and HRM dimensions of the organization in direct alignment (See Briscoe & Schuler, 2012) while being respectful of local country laws or regulations.

GLOBALIZATION AND IMPLICATIONS
AND IMPACTS FOR HRM IN THE FUTURE

Entry into international markets creates a host of HRM issues, challenges, problems, and opportunities that must be addressed by HRM professionals and other organizational members if a company is to not only survive but also thrive in a global environment. Once the choice has been made to compete in a global arena, companies must seek to manage employees who are sent to foreign countries as well as local employees. And this results in another issue facing international organizations, the extent to which their HRM practices should either 'converge' worldwide to be basically the same in each location, or 'diverge' to be differentiated in response to local requirements. There is a natural tendency for managerial traditions in the parent company to shape to the nature of key decisions, but there are strong arguments for giving as much local autonomy as possible in order to ensure that local requirements are sufficiently taken into account. (This is known as the global/local dilemma) (see Andrews, 2011). Convergence may be increasing as a result of the following factors:

- The power of markets
- The importance of cost
- Quality and productivity pressures
- The development of like-minded international cadres
- The widespread practice of benchmarking 'best practices.'

However, before focusing on these challenges it is important for HRM professionals to first understand what is meant by international human resources management (IHRM) and the different levels of participation in international markets. This is especially important because as noted previously a company becomes more involved in international trade, different types of HRM issues, challenges, problems, and opportunities arise.

Broadly defined, global or IHRM is the process of procuring, allocating, and effectively utilizing human resources in an international business. More specifically, global or international human resource management (IHRM) is the process of employing, developing and rewarding people in international or global organizations. It involves the world-wide management of people, not just the management of expatriates. An international organization or firm is one in which operations take place in subsidiaries overseas, which rely on the business expertise or manufacturing capacity of the parent company. Such companies or organizations bring with them their own management attitudes and business styles. HRM professionals of such organizations cannot afford to ignore the international influences on their work.

IHRM involves a number of issues not present when the activities of the company or organization are confined to one country. For example,

- The variety of international organizational models that exist
- The extent to which HRM policy and practice should vary in different countries. (This is also known as the issue of Convergence and Divergence).
- The problem of managing people in different cultures and environments.
- The approaches used to select, deploy, develop and reward expatriates who could be nationals of the parent company or 'third-country nationals' (TCNs)—nationals of countries other than the parent company who work abroad in subsidiaries of that organization.

How Does Globalization Affect HRM?

Globalization has made us a multicultural society which has implications on HRM professionals and their function in a company's host and other countries. There are four theoretical frameworks that can help HRM professionals and other company employees explore the influences on HRM across international bound-aries, including: cultural, institutional, universal and contingency perspectives (White, 2015).

The cultural perspective suggests there are clear cultural differences between nationalities and these should be recognized. International corporations which accept and recognize these cultural differences in managing employees through HRM practices will be successful in their host countries.

The institutional perspective accepts there are differences that need to be understood and recognized within societies and these have an impact on the HRM practices, but it rejects the concept that certain practices, such as recruitment and selection, performance management and reward lead to improved organizational performance as these practices may mean different things within different societies.

The universal perspective approach claims that certain HRM practices, such as performance management, recruitment and selection and reward lead to higher organizational performance. It has been suggested that HRM practices that are successful in the home country should be adopted into the host country (Marchington & Wilkinson, 2012). A criticism of this viewpoint is that it does not take into account internal and external factors, such as the characteristics of the organization or the culture of its host country (White, 2015).

Finally, the contingency perspective depends on both the internal and external factors of an organization for the take up of HR practices. The key features for HRM are the location of the organization, the product market, the organizations life cycle stage and if the organization is privately owned or a joint venture. Each of these factors will have an effect on HRM, for example where the organization is based will depend on the HR practices and policies it deploys.

Impacts and Implications on HRM

Given the above one can argue that the impacts and implications on HRM in global or international or multinational corporations depends on the type of organization, it's product life cycle and the core belief of its hierarchy (Marchington & Wilkinson, 2012). Edwards (2011) takes this view further and outlines that the influences are categorized into home country/country of origin effects, dominance effects, international integration effects and host country effects.

The home country/country of origin view supports the enforcing of headquarter HRM practices from the home country across all countries where there is a subsidiary. All countries where there is a subsidiary for the multinational corporation will adopt a single approach to HRM practices, such as recruitment and selection, reward and performance management. Using this model means the global or multinational or international company doesn't take into account local culture and practice when implementing HRM practices.

The dominance effect supports a standard approach of HRM practices across all countries for the multinational, global or international corporation as this is seen to be best practice internationally. Again this doesn't take into account local culture and practices in which the international corporation operates.

The international integration effect relates to the extent at which the international, global or multinational corporations build closer relationships across different borders. In some instances, the corporation may move their headquarters from their home country to other regional countries, adopting their exiting HRM policies while also bringing some best HRM practice from the home country.

The host country effect adopts the HRM practices and policies of the host country in which the corporation operates in. This could be due to it being too difficult to enforce the home country HRM practices and policies due to cultural differences or the practices and policies in place do not need to be changed.

Globalization is seen to be a complex and controversial subject with many supporters and critics. As briefly discussed earlier, the implications on HRM professionals and their functions for international corporations are dependent on a variety of factors. Market pressures and local influences, such as culture, have strong implications on HRM practices implemented by global corporations with research supporting the view of the complexities and different influences. It can be argued therefore that there is no one best fit for HRM practices for all organizations across the globe, but there are some best fit processes that can be incorporated along with the local culture and business practice.

Today's organizations are becoming more international and having systems, policies and process in place to be able to deal with this changing landscape of a host companies' workforce is paramount. A system, for example, for employees that supports multiple language and different data formats will help improve engagement as employees can manage their own data in their native language. This also enables organizations to roll out employee self-service access to other countries, as well as providing non-host country nationals who work for the corporations to use the application in their chosen language.

Global HRM is an umbrella term that includes all aspects of an organization's HRM, payroll, and talent management processes operating on a global scale. As technological innovations make it easier for organizations to conduct business across the world, global expansion and accompanying HRM policies and procedures as noted earlier has become an increasing reality—if not necessity. Operating human resources across geographic and cultural boundaries can often prove difficult for global organizations. Nonetheless, with the widespread use of technology, the ability to communicate with anyone around the world and access to new and varied markets, international HRM issues like those briefly discussed below are important for HRM professionals to grasp.

Language. As briefly noted earlier, one of the more obvious effects of workforce globalization is the need for language services such as translation. Employees from foreign countries who speak different languages often must travel to meet or communicate with others inside the organization. This has caused more companies to hire foreign language translators. Translators help employees from different countries communicate during meetings or at events. They also help U.S. employees traveling to foreign countries interact with the local employees, partners and customers.

Culture. Developing a global organizational culture is much more complex than building one domestically. The point of a common culture is that employees share norms and values. When a corporation's employees come from varying cultures themselves, they inherently have distinct differences in their own view of work, communication and other aspects of the company. Thus, HRM professionals must work diligently to train employees on cultural sensitivity and find common points shared by employees throughout the organization. Virtual work teams often are used to promote cross-cultural teamwork.

Localization. Even while trying to create a global culture, HRM professionals often have to emphasize localization in each country. This correlates with strategies used by companies as they enter foreign markets and try to build good rapport with local communities. This means having strong hiring and training processes at national and local levels and compensation and motivation systems that fit well with each country of operation.

Compliance with International Laws. One effect of globalization on HRM is the need for businesses to understand and apply the laws of many different jurisdictions to the particular business. The federal government sets out a number of tax and labor laws that businesses operating in the United States must comply with, but there may also be local and regional laws that apply to companies that operate in different states or different countries.

As companies decide to expand into the global marketplace or as they hire employees from diverse geographic and cultural backgrounds, they may have to adapt to new labor laws and tax liabilities. Doing business in Europe, for example, will require the firm to pay value added tax. Hiring employees at branch locations in different locations might change the requirements on minimum wage, tax allowances or working hours. Also, hiring employees who are non-naturalized US citizens might require HRM to apply for work visas and report economic data to the federal government. Compliance with international law can be an issue for companies that have little to no experience in the global environment, because these laws tend to be complex and sometimes difficult to implement. Keeping well-informed of the legal requirements for the business's operations can help alleviate some of this complexity. Therefore, understanding a countries' laws is vitally essential to the organization because any breach of them will have a serious impact not only on the business's financial well-being but also on its reputation.

Diversity Recruitment & Cultural Diversity. Globalization makes for a larger labor pool from which to choose, but it also increases the possibility of language and cultural barriers in the recruitment process. If the company does not address such barriers, it can make the recruitment process increasingly time-consuming and difficult. HRM professionals must adapt to the different customs and cultures when hiring employees in different countries. Language barriers also may necessitate hiring bilingual employees and adapting employee documents, such as employee manuals and training materials, into different languages.

Globalization also means that companies of all sizes are now interacting with customers and stakeholders from diverse cultures, languages and social backgrounds. In response, many HRM professionals seek to hire employees from equally diverse backgrounds. Companies engaging in this diversity recruitment recognize the value of having people on staff that their customers can relate to, and they know that having a team of diverse people contributes to the range of ideas and influences within the organization.

Successful diversity recruitment in international HRM is dependent upon understanding and maintaining cultural diversity. Working with people from different locations or from different cultural backgrounds means adapting the company's work style to new ideas, new ways of communicating and unfamiliar social practices. If the company hires an employee from England, for example, the employee might have different ideas about how to manage employees or on how to run technology processes based on their own experiences back home. Being open to new work styles and cultural differences is the hallmark of cultural diversity in HRM.

Benefits and Compensation. Benefits and compensation are the backbone of any HRM strategy, but in international HRM, benefits and compensation are even more important in focusing on the work-life balance of employees. The idea behind work-life balance is to provide employees with programs and initiatives that improve both their personal and professional lives. This is considered part of international HRM, because many multinational companies have already implemented programs such as flexible working time, paternity leave, extended holidays and on-site childcare. In fact, many nations around the world, including much of Europe, mandate these programs by law. Implementing them on the local scale is one of the challenges and, ultimately, rewards of international HRM.

Training and Development. Related to the idea of benefits and compensation in international HRM are training and professional development programs. Training programs typically encompass in-house seminars and meetings designed to give employees on-the-job knowledge of skills that are important to doing business globally. HRM might offer language classes to expatriates, for example, or a company might host language classes to give its call center staff an edge in telephone sales. It might also teach its employees how to use a new global software platform. This emphasis on training seeks to give the company a competitive edge in the global marketplace by honing the employees' diversity emphasis.

Professional development is concerned with providing employees opportunities to achieve their career-related goals and very often encompasses the "extra" training that HRM provides to its employees, such as providing them resources to earn a college or university degree, allowing them to attend networking events and conferences, global training seminars and other specific competency-based programs. Professional development also helps expatriates, for example, to hone their skills in global marketing, international business development and finance trends. Professional development is important to globalization because it creates a win-win situation. The employees feel as though the organization is concerned with providing a range of skills and competencies for their employees. Likewise, the organization benefits from the added skills and connections that the employees who take advantage of professional development programs acquire.

Impact of Globalization on the HRM Function and Professionals

As globalization continues to expand, the functions within global or international companies all are impacted. It is not unusual for employees to fear being replaced by a cheaper workforce overseas and executives are required to learn the various cultural differences and regulatory environments in which they operate. But in the author's view none of the departments and employees are affected as much as HRM and professionals that must manage the workforce at home and abroad. Technology is available that can help HRM professionals manage the processes involved in globalization, but there are downsides for HRM professionals and other leaders and managers who must deal with languages, time differences and employment rules around the world.

Job and Roles Redefined. One of the positive aspects of globalization on HRM is redefining the role of the HRM professional within global organizations. Instead of managing the minutia involved with the administration of employee benefits and payroll, which continues to be outsourced, HRM professionals increasingly play a larger role in the company by being involved with strategic planning and developing strategic HRM programs to, for example, train and improve the diverse and global workforce.

The Potential for Recruitment Grows Substantially. Like in many of their domestic organizations HRM professionals are no longer bound by the physical boundaries of their local area when their company moves into the global playing field. As a result, HRM's recruitment efforts become easier and more diverse as they have a wider pool of talent from which to draw. The larger employee pool is especially notable in the higher-skilled categories where there often is a gap between supply and demand. Businesses may thrive with competitive products and services, but cannot survive globally without the right mix of talented employees that HRM professionals are responsible for identifying, recruiting, selecting, onboarding, training and developing, and compensating, and so on.

Critical HRM Technology Changes Occur. For companies that retain benefits, compensation, payroll deductions, employee training and performance evaluations in-house, HRM professionals increasingly are tasked with operating new computer systems required to manage a global workforce. Hundreds of vendors can provide global companies with the appropriate software programs to deal with the numerous HRM tasks, but someone still has to evaluate the appropriate fit for the corporation and operation of the systems. HRM professionals have to expend considerable time and effort to learn new platforms when their companies rely on the latest software to manage a worldwide workforce.

Challenging Cultural Differences. Perhaps one of the most challenging aspects of globalization on HRM professionals is the need to discover and learn the cultural differences at play with their new global workforce. HRM professionals must learn how best to communicate company goals and missions, integrate diverse value systems into their companies and coordinate the activities of all their employees to achieve their goals. HRM professionals in the home office must also build working relationships with frontline managers to communicate company policies, ensure new hires understand the parameters of their employment and translate company directives for workers. HRM professionals need to develop an understanding of the living conditions and training processes in other countries and follow foreign employment regulations, labor relations laws and organized labor issues, as well as figure out how to create effective performance appraisals often from afar. More than ever, HRM professionals must partner with and rely on the local supervisors or managers on the ground to communicate vital HRM information, rather than relying on their own training and abilities.

CONCLUSION

Globalization is a polarizing subject that is not easily defined. Globalization allows for increased competition, lifts barriers to entry for developing countries, helps to promote economic growth and works to unify the world's economies. Globalization provides opportunities for businesses to invest in foreign markets and to gain access to new capital. A key concern in achieving financial results through globalization is the effect it has on a firm. Bringing employees together despite distance and cultural differences is a challenge company leaders and HRM professionals must continue to tackle.

As is the case with domestic organizations, the HRM of company is an integral party of its success. HRM for todays and tomorrow's global corporation that operates in multiple countries presents many cultural and socio-economic challenges. Globalization has many positive and negative effects on any global or international corporation's HRM function and professionals.

Global HRM efforts will continue to present particular issues, challenges and opportunities for HRM professionals. There are a number of best practices available to HRM professionals and other organizational leaders for managing an organization's most valuable resource—it's people at work. Much of what has been discussed throughout this chapter and others in this book on HRM can be applied to both domestic and internationally successful organizations that are able to sustain and prolong their success through the way they manage their human resources.

While there are many similarities, global HRM is distinct from domestic HRM because of its broader perspective, the greater scope of activities included in global HRM, and the higher level of risk associated with global HRM activities.

Today's and tomorrow's global organizations will continue to take any one of a number of different approaches to HRM, with the choice depending on political and legal regulations; the managerial, educational, and technological development in the host country; and differences between the home and host cultures.

HRM professionals will need to increase their skill and competence in working with other organizational members to successfully coordinate global or international HRM operations in a variety of countries, each with its own local cultural, legal, and traditional influences. In the years to come HRM professionals must ensure that their organization's policies are flexible enough to allow for these local variations while not losing sight of the fact that such policies also must be developed to help achieve the overall strategic global objectives of the corporation.

Increased care must be taken by HRM professionals in developing the various HRM activities to ensure that they take into consideration each local country's cultural and legal nuances. Staffing, training and development, performance appraisal, compensation, workplace safety, management of labor relations and the use of expatriates versus locals are of paramount concern to successful global HRM (see Cascio, 2019; Mello, 2019; Mathis et al., 2017; Noe et al., 2019; Snell & Morris, 2019).

Like all of the other HRM activities discussed in this book, HRM professionals and other managers and leaders must recognize the important role that globalization and its impact and implications for its employees can have on their organization's success in the international arena. The collective HRM activities all play important roles in developing and sustaining competitive advantages for a global organization. Today and in the future the organization's ability to attract, develop, and retain a talented workforce will be a critical factor in developing a high-performance, successful international organization.

The 'universalistic' approach to HRM must be rejected by HRM professionals as the basic functions of HRM are given different weights among countries and are carried out differently. In addition, the cultural differences among countries have produced the slogan in global or international HRM "Think GLOBALLY and act LOCALLY." This means that an international balancing act is required by HRM professionals and their organizations, which leads to the fundamental assumption made by Bartlett and Ghoshal (1991) that balancing the needs of coordination, control and autonomy and maintaining the appropriate balance are critical to the success of the multinational company.

In concluding this chapter it is important for HRM professionals to remember that the recent uncertainty in global politics and the continued business risks mean that global companies and their HRM professionals will continue to face some difficult challenges in the coming years. HRM professionals will need to increasingly be aware of the many factors that significantly affect HRM in a global environment, such as political, economic, sociocultural, and technological, and that they understand how these factors come into play in the various levels of global participation. Finally, it requires that HRM professionals be adept at understanding the impact and implications of globalization on the broader corporation, its employees and on their role in helping to effectively manage the company's most important resource, its people, to gain and sustain competitive advantage in today's and tomorrow's global marketplace.

REFERENCES

Adler, N. (2008). *International dimensions of organizational behavior* (5th ed.) Boston, MA: PWS-Kent.

Amadeo, K. (2018a, June 2). *Brexit consequences for the UK, the EU, and the United States.* Retrieved from https://www.thebalance.com/brexit-consequences-4062999

Amadeo, K. (2018b, June 13). *What happens if Trump dumps NAFTA: The key points of NAFTA renegotiations.* Retrieved from https://www.thebalance.com/donald-trump-nafta-4111368

Amadeo, K. (2018c, April 21). *WTO members, categories, and benefits: 3 reasons why WTO membership is so important.* Retrieved from https://www.thebalance.com/wto-membership-benefits-and-importance-3306364

Andrews, L. (2011, March 28). *The global vs local dilemma.* Retrieved from http://source.ethicalfashionforum.com/article/the-global-vs-local-dilemma

Bartlett, C. A., & Ghoshal, S. (1991). *Managing across borders: The transnational solution.* London, UK: London Business School.

Briscoe, D. R., & Schuler, R. S. (2012). *International human resource management* (4th ed.). London, UK: Routledge.

Cascio, W. R. (2019). *Managing human resources: Productivity, quality of life, profits* (11th ed.). New York, NY: McGraw-Hill Education.

Choi, C., & Schreiner, B. (2014, January 14). *Beam being acquired by Japan's suntroy.* Associated Press, Retrieved from http:// ap.org

Dewhurst, M., Harris, J., & Heywood, S. (2012, June). The global company's challenge. *McKinsey Quarterly.* Retrieved from https://www.mckinsey.com/business-functions/organization/our-insights/the-global-companys-challenge

Dreyfuss, E. (2017, February 9). *Trump can't stop the globalization of work—The Internet will see to that.* Retrieved from https://www.wired.com/2017/02/trump-cant-stop-globalization-work-internet-will-see/

Duprey, R. (2013, June 5). *A-B InBev completes Modelo acquisition.* Retrieved from https://www.fool.com/investing/general/2013/06/05/a-b-inbev-completes-modelo-acquisition.aspx

Edwards, T. (2011). The nature of international integration and human resource policies in multinational companies, *Cambridge Journal of Economics, 35*(3), 483–498.

Elliott, L., & Wearden, G. (2017, January 17). Xi Jinping signals China will champion free trade if Trump builds barriers, *The Guardian.* Retrieved from https://www.theguardian.com/business/2017/jan/17/china-xi-jinping-china-free-trade-trump-globalisation-wef-davos

Friedman, T. L. (2016). *Thank you for being late: An optimist's guide to thriving in the age of accelerations.* New York, NY: Farrar, Straus & Giroux.

Gunther, M. (2005, June 27). Cops of the global village. *Fortune,* 158–166.

Higginbottom, K. (2017, December 28). *Top challenges facing HR directors of global firms in 2017.* Retrieved from https://www.forbes.com/sites/karenhigginbottom/2016/12/28/challenges-facing-hr-directors-of-global-firms-in-2017/#2b530a554f95

Johnson, R. (2011, June 16). 17 awesome McDonald's dishes you can't buy in America. *Business Insider*, Retrieved from http://www.businessinsider.com/mcdonalds-meals-around-the-world-2011-6

Lioudis, N. (2018, March 16). *How does the foreign exchange market trade 24 hours a day?* Retrieved from https://www.investopedia.com/ask/answers/how-forex-market-trade-24-hours-day/

Mann, T., & Spegele, A. B. (2017, June 30). Why GE builds more factories overseas. *The Wall Street Journal*, A1, A9.

Marchington, M., & Wilkinson, A. (2012). *Human resource management at work: People management and development*. London, UK: CIPD.

Mathis, R. L., Jackson, J. H., Valentine, S. R., & Meglich, P. A. (2017). *Human resource management* (15th ed.). Boston, MA: Cengage,

Mello, J. A. (2019). *Strategic human resource management* (5th ed.). Boston, MA: Cengage.

Noe, R. A., Hollenbeck, J. R., Gerhart, B., & Wright, P.M. (20190. *Human resource management: Gaining a competitive advantage* (11th ed.). New York, NY: McGraw-Hill Education.

Partington, R. (2018, January 15). *No-deal Brexit would cost EU economy £100bn, report claims*. Retrieved from https://www.theguardian.com/politics/2018/jan/15/no-deal-brexit-would-cost-eu-economy-100bn-report-claims

Post, J. (2017, June 22). What is a PEST analysis? *Business News Daily*. Retrieved from https://www.businessnewsdaily.com/5512-pest-analysis-definition-examples-templates.html

Quora. (2017, August 28). Is globalization creating a single world culture? *Forbes.* Retrieved from https://www.forbes.com/sites/quora/2017/08/28/is-globalization-creating-a-single-world-culture/#754d89763bd3

Romei, V. (2018, January 22). What will the EU look like after Brexit? *Financial Times*. Retrieved from https://www.ft.com/content/dec6968c-f6ca-11e7-8715-e94187b3017e

Sato, K. (2014, February 10). *The next ten years of the world in the era of globalization and the internet.* Retrieved from https://www.huffingtonpost.com/katsuakisato/the-next-ten-years-of-the_b_4761714.html

Shen, L. (2016, December 18). Here are the 5 biggest M&A deals of 2016. *Fortune*. Retrieved from http://fortune.com/2016/12/28/mergers-and-acquisitions/

Sheng, E. (2016, December 21). The five biggest Chinese investments in the U.S. in 2016. *Forbes*. Retrieved from http://www/forbes.com

Siegel, J., & Larson, B. Z. (2009). Labor market institutions and global strategic adaptation: Evidence from Lincoln Electric. *Management Science, 55*(9), 1527–1546,

Snell, S. A., & Morris, S. S. (2019). *Managing human resources* (18th ed.). Boston, MA: Cengage.

Stoll, J., & Colias, M. (2017, February 80. Mexico is key cog in GM's profit machine. *Wall Street Journal*. Retrieved from https://www.wsj.com/articles/gm-says-it-supports-tax-reform-but-border-tax-is-complicated-1486473480

Tarique, I., Briscoe, D. R., & Schuler, R. S. (2010). *International human resource management* (5th ed.). New York, NY: Routledge.

Tulshyan, R. (2010, March 18). Quirkiest cultural practices from around the world, *Forbes*. Retrieved from https://www.forbes.com/forbes/welcome/?toURL=https://www.forbes.com/2010/03/18/business-travel-etiquette-forbes-woman-leadership-global&refURL=https://www.google.com/&referrer=https://www.google.com/

Tung, R. L. (2016). New perspectives on human resource management in a global context. *Journal of World Business, 51*(1), 142–152.

U.S. News & World Report. (2016). Best countries. Retrieved from http://worldnews.com

Vollmer, S. (2015). How to mind your manners in the Middle East: CPAs who do business in the region need to know the cultural rules. *Journal of Accountancy, 219*(1), 42.

White, G. (2015, June 24). *How has globalization affected HRM?* Retrieved from https://www.thehrdirector.com/features/expatriates/how-has-globalisation-affected-hrm/

CHAPTER 3

ORGANIZATIONAL DRIFT

Why Organizations Drift Off Keel and What Human Resource Professionals Can Do About It

James P. Eicher and William J. Mea[1]

Well-intentioned organizational efforts of recent decades (BPR, M&A, ERP, etc.) often have unintended consequences that sub-optimize results. At times, they lead to declining profits and serve the firm's many stakeholders poorly. This chapter identifies the symptoms of what we call *Organizational Drift* and provides human resource professionals with a guide for recognizing and correcting the issue.

Organizations typically begin with a clear mission and clear processes about how to serve their core customer. Shifts in the business climate since the late 1980s have pushed firms to make dramatic changes. Organizational drift is the frequent result of new-era competitive shifts. The changes are meant to respond to external factors, but these efforts sometimes leave organizations unfocused. Orga-

---

[1] Text of OMB-required Standard Disclaimer and Author Bios.

The views expressed in this chapter are solely those of the authors and do not necessarily represent the views of the Office of Management and Budget, the Administration, or the United States. The authors have no financial interest in or ownership of any companies mentioned in the chapter.

Human Resources Management Issues, Challenges and Trends:
"Now and Around the Corner", pages 53–79.
Copyright © 2019 by Information Age Publishing
All rights of reproduction in any form reserved.

nizational drift, or reorganizing over time without deliberate, conscious intention is like a ship responding to heavy winds. The organizational changes sometimes push the firm off course, leaving it less profitable and less capable of serving its core stakeholders.

For example, over time all organizations organically restructure. The changes can create inappropriate spans of control and add unnecessary levels of hierarchy. In some cases, firms develop duplicate support or "shadow" departments across the company (Chang, Buchanan, Spiegel, Martin, Uchida, Schira, & Staub, 2003; Duperrin, 2011; Neilson, Pasternack, Mendes, & Tan, 2004). They may decentralize processes to the point of fostering a culture of unaccountability, leaving in place "legacy" staff that solve new business problems with dated methodologies, technologies and thinking (Greesonbach, 2017; Mandis, 2013; Miliard, 2017; Sternberg, 2014).

In addition to making a poor use of talent, research indicates that many cost saving and revenue generating efforts to increase shareholder return and productivity rarely succeed other than enriching consultants. For example, only 25 percent of downsizing efforts improve return on investment (ROI) (Paterson, 2016). Similar results are reported for merger and acquisition (M&A)—the ensuing integration of organization structure, processes and culture sometimes yields "no improvement in financial performance of acquirer companies after merger" (Rashid & Naeem, 2017). The success of technology investments to improve performance remains cloudy at best. A recent analysis of 250 global companies to determine whether increased technology spending could lead to improved financial performance showed: "…no direct correlation between technology investments and profitable growth" (Krishnamurthy, Sharma, & Sarangarajan, 2015).

In some cases, organizational change efforts can create long-term financial benefits and deliver sustainable competitive advantage. What are some possible differences? We discuss ways in which Human Resource (HR) professionals can discover the dynamics that contribute to improving organization performance. We also illustrate how an understanding of organizational drift can help managers make deliberate choices that avoid drift. Paired with big data and predictive analytics, managers can mitigate the unintended consequences of change and achieve competitive advantage (Blenko, Mankins, & Rogers, 2010).

The game of poker is comparable to firm strategy and understanding how organizations anticipate the future without recognizing with full awareness. We borrow the term "tell" from poker throughout the chapter to describe signs or symptoms of organizational drift. A tell is a shift in a player's actions or appearance that gives an indication of advantage or weakness.

The chapter has four sections. The first section provides assessment questions and a framework for organizational drift. The second section describes the signs of organizational drift. It describes "*the tells*" for each component of the organizational drift framework and how the tell is a symptom of organization dysfunction that may adversely affect organization performance. The third section explains why well-intended organizational changes fail to yield good results. Finally, the last section provides guidelines to avoid organizational drift. It offers guidance on how to create organizational alignment in a way that can mitigate the underlying causes of organizational drift.

I. ORGANIZATIONAL DRIFT: LEARNING TO RECOGNIZE WHAT YOU MAY ONLY SUSPECT

Recognizing organizational drift provides both a diagnosis for understanding organizational performance and a solution for improving competitive advantage. HR professionals—with the knowledge of their organization's hierarchy, competencies and compensation plans—are well-positioned to influence their organization's corporate-level (C-level) executives and financial performance. We ask executives the following questions.

1. Do many of your managers have few or no direct reports?
2. Do you have excessive levels of management reporting?
3. Are there employees performing tasks not aligned to their competencies?
4. Are HR, IT, Finance and other support functions duplicated throughout the organization?
5. Are key customer, development and operational processes "owned" by multiple leaders?
6. Is the relationship between effective performance and appropriate rewards unclear?

If one answers "yes" to two or more of the symptoms, these are signs of organizational drift. The tells can be difficult to detect, especially in large, multinational organizations as organizational drift is the product of cumulative small changes to discreet parts of the organization. Often the changes take place in geographically far-flung departments and functions, making detection a challenge. Our experience is that leaders often grapple with the negative financial outcomes of organizational drift long after it has occurred. They do not have an accurate assessment of the tells - and their cumulative financial impact on the enterprise - until financial difficulties appear on balance sheets, long after organizational drift has been in play (Sherman & Young, 2016).

When there are perceived organization financial challenges, leaders often address structure and/or operations as defined by the authors by issuing some type of reduction in the workforce (reductions-in-force, labor arbitrage, resource actions, etc.) (Todrin, 2011); or by redesigning processes (reengineering, developing lean processes, agile development, etc.) (Bain & Company, 2018). These well-meaning but tactical responses can initiate cycles of destabilizing layoffs, mergers, acquisitions and costly enterprise-wide technology solutions. These solutions often provide only temporary financial cover when the outcomes of process redesign and cutting headcount fail to provide long-term financial improvement (Blenko, Mankins, & Rogers, 2010).

As in poker, the "tells" indicate organizational drift. With the advent of big data and predictive analytics these tells can be more easily identified and managed through organization data mining and other efforts. This chapter identifies the symptoms or tells of organizational drift, providing HR leaders with guidance to help their organizations maintain a sustainable competitive advantage. Thus, the purposes of Organizational Drift Framework discussed in this chapter are to:

- Illustrate the structure and operations of an organization;
- Recognize the tells of organization drift and mitigate their negative impact; and
- Guide and align organization structure and operations to realize better long-term ROI.

II. WHY YOUR ORGANIZATION IS NOT DOING WHAT IT IS SUPPOSED TO DO—THE TELLS OF ORGANIZATIONAL DRIFT AND THEIR POTENTIAL IMPACT

For the purposes of readily identifying the behavior and impact of each organizational drift tell, the authors have developed a framework that "deconstructs" an organization into two connected *levers* - structure and operations - each of which has three subcomponents.

Briefly, spans of control, organizational levels and talent leverage form the structural levers (scope of decision-making, decision authority and what competencies, experience and skills are needed for successful execution). Work functions, business processes and metrics form the operational levers that dictate how fast or slow tasks are executed in support of functional products or services (e.g., the sequence of the tasks, the aggregation of task sequence into processes, and to what quality/service and/or product measurement they are produced).

Each of the six components of the framework (along with the constructs of structure and operations) has a corresponding tell that signals organization performance challenges. We describe the corresponding tells in the section that follows.

Structure

The description of the first three tells of organizational drift relate to the structure portion of the framework: spans of control, levels and leverage.

Tell #1: Span Contraction

Span contraction is the result of having many of your management personnel having few (or no) individuals reporting to them. The underlying construct is *span of control* or the ratio of direct reports to each previous organization level. The key question to ask regarding effective spans of control is, "*Do people in your organization supervise too few or too many people?*"

Although spans of control vary, when span contraction occurs the aggregate average many vary wildly, without any apparent financial "logic." One manager for every three employees versus one manager for every seven employees represents two very different cost structures. For example, over time areas of work can be carved up into small sets of activities that would be financially better served if they were aggregated into larger segments and held accountable to fewer managers.

In the authors' framework, span contraction indicates that the opposite has occurred. Large segments of responsibility become divided up into small organization components (departments, projects, etc.) across the organization. This narrows the scope of roles and increases the number of work-related hand-offs from department to department, with more managers managing fewer employees at greater cost per manager (Gupta, 2010; Myatt, 2012).

- Potential Financial Impact: Dilution of manager per employee cost.

Tell #2: Pan-Caked Levels

Pan-caked levels are the result of excessive levels of supervisory personnel. The underlying construct is *organizational levels* or distinct reporting relationships in the structure of the organizational hierarchy. The key question to ask regarding efficient organizational levels is, "*Is decision making slowed by unnecessary levels of review or approval?*"

Many organizations assume that their organizational levels are arranged over time in a classic hierarchy or "pyramid." The objective is clearly defined criteria for approvals, enabling efficient and effective decisions. With pan-caking the organization becomes mid- to top-heavy. A careful analysis of one's organizational charts may reveal a disproportionate number of mid-level managers. When managerial and executive titles exceed the number of direct reports they merit; it results in a picture of the organization that looks more like a "diamond" than a pyramid. This can inhibit the real-time flow of mission-critical information. Chandler (2015) states:

> Large, complex organizations tend to add new specialisms over time. Rather than using a formal 'design process' a more organic change typically unfolds- usually based around people. From an organization shape perspective this tends to produce rather steep sided hierarchal pyramid structures or even worse diamond shaped structures with too many people in the middle and too few at the base. The high number of organizational layers coupled with managers who have very few direct reports produces a number of organization effectiveness issues such as a slowing of decision making and difficulties coordinating and cascading. (p. 1)

One may have few individual contributors reporting to many managers each of whom controls a small portion of critical business processes. To be competitive, organizations have driven decision-making authority down to the lowest levels possible to facilitate the speed and quality of business execution. Roles that were once played exclusively by management—for example, the authority to halt automobile manufacturing assembly lines—is now played by hourly assembly line workers.

- Potential Financial Impact: Reduced cycle time of key product/service, customer and operational execution.

Tell #3: Leverage Gaps

Leverage gaps refer to how well your organization utilizes the performance of the existing talent pool (Majdalani, Sfeir, Nader & Omair, 2014; Yarnall, 2011). Pratap (2016) states:

> …in this new war for talent, companies must look for new and innovative ways to attract, develop and retain people. The question is: are they ignoring and under-leveraging the internal pool of talent that lies within? (p. 1)

Specifically, leverage gaps are the mis-alignment between personnel with management titles—and associated compensation—not performing management duties. The underlying construct is *leverage capability* or the mix of title-driven levels such as Manager, Senior Manager, Director, Vice President, etc. within a function aligned to optimal competency/compensation mix. This alignment is necessary to maximize performance. Mascarenhas (2015) states:

> An assessment and alignment of job responsibilities, salaries and actual work being done in positions is required to recognize good performance and to monitor and report the achievement of employee goals. (p. 1)

The key question to ask regarding leverage capability is, *"Are individuals performing tasks that could be performed by less senior and/or experienced individuals with different competencies and skills?"*

With leverage gaps, talent is not fully optimized relative to title, role, experience and compensation. For example, supervisors, managers, directors and vice presidents may have maintained their title—and accompanying compensation—but either perform tasks that are no longer needed by the business to operate or do not require the level of expertise of the current management (LeBlanc, 1992). Often this can be the result of multiple mergers and acquisitions, where organizations do not align accountability to experience. This can lead to what many organizations refer to as "legacy staff/jobs" where individuals are not held accountable to any specific performance reflective of appropriate compensated (Greesonbach, 2017; Miliard, 2017; Sternberg, 2014).

As a result, there may be disparity between pay and job responsibility. Bidwell (2015) states:

> We are highly attuned to things we think are unfair…as workers, we look at the ratio of what we're putting in, versus what we're getting out, and we compare that to the ratio of what other people are putting in and getting out…. [It's only] natural to think: Is this fair? (p. 1)

- Potential Financial Impact: Pay band inequity.

Operations

The description of the second three tells of organizational drift relate to the operations portion of the framework: functions, processes and metrics.

Tell #4: Functional Fragmentation

Functional fragmentation is the result of duplicated function clusters positioned in "fragments" across multiple organizational groups. The underlying construct is *support activities* or functionally defined groupings of tasks positioned across multiple organization units (e.g., Human Resources, Finance, Procurement, Legal, IT, Marketing, etc.). The key question to ask regarding support activities is, *"Are activities being performed across the organization that could be repositioned in a central function either inside or outside (e.g., outsourced) the organization?* (Campbell, Kunisch, & Müller-Stewens, 2011). Bizarro (2017) states:

> Centralization should always be the first consideration because of the capacity to gain control—you have the ability to regulate your employee's time, activity, and quality. If centralization isn't right for you, consider outsourcing… Many companies chose to outsource in areas of human resources, finance, marketing, and information technology. (p. 1)

Functional fragmentation can arise because, over many years, individuals form relationships based on what specific individuals can do for them. For example, you may have an associate in information technology (IT) that has solved many critical problems that creates a service expectation. The same service expectation can be said for HR, Legal, Finance or Marketing support. As organizations grow larger, they need to scale AND control costs. Thus, support functions can become centralized. With functional fragmentation, actions executed by the centralized function fail to meet the prior service expectations of internal customers.

Organizations may then be tempted to create their own support functions (such as training) in addition to centralized corporate support functions. These redundant functional activities are often referred to as *"shadow staffs"* where entire functional areas are duplicated in an organization. Note that in some cases organizations shift functions to other suppliers only to realize months later that they have "reappeared" inside the company. They are now paying for both outsourcing and an internal function they originally outsourced, duplicating support costs. Mountain and Saenz (2009) state:

> When cost reduction becomes a priority, one of the first places executives look for savings is general and administrative (G&A) expenses-the cost centers that provide front-line support and back-office functions such as finance, information technology and human resources. There are good reasons why G&A represents such an attractive target. When business is growing, companies tend to add support services. But in a downturn, it becomes painfully apparent that some incremental support services don't contribute enough to sales or earnings, and many executives react with across-the-board cuts in G&A. (p. 1)

- Potential Financial Impact: Duplication of support costs.

Tell #5: Process Isolation

Process isolation is the result of redundant or duplicated business processes performed independently across the organization. It is a pattern like functional fragmentation, except this involves processes (e.g., supply chain, purchasing, order management, etc.) duplicated across geographically dispersed areas. The duplicated processes may have different process steps (IT applications support, database repositories, quality standards, customer masters, shipping locations, etc.) that make consistent business outcomes difficult. One common "solution" is to integrate disparate processes under a common global IT platform.

The underlying construct is *process clustering,* or defined, aggregated sequences of activities that directly contribute to achieving strategic objectives. Examples of objectives would include operational effectiveness, customer experience or innovation of products and services. These processes—operational effectiveness, innovation and customer experience—are often referred to as *core processes* (Treacy & Wiersma, 1997), critical to an organization's financial success. With process isolation, organizations duplicate their core processes across the enterprise, each with its own separate leadership, metrics, staffing levels, etc. Like functional fragmentation, key processes are unnecessarily duplicated. Jeston and Nellis (2008) state:

> Process governance is arguably one of the most important dimensions for the continued and long-term (sustainable) success in creating a process-focused organization. Without a level of leadership commitment to the establishment of a governance structure based around business processes, it will be extremely difficult to achieve anything except isolated business process improvement projects and activities. (p. 105)

The key question to ask regarding process clustering is, *"Are there mission critical processes disconnected and working in isolation that unnecessarily compete for limited resources?"*

As organizations scale up, processes that once were managed by a single department now become threaded throughout the organization's structure. They become distributed in small sequences of activities throughout hierarchies, creating (like shadow staffs) shadow processes. With process clustering one creates excess steps in one's critical core business processes, resulting in lost opportunities (Hendriks, 2015; Lette, 2016). Too many hands must touch the process and too many eyes must see information before executing key activities. Ownership and accountability for important manufacturing, customer, service and design decisions becomes isolated across the globe, and this in turn creates process inefficiencies.

- Potential Financial Impact: Opportunity costs.

Tell #6: Metrics Severing

Metrics severing is the result of a large amount of unnecessary work that is rewarded and large amounts of necessary work that is not incentivized. The underlying construct is *metric calibration*, or measurements and financial rewards that are linked in a meaningful way to providing customer, employee and shareholder value. Metrics severing often becomes a performance concern when rapid technological change requires new skills and competencies. Updated measurements of success therefore incent new behavior in growth areas (e.g., the recent drive to cloud computing and artificial intelligence (Forbes Technology Council, 2017). The key questions to ask regarding metric calibration are, *"Are individuals over compensated for work that is no longer necessary and under compensated for work necessary for long-term financial growth?"*

As competitive pressures mount on maturing organizations there is a common push to invest in new areas. It may involve new streams outside of what brought in past revenue and increased shareholder value. The demand for strategic, long-term investment—in both capital and labor—necessitates a re-evaluation. Leaders need to update the competencies and the measurements that incentivize new behaviors and technologies. Ballowe (2018) states:

> As a leader in your organization who has put the time and effort into building your strategic plan, you want to be sure your employees adopt your vision and sense of purpose...A common trend in compensation plans is to pay for performance. Remember the purpose of incentive plans is to change behavior and move your whole organization as a team toward your vision. Make sure that your incentive plans clearly link performance to business goals. (p. 1)

With metrics severing, the link between what people currently do and what they need to do is broken. Performance may be dissociated from future financial growth and instead linked to current roles. This results in a disconnect between performance measurements and successful outcomes for financial objectives. This can sometimes create employee "angst" inside an organization where individuals

TABLE 3.1. Organizaitonal Drift Framework and Tells Summary

Organizational Drift Framework					
Structure			Operations		
Spans of Control	Levels	Leverage	Functions	Processes	Metrics
:"Tells" Span Contraction	Pan-Caked Levels	Leverage Gaps	Functional Fragmentation	Process Isolation	Metrics Severing

think: "I am being paid to do job x, but you really need me to do job y; and I don't know if I have the skills and competencies to do job y" (Bessen, 2014).

- Potential Financial Impact: Strategic pay for performance.

We should highlight the difference between leverage gaps vs. metrics severing. Leverage gaps assume that employees have the requisite experience and skills but are misaligned with level, position and compensation. Metrics severing assumes that current employees do NOT necessarily have the requisite skills AND the organization has not developed the metrics to incentivize future, strategic growth.

In Table 3.1 we summarize the organizational drift framework and accompanying tells.

There are significant potential financial impacts for each organizational drift tell. In summary they include:

- Dilution of manager per employee cost;
- Reduced cycle time of key product/service, customer and operational execution;
- Pay band inequity;
- Duplication of support costs;
- Opportunity costs; and
- Strategic pay for performance.

Knowing tells of organizational drift may validate one's intuitions about an organization that is not performing as it "should."

III. WHY THE ORGANIZATION IS NOT DOING WHAT IT IS SUPPOSED TO DO—SOME UNINTENDED CONSEQUENCES OF WELL-MEANING TRANSFORMATION "SOLUTIONS"

As an informed leader, one may now have a sense that the enterprise is not performing the way it "should" as a result of organizational drift. At this point one may determine that you need to take some type corrective action. This may take the form of a reduction of employees in your organization's workforce, or *riffing*

(RIF), and/or the redesign of key business processes, or *business process reengineering* (BPR). Both RIFs and BPR can be well-intended programs to improve the financial performance of the organization, realign competencies and priorities, and provide customers with better products and services. Unfortunately, RIFs and BPR are sometimes not long-term solutions. They can initiate cycles of destabilizing layoffs, mergers, acquisitions and costly enterprise-wide technology solutions that diminish long-term financial benefits. They also create fear that sub-optimizes performance (Bain & Company, 2018; Todrin, 2011).

In this section, we use the organizational drift framework to illustrate how the initial positive results of riffing and business process re-engineering may diminish over time. These solutions often provide only temporary financial cover when the outcomes of process redesign and/or cutting headcount fail to provide long-term financial improvement. Let us understand how this happens.

One's organization's pre-RIF and/or BPR story may begin with a scenario as follows. You have identified your organization's thinning profit margins, cost of sales compared to your competitors and diminished revenue. This suggests a major cost reduction effort. You have identified that your organization's service levels are lower compared to competitors, there is a declining free cash flow, and inventory supply-demand are completely unbalanced. These would appear to suggest a major re-design and reengineering effort is needed. Observations and initial analysis may reveal:

- …we have too many managers per employee; we're too top heavy…
- …we have too many levels in some of the departments, and it's seems to be slowing down decision making…
- …we are not leveraging our talent based on experience, competencies and assignments but to some degree simply based on who we're comfortable with and who's been in a department the longest…
- …we have 5 training organizations outside of HR, 3 legal groups, and 2 controllers, and we haven't even analyzed our European, Asian or Mid-Eastern headcount yet…
- …we have customer service and call center functions that have sprung up throughout the company, all in high cost urban and suburban locations…
- …we are measuring and compensating people for jobs in areas of declining sales, and need to set new measurements, hiring the right people in our strategic growth are even if it means "eating our children …

Does this sound absurd? Welcome to organizational drift! Using the organization drift framework, let us visualize and deconstruct how both a RIF/BPR would work. For illustration purposes, the authors use a generic organization chart that depicts customary departments for an Order Management System. Note that in Figure 3.1 below we have identified the informally connected sequence of tasks—the roles and "hand-offs"—involved in an order management system. They may

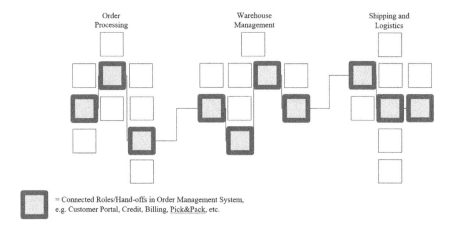

FIGURE 3.1.   Customary Departments Involved in an Order Management System

include but are not limited to: Customer Portal, Credit, Billing, Inventory Management, Pick&Pack, etc.

In Figure 3.1 and going forward, the gray outlined boxes represent the roles and hand-offs threaded throughout Order Processing, Warehouse Management and Shipping/Logistics. In the authors' sample scenario there are 10 key connected roles and hand-offs for executing Order Management: three in Order Processing, four in Warehouse Management and three in Shipping/Logistics.

Note that roles and hand offs from one individual or department to the next in the sequence of tasks are NOT to be mistaken for a formal business process. There is no documentation (no Visio charts, no training materials, or published Standard Operating Procedures (SOPs), etc.) for these activities. This is a string of informal activities that has grown organically over the years based on tribal knowledge and informal relationships of "who has learned what, and when," sometimes over decades. Freifled (2013) states:

> We're all familiar with the phrase, "Knowledge is power." But an often-overlooked source of power is "tribal knowledge"—the collective knowledge of the organization contained within the context and boundaries of the various "tribes" (business units, functions, product teams, and project teams) that make up the organization. The knowledge developed within these tribes typically is transmitted by those with the deepest domain expertise through conversation or demonstration and learned over time through experience. It continues to evolve and becomes part of the tribe's language and way of doing business. To newcomers and those outside the tribe, it can be difficult to grasp. Some of the information and data is documented, but a considerable portion of it is not. And the tribal knowledge that is documented often is challenging and time consuming to find and access. Depending on the tribe and its purpose, the knowledge may be willingly shared, it may be carefully guarded

as a source of power, or it may be rightfully protected (as in the case of classified information). (p. 1)

These informal sequences of roles and tasks can be *a major outcome* of *organizational drift,* of the organic reorganizing and changes without deliberate, conscious intention. Freifeld goes on to state (2013):

> While the instinct to form tribes goes back hundreds of thousands of years, the recognition of challenges associated with the sharing of tribal knowledge across an enterprise is starting to spread…Tribes aren't inherently problematic. In fact, they are powerful and necessary for business success. But tribal behaviors can impede productivity, particularly in complex organizations, because the full complement of knowledge contained within one tribe is not systematically shared with or understood by other tribes. (p. 1)

Now that one has determined to execute a RIF to this organization, let's look at how to one might proceed. In the standard RIF management typically looks at headcount reduction without analyzing the impact on operations. This is often an across-the-board cut that focuses on broadening spans of control and eliminating some management levels. There are often "gut based" decisions made without analytic information or thinking through the consequences to operational performance (Bonabeau, 2003; Dishman, 2015). It reflects the sense that, "We're paying too much to some people for some of the work done." Let us look at executing a RIF recognizing the structural tells of organizational drift.

In this riffing scenario (based on identifying and responding to tells 1–3, Figure 2), the increase in span of control is represented by the *upward arrows.* Reduction of levels/headcount is represented by the "X"'s and the leveraging and alignment of compensation to responsibility is represented by the "L."

In Figure 3.3, we visualize the results of the riffing effort, that is, what the organization "looks like" after the RIF has taken place.

Note that post-RIF, five of the shifted/eliminated roles are from the 10 key steps of the informal connected sequence of tasks that form the foundation of the Order Management System. An across-the-board cut seems a sure and fair way for everyone to share the pain. For several quarters there may be financial improvement to the bottom line, primarily due to reduced labor costs/headcount. Then an unexpected uptick in costs appear and initial cost savings begin to diminish. The declining performance is brought about by the disruption of five of the 10 roles/hand-offs of the tribal network of the Order Management System. Negative performance due to the disruption of informal, tribal knowledge is a well-recognized phenomenon. Wortman (2017) states:

> When an experienced employee leaves the company or suddenly goes out on leave due to a personal illness or emergency, the tribal knowledge gap can bring operations to a grinding halt. (p. 1)

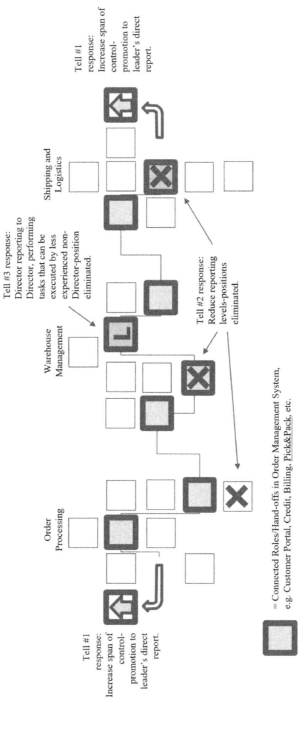

FIGURE 3.2. Org Drift Solutions Scenario—RIF: Tells 1–3.

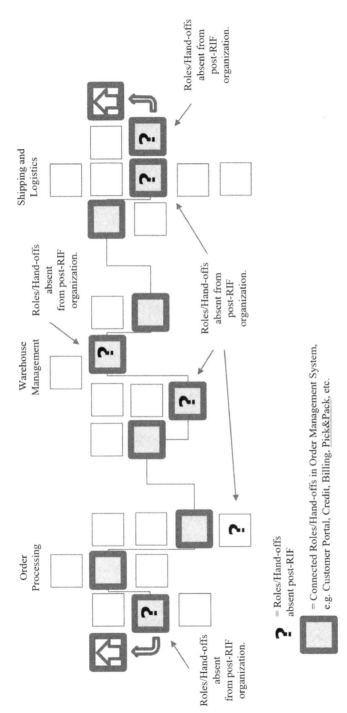

FIGURE 3.3.   Org Drift Solutions Scenario—Post RIF Organization

Carey (2014) goes on to state:

> Whether it is the corporate knowledge, intellectual capital, tacit knowledge, or tribal knowledge that your employees have, once they walk out the door and don't come back, the loss of that corporate knowledge can have an enormous negative impact on your operation. (p. 1)

Another alternative in this situation is to conduct a series of BPR actions to streamline the organization and its operations. In a customary BPR effort management may look at process optimization without necessarily analyzing the impact on the decision-making abilities, management competencies and roles in the hierarchal structure. This is often an efficiency exercise that focuses on simplifying executable steps and consolidating organization functions without considering levels of approval necessary to execute redesigned processes. The organization may have "too many finance people" located throughout the organization that could be shifted to a lower cost provider, taking the undocumented processes in a "lift and shift" exercise without clear understanding of tasks and roles. Similarly, duplicated functions and related processes (e.g., HR, Sales, etc.) can be centralized into a corporate, global function located in a single geography. Similarly, you may have retained a rewards system that still compensates business that are not growing at the expense of strategic growth initiatives that build long-term profits. Like RIFs, these are often "gut based" structural decisions made without analytic information or consideration of the consequences to operational performance (Bonabeau, 2003; Dishman, 2015).

Let us look at executing BPR using the operational tells of organizational drift as represented in Figure 3.4.

In a BPR scenario based on identifying and responding to tells 4–6, the centralizing of duplicated functions is represented by "C"; the consolidation of processes to a lower cost center is represented by "O"; and the alignment of metrics to future business, and experienced employee redundancy, is represented by "X."

In Figure 3.5, we visualize the results of the BPR effort, that is, what the organization "looks like" after BPR has taken place.

Note that in the post-BPR (like the post-RIF results), five of the shifted, consolidated or eliminated roles are from the 10 key steps of the informal connected sequence of tasks that form the foundation of the Order Management process. Streamlining one's organization seems a "cannot lose proposition" that is backed up by solid financials. Again, for several quarters there may be topline improvement, but later revenues remain flat or begin to trend downward. As is the case for the post-RIF scenario, the declining performance is brought about by the disruption of five of the 10 roles/hand-offs of the tribal network. Informal processes may get things done, but they can throw off the effort when they follow unrecognized paths from knowledge and behaviors that happen outside of formal organizational processes. Nelson (2015) states:

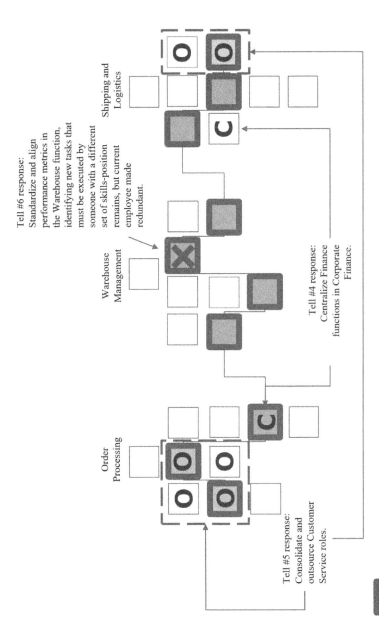

FIGURE 3.4. Org Drift Solutions Scenario—BPR: Tells 4–6.

Tell #6 response: Standardize and align performance metrics in the Warehouse function, identifying new tasks that must be executed by someone with a different set of skills-position remains, but current employee made redundant.

Shipping and Logistics

Warehouse Management

Tell #4 response: Centralize Finance functions in Corporate Finance.

Order Processing

Tell #5 response: Consolidate and outsource Customer Service roles.

= Connected Roles/Hand-offs in Order Management System, e.g. Customer Portal, Credit, Billing, Pick&Pack, etc.

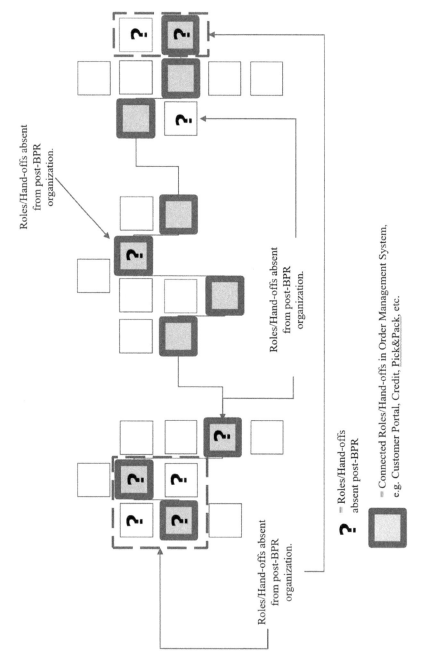

FIGURE 3.5.   Org Drift Solutions Scenario—Post BPR Organization.

The traditional village has a bunch of elders—story tellers who pass on histories, genealogies and values. The "villages" of today are called business units or functional operations, and the "elders" are curators of tribal knowledge who understand business process and how work gets done... We all subscribe to the importance of process reengineering and process documentation. However, the reality is that most organizations still depend on seasoned employees who understand and control operations to ensure the continuous and smooth delivery of products and services. These holders of tribal knowledge are critical to Business Continuity... This operating system ensures that when something does go wrong the village elders are there to swoop in to resolve the crisis and perpetuate themselves as heroes whose jobs cannot possibly be altered or eliminated. (p. 1)

IV.   ORGANIZATIONAL ALIGNMENT: GUIDELINES TO AVOID ORGANZATIONAL DRIFT AND ITS UNINTENDED CONSEQUNECES

Organizational drift implies numerous impediments to efficient cost structures and successful organization performance. Common solutions—notably RIF and BPR actions—are reactive efforts to stem short term financial bleeding. In an ideal world, HR professionals in support of C-level management would develop an enterprise where organizational drift never occurs. Therefore, tactical BPR and RIF efforts would not be necessary.

The purpose of analyzing organizational drifts component pieces is to reveal sources of hidden costs and unaccountable results. When uncovered and mitigated, this can lead to sustained competitive advantage in the face of both anticipated threats and unexpected change. How can one avoid the problems that lead to organization drift? The following are organization drift avoidance guidelines. They inform a framework in which HR professionals can create a versatile, aligned organization that continuously reinvents itself to sustain competitive advantage.

To overcome organization drift it is useful to envision how one can intentionally link structure and operations to the framework. This provides HR professionals with a high-level definition of "what good looks like." It informs discussions with C-level management. The linkage helps to promote organizational *alignment* (as opposed to *drift*) and can result in a *versatile cost structure* (Trevor & Varcoe, 2017).

TABLE 3.2   Overview of Aligning Structure to Operations in the Organizational Drift Framework

Organizational Alignment		
Structure	**Interdependent with**	**Operations**
Span of Control	*linked to*	Functions
Levels	*linked to*	Processes
Leverage	*linked to*	Metrics

Organization alignment begins by understanding how spans of control, organizational levels and capability leverage work together with functions, processes and metrics. It focuses on the interdependencies in a unique way so that duplication, rework, and decision paralysis are eliminated. One-time savings from tumultuous layoffs, process and technology changes have the possibility to turn into ongoing, continuous efficiencies. Let us look at some organization design guidelines that can enable you to avoid each pair of symptoms and link the levers in a way to achieve sustainable performance.

Span contraction and functional fragmentation can be avoided by assessing the transactional characteristics of activities. If activities are largely repeatable, readily scalable and sustainable through easy access to knowledge and skills, then these activities are probably less complex than others. They *require less supervision to execute*. Individual contributors will be able to make autonomous decisions to solve problems and require little direction.

For example, IT call centers are an example where wide span of control is customary. Individuals repeat similar activities on a day-to-day basis and are empowered to solve caller problems. They have a wide span of control—in some instances up to about a hundred employees for every supervisor/manager. On the other hand, a technology R&D group that works on a "never-been-invented product" may need constant direction and feedback from a senior leader. The activities (research, tests, materials, etc.) have no prior track record and are not repeatable. Scalability is unknown. In this case, the work may require a narrow span of control; let us say one leader to three to four scientists.

The action of linking spans to complexity results in a ratio of leaders to activities that can be "rationalized," calibrating work to supervisory pay in a way that is not arbitrary. Support activities are less likely to be duplicated or fragmented across an organization in a *peanut butter spread* if leadership is deliberately aligned to the complexity of executing tasks. Proper spans of control free up both leaders and employees to focus on activities that require rapid, innovative responses when needed.

It is possible to avoid isolating key processes by creating networks of individuals whose purpose is to execute on innovation, operational excellence and customer service. One assembles individuals in teams with clearly defined roles, responsibilities and outcomes connected to core processes. The team is not part of a functional department but is an autonomous organization with sole purpose of executing a process. Teams and team leaders approve decisions. This reduces cycle time and maximizes internal and external opportunities. Networks of teams can aggregate as needed into larger networks managed by fewer leaders.

For example, project teams assemble using subject matter experts to execute on a defined deliverable or deliverables set to specific customer expectations. Each team member's role is defined at the start to link to a specific deliverable (not an ongoing functional role). This contrasts with employees in a function whose task it is to carry out segments of a process threaded through other functions. Layers of approval to carry out requests delay a process far from the customer's input in the latter case. Project teams represent one model for creating organizational networks that rely on coordinated expertise. They produce specific deliverables as opposed to managing isolated segments of processes to meet a goal.

Linking siloed departments to strategic processes results in significantly less downtime; fewer approvals are necessary to execute key work actions. Time-to-opportunity is decreased and feedback arrives in time to make corrections. It helps perfect products, services, operations and the customer experience. Networks of teams are more "proximate" to customer feedback and can change in response to requests for improvement. This supports a culture of performance

Leverage capabilities severed or disconnected from metrics can be avoided by assigning performance-based measurements to proven competencies, skills and experiences. Work performance becomes deliverables based, and once a deliverable is completed, new ones are assigned. Deliverables assignments are based on meeting the organizations strategic and tactical product/service, operational and customer objectives.

The action of assigning measurable deliverable or multiple deliverables commensurate with abilities allows leaders to assess the link of employee pay to performance. A deliverable-based model compels an individual in a role to execute to a specific action. Guidelines Two and Three stress the importance of assigning deliverables to both teams and individuals to facilitate overall organizational alignment and to mitigate organizational drift.

Table 3.3 provides a summary of the Guidelines for linking structure and operations. It can help mitigate the impact of organizational drift going forward.

Table 3.4 summarizes the symptoms, constructs, impacts and guidelines that lead to organizational calibration. It can be used to help guide the creation of a versatile cost structure that withstands market vicissitudes and technology revolutions. Organizations need to deliberately calibrate structure with the three components of its operations.

TABLE 3.3.   Competitive Advantage Guideline Summary: Calibrate Structure and Operations

Organizational Alignment		
Structure	**Calibrated to**	**Operations**
Span of Control	Link spans of control relative to the complexity of the functional activities	Functions
Levels	Replace organizational levels with networks that link to executing strategic processes	Processes
Leverage	Assign metrics equal to proven capabilities that accurately leverage pay, skills, and title	Metrics
Objective: Versatile Cost Structure		

TABLE 3.4. Symptoms and Alignment

Tell	Quiz Question	Construct	$$$ Impact	Guideline
1. Span Contraction	Do a majority of your managers have few or no direct reports?	Span of control	Dilution of manager/ employee cost	Link spans of control relative to the complexity of the functional activities
4. Functional Fragmentation	Are HR, IT, Finance and other support functions duplicated throughout the organization?	Functions	Duplication of support costs	
2. Pan-caked levels	Do you have excessive levels of management reporting?	Organizational levels	Reduced cycle time	Replace organizational levels with networks that link to executing strategic processes
5. Process isolation	Are key customer, development and operational processes "owned" by multiple leaders?	Process clustering	Lost opportunity costs	
3. Leverage gaps	Are there employees performing tasks not aligned to their competencies?	Leverage capability	Pay band inequity	Assign metrics equal to proven capabilities that accurately leverage pay, skills and title
6. Metrics severing	Is the relationship between effective performance and fair rewards unclear?	Metrics calibration	Lack of pay for performance	

When calibrating structure and operations, one's organization will take on the following characteristics:

- Flat, networked structure with shared roles;
- Organization and individual capability rewarded/compensated for outcomes/deliverables; and
- A scorecard of metrics aligned with strategy.

When planning and executing toward an aligned organization, the authors assume that our HR readers can take on a major role in designing and executing organizational change. Their knowledge of the organization, its labor rules and payroll costs are a key competency that has a role in the firm's success. Some recommendations and considerations are listed below.

- Align objectives to the strategic intent. That may include innovation of product/services, excellent customer experience, and operational efficiency and effectiveness.
- When considering a change effort, employ hard data and an analytical approach based. One needs to use accurate financial and human resources data, both internal (a "single source of internal truth") and external (market, competitor) to the firm.
- Anticipate that the reaction to this approach to organization management may be perceived as counter to your organization's current culture

- Acknowledge that one's organization may not have the current capabilities needed to execute an aligned organization. A new emphasis on learning and development may be required to succeed.
- A thorough and aggressive change management process is needed to accomplish major changes. Technology changes need to consider the process and the people in an integrated way.

An organization's profitability and top line revenue targets can be dramatically affected by addressing both structural and operational interdependencies. Taking coordinated management action can lead to organizational excellence. Specifically, by implementing the Organization Drift Framework, HR leaders' organizational expertise and knowledge can enable C-levels leaders to be fully aware of the financial benefits of positive organization change.

SUMMARY & CONCLUSION

HRM continues to partner with C-level executives to provide strategic direction to the organizations business and operations, far beyond its tactical roles of the past (Delery & Doty, 1996; Gorman, 2015). The Society for Human Resource Management (2016) states:

> HR can have a direct impact on the organization's strategy through its input into the organizational strategic process and through its own strategic initiatives. (p. 10)

The Society for Human Resource Management (2016) specifically calls out the importance of HR leaders addressing and mitigating the impacts of Organizational Drift:

> …drift happens when an organization keeps doing what it is used to, perhaps making incremental changes, until it is no longer on track toward its desired destination. When this happens, an organization may have to transform itself and its plans. HR must actively resist satisfaction with the status quo, challenging the strategic effectiveness and efficiency of all its policies and processes and amending them as needed. (p. 9)

As Human Resource practitioners supporting organization leadership, we often have a disquieting combination of data and intuition that an organization is not functioning "as it should." That is, it does not meet business and financial objectives. This resulting discomfort can lead to organizational behavior that undermines long-term business needs. We believe that an understanding of the Organizational Drift Framework (with tells and alignment principles) is a useful tool. It helps equip HR practitioners with a set of objective analytics to solve problems at the root of sub-optimized business performance.

The use of organizational drift tells answers the question, "What's going on here; am I imaging this stuff?" Armed with this approach, HR practitioners can have more meaningful impact on C-level decisions. Transformative change efforts can be more deliberate, and the decisions can be more conscious rather than akin to gambling with one's most, important resource—the people—creating a truly strategic role of HR leaders.

REFERENCES

Bain & Company. (2018, April). Business process reengineering. *Insights Management Tools.* Retrieved from http://www.bain.com/publications/articles/management-tools-business-process-reengineering.aspx

Ballowe, T. (2018). Paying for performance—The right way. *On Strategy.* Retrieved from https://onstrategyhq.com/resources/paying-for-performance-the-right-way/

Bessen, J. (2014, September). Workers don't have the skills they need—And they know it. *Harvard Business Review.* Retrieved from https://hbr.org/2014/09/workers-dont-have-the-skills-they-need-and-they-know-it

Bidwell, M. (2015, June). The uncomfortable questions you should be asking about pay equity. *Knowledge@Wharton.* Retrieved from http://knowledge.wharton.upenn.edu/article/the-questions-you-should-be-asking-about-pay-equity/

Bizarro, D. (2017, August). Outsourcing vs. centralizing vs. offshoring: Which is best for your business? *VCFO.* Retrieved from https://www.vcfo.com/blog/outsourcing-vs.-centralizing-vs.-offshoring-which-is-best-for-your-business

Blenko, M., Mankins, M., & Rogers, P. (2010, June). The decision-driven organization. *Harvard Business Review.* Retrieved from https://hbr.org/2010/06/the-decision-driven-organization

Blenko, M., Mankins, M., & Rogers, P. (2013, August). The five steps to better decisions. *Bain & Company.* Retrieved from http://www.bain.com/publications/articles/the-five-steps-to-better-decisions.aspx

Bonabeau, E. (2003, May). Don't trust your gut. *Harvard Business Review.* Retrieved from https://hbr.org/2003/05/dont-trust-your-gut

Campbell, A., Kunisch, S., & Günter Müller-Stewens G. (2011, June). To centralize or not centralize? *McKinsey Quarterly.* Retrieved from https://www.mckinsey.com/business-functions/organization/our-insights/to-centralize-or-not-to-centralize

Carey, C. (2014, December). Protecting your tribal knowledge isn't an event, it's an ongoing process. *Compendian.* Retrieved from http://www.compendian.com/2014/12/protecting-your-tribal-knowledge-isnt-an-event-its-an-ongoing-process

Chandler, A. (2015, March). Spans & Layers—An ongoing organization design challenge. *Linked In.* Retrieved from https://www.linkedin.com/pulse/spans-layers-ongoing-organization-design-challenge-andrew-chandler/

Change, J., Buchanan, I., Spiegel, E., Martin, P., Uchida, A., Schirra, W., & Staub, C. (2003, May). Shining the light on shadow staff: Understanding and minimizing hidden staff costs. *Booz&Co.* Retrieved from https://www.strategyand.pwc.com/media/uploads/ShiningtheLightonShadowStaff.pdf

Delery, J., & Doty, H. (1996, August). Modes of theorizing in strategic human resource management: Tests of universalistic, contingency, and configurational performance predictions. *Academy of Management Journal, 39*(4), 802–835.

Dishman, L. (2015, July). Scientific proof that your gut is best at making decisions. *Fast Company.* Retrieved from https://www.fastcompany.com/3049248/scientific-proof-that-your-gut-is-best-at-making-decisions

Duperrin, B. (2011, August). Getting rid of unproductive shadow organizations. *Bertrand Duperrin's Notepad.* Retrieved from http://www.duperrin.com/english/2011/08/30/getting-rid-of-unproductive-shadow-organizations/

Forbes Technology Council. (2017, December). 13 top tech skills in high demand for 2018. *Forbes.* Retrieved from https://www.forbes.com/sites/forbestechcouncil/2017/12/21/13-top-tech-skills-in-high-demand-for-2018/#19ea87761e5c

Freifeld, L. (2013, December). Unlocking tribal knowledge to transform your organization. *Training.* Retrieved from https://www.google.com/search?biw=703&bih=615&ei=yPMiW-ruKsTSgAafw6O4BA&q=Unlocking+tribal+knowledge+to+transform+your+organization.+&oq=Unlocking+tribal+knowledge+to+transform+your+organization.+&gs_l=psy-ab.3...5842.5842.0.8649.1.1.0.0.0.0.341.341.3-1.1.0....0...1..64.psy-ab..0.0.0....0.dFDZU4My3gc

Gorman, C. (2015, March). Why strategic HR matters and how HR can become more strategic. *A great place to work.* Retrieved from https://www.greatplacetowork.com/resources/blog/why-strategic-hr-matters-and-how-hr-can-become-more-strategic

Greesonbach, S. (2017, December). 4 ways to re-energize a legacy culture without alienating original employees. *Culture Summit.* Retrieved from https://www.culturesummit.co/articles/4-ways-to-re-energize-a-legacy-culture-without-alienating-original-employees/

Gupta, A. (2010, January). Organizations size and span of control. *Practical Management.* Retrieved from http://www.practical-management.com/Organization-Development/Organization-s-size-and-span-of-control.html

Hendriks, J. (2015, September). Are your business processes stifling your market opportunity? *IDC.* Retrieved from https://www.linkedin.com/pulse/your-business-processes-stifling-market-opportunity-print-belgium/

Jeston, J., & Nelis, J. (2008). *Management by process: A roadmap to sustainable business process management.* Oxford, UK: Butterworth-Heinemann.

Krishnamurthy, K., Sharma, V., & Sarangarajan, R. (2015, November). Maximizing the value from technology investments: Spending smart instead of just spending big. *Strategy&.* Retrieved from https://www.strategyand.pwc.com/reports/maximizing-value-technology-investments

LeBlanc, P. (1992, Summer). Pay-banding can help align pay with new organizational structures. *Global Business and Organizational Excellence.* Retrieved from https://onlinelibrary.wiley.com/doi/pdf/10.1002/npr.4040110304

Lette, E. (2016, October). What are lost opportunity costs and how do I measure them? *Business Bank of Texas.* Retrieved from https://www.businessbankoftexas.com/business-resource-center/what-are-lost-opportunity-costs-and-how-do-i-measure-them

Majdalani, F., Sfeir, F., Nader, P., & Omair, B. (2014). Leveraging an untapped talent pool: How to advance women's role in GCC family businesses.. *Strategy&.* Retrieved from Leveraging an untapped talent pool.

Mandis, S. (2013). *What happened to Goldman Sachs: An insider's story of organizational drift and its unintended consequences.* Cambridge, MA: HBR Press.

Mascarenhas, M. (2015, April). Positions and job responsibilities: Are they aligned? *Linked In.* Retrieved from https://www.linkedin.com/pulse/does-your-position-description-match-job-title-mascarenhas-cmc/

Miliard, M. (2017, January). Tips for managing legacy employees during big EHR implementations. *Heatlthcare IT News.* Retrieved from http://www.healthcareitnews.com/news/tips-managing-legacy-employees-during-big-ehr-implementations

Morden, T. (2007). *Principles of Strategic Management.* New York, NY: Routledge.

Mountain, D., & Saenz, H. (2009, April). For cost reduction, streamline support services. *Bain and Company.* Retrieved from http://www.bain.com/publications/articles/for-cost-reduction-streamline-support-services.aspx

Myatt, M. (2012, November). Span of control: 5 things every leader should know. *Forbes.* Retrieved from https://www.forbes.com/sites/mikemyatt/2012/11/05/span-of-control-5-things-every-leader-should-know/#4f37439028c8

Neilson, G., Pasternack, B., Mendes, D., & Tan, E-M. (2004, February). Profiles in organizational DNA research and remedies. *Strategy+Business.* Retrieved from https://www.stratcgy-business.com/article/rr00004?gko=d84d0

Nelson, C. (2015, October). RPA and the demise of tribal knowledge and the village elders. *LinkedIn.* Retrieved from http://isg-one.com/index/module-article-detail/rpa-and-the-demise-of-tribal-knowledge-and-the-village-elders

Paterson, C. (2016, June). Why downsizing fails: A case study. *CEOworld Magazine.* Retrieved from Retrieved from https://ceoworld.biz/2016/06/21/why-downsizing-fails-a-case-study/

Pratap, A. (2016, October). Why HR must leverage internal talent pools. *People Matters.* Retrieved from https://www.peoplematters.in/article/recruitment/why-hr-must-leverage-internal-talent-pools-14308

Rashid, A. & Naeem, N. (2017, March). Effects of mergers on corporate performance: An empirical evaluation using OLS and the empirical Bayesian methods. *Borsa Istanbul Review.* Retrieved from https://www.sciencedirect.com/science/article/pii/S2214845016300163

Sherman, H., & Young, S. (2016, July/August). Where financial reporting still falls short. *Harvard Business Review.* Retrieved from https://hbr.org/2016/07/where-financial-reporting-still-falls-short

Society for Human Resource Management. (2016). Strategic management. Retrieved from https://learnhrm.shrm.org//wp-content/uploads/2015/12/text_excerpt_for_demo_2016.pdf

Sternberg, L. (2014, January). How should you deal with legacy employees? *Talent+.* Retrieved from https://www.talentplus.com/talent-plus-viewpoint-blog/35-leadership/450-how-should-you-deal-with-legacy-employees

Todrin, D. (2011, July). The six biggest downsizing mistakes. *Entrepreneur.* Retrieved from https://www.entrepreneur.com/article/220074

Treacy, M., & Wiersma, M. (1997). *The discipline of market leaders.* New York, NY: Perseus.

Trevor J., & Varcoe, B. (2017, February). How aligned is your organization? *Harvard Business Review.* Retrieved from https://hbr.org/2017/02/how-aligned-is-your-organization

Wortman, J. (2017, January). Is your business at risk from hidden pockets of tribal knowl-edge? *Integrify.* Retrieved from https://www.integrify.com/blog/posts/business-risk-hidden-pockets-tribal-knowledge/

Yarnall, J. (2011). Maximizing the effectiveness of talent pools: A review of case study literature. *Leadership & Organization Development Journal,* 32(5)510–526.

CHAPTER 4

WATERING THE ORGANIZATIONAL LANDSCAPE

Meeting Employee Needs through HRM Flexibility

Alexandra E. MacDougall, Zhanna Bagdasarov, and M. Ronald Buckley

Change has always been with us, but it seems that the pace of change is accelerating.

—*Yehuda Baruch* (2004, p. 58)

Today's human resource professionals are tasked with meeting the needs of an increasingly complex and diverse workforce. Socio-demographic changes such as an aging workforce (Morris & Venkatesh, 2000), increased ethnocultural diversity (Ng & Johnson, 2015), more women in the workforce, and an increasing number of dual-career households (Baltes, Briggs, Huff, Wright, & Neuman, 1999) require that companies remain ahead of legislative mandates with HR-initiated diversity and inclusion programs (Kelliher & Anderson, 2010). Growing expectations and felt pressure for work-life balance (Allen, Johnson, Kiburz, & Shockley, 2013), moreover, suggests that to remain competitive, firms need to be responsive to workforce needs (Matz-Costa & Pitt-Catsouphes, 2010). Rapid technological

Human Resources Management Issues, Challenges and Trends:
"Now and Around the Corner", pages 81–101.

advancements have led to a greater reliance on technology in business while drastically shifting the organizational landscape and the conditions in which work is completed (Parker, Wall, & Cordery, 2001).

These observations indicate Baruch's (2004) above commentary on change resonates across societal, demographic, and technological realms, especially as they relate to business. Such external factors have drastically changed the world of work (Burke & Ng, 2006), with careers becoming more open, multidirectional, and individualistic, while losing stability, structure, and employer control (Arthur & Rousseau, 1996; Baruch, 2004, 2006). Accompanying this transition is a shift in employee expectations and preferences (Matz-Costa & Pitt-Catsouphes, 2010) that calls for rethinking the psychological contract as well as the effective management of people at work (Lyons, Schweitzer, & Ng, 2015).

The current effort is intended to shed light on the changing organizational landscape and the corresponding implications for contemporary human resource management. Specifically, we begin with a brief description of how socio-demographic and technological changes are influencing employee expectations. In light of this discussion, and in line with the new career model (e.g., Lyons et al., 2015), we will make the case for flexible work arrangements that grant employees agency in deciding how, when, and where their work tasks are completed. Finally, we will provide a detailed review of four key types of flexible work arrangements that may be capitalized on by human resource professionals.

THE CHANGING ORGANIZATIONAL LANDSCAPE

Socio-Demographic Changes

Over two decades ago, Jackson and Schuler (1995) highlighted the evolution in the U.S. labor market towards greater diversity, a trend we have continued to witness well into the 21st century. Workplace diversity "acknowledges the reality that people differ in many ways, visible or invisible" (Shen, Chanda, D'Netto, & Monga, 2009, p. 235). Although human resource managers have historically attended to more visible, conventional forms of diversity such as age, gender, and ethnicity, new concerns have emerged regarding other hidden forms of diversity including disability, sexual orientation, religion, individual differences, and cultural background, among others (Baruch, 2004; Ely & Thomas, 2001; Kossek, Lobel, & Brown, 2006; Shen, et al. 2009).

The changing demographic composition of the workforce calls for human resource departments to proactively manage diversity and inclusion so as to empower all members in their respective workplaces (Kossek et al., 2006). Likewise, given that a diverse workforce is necessarily comprised of individuals with varied values and beliefs, frames of references, experiences, and information (Shen et al., 2009), human resource professionals should be cognizant of the potentially distinct experiences and expectations of all employees. The following discussion breaks out some of these patterns for age, gender, and ethnicity.

Today's workforce is comprised of younger representatives from the Silent Generation (born 1925–1945) along with the Baby Boomers (born 1946–1964), Generation X (born 1965–1979), Generation Y or Millennials (born 1980–1994), and older members of Generation Z (born 1995–2012) (Ng & Parry, 2016). This multigenerational composition of the workforce, moreover, means employees in certain industries may be working with others who are nearly fifty years their senior or junior (McDonald, 2006). Accordingly, understanding how and if generations differ with respect to work values, attitudes, and expectations could prove immensely useful in initiating HRM policy change (Ng & Parry, 2016). For example, members of the Silent Generation tend to place emphasis on intrinsic values such as prestige, autonomy, and work centrality, whereas younger generations tend to appreciate extrinsic and social values such as working conditions, compensation, and their network of coworkers (Ng & Parry, 2016).

As compared to the Baby Boomers, members of Generation X value work-life balance, autonomy, and independence over organizational loyalty (Festing & Schafer, 2014). Known for their "work hard, play hard" mentality (Doverspike et al., 2000), Generation Xers are most attracted to firms that value personal and leisure time. Although Millennials share Generation X's values regarding leisure time and work-life balance, Millennials value extrinsic, materialistic rewards to a greater extent (Ng & Johnson, 2015; Ng & Parry, 2016; Smola & Sutton, 2002). Moreover, in the wake of increasing protean and boundaryless careers, Millennials are concerned with corporate social responsibility, continuous learning opportunities, and opportunities for mobility (Festing & Schafer, 2014). To summarize, younger generations, including Gen X, Gen Y, and Gen Z, tend to be more individualistic than are their older counterparts (Festing & Schafer, 2014). They value leisure time to a greater extent than did past generations (Lyons & Kuron, 2014), and tend to be technologically savvy having grown up with various technologies readily available to them.

Beyond generational values, it is also important to note the impending change to the organizational landscape as the roughly 77 million workers to be aged 65 or older by 2040 near retirement (Johnson, 2004). As noted by Beinhocker, Farrell, and Greenberg (2008), "the twilight of the U.S. baby boom generation is approaching, and with it deep, structural economic shifts whose impact will be felt for decades to come" (p. 1). This comes as little surprise, given that the youngest members of the Silent Generation and Baby Boomers are now 73 and 54, respectively. Yet, many individuals from these older generations would actually like to continue working, and in doing so, would face a number of barriers related to health care, labor law, retirement regulations, as well as negative perceptions regarding older workers (Beinhocker et al., 2008; Matz-Costa & Pitt-Catsouphes, 2010). In searching for best HR practices, then, practitioners must be cognizant of employee values and attitudes as well as potential constraints on the employment context.

Another change to the organizational landscape is the rising percentage of women in all sectors of the U.S. workforce (Greenhaus & Kossek, 2014; Harel, Tzafrir, & Baruch, 2003). In fact, there is an apparent "cracking" (albeit not breaking) of the glass ceiling (Baruch, 2006), which is beneficial to organizations for a number of reasons. Perhaps most notably, the integration of women into managerial positions not only signals fairness in selection and promotion processes, but also high-quality HRM practices and overall organizational effectiveness (Harel et al., 2003). Nevertheless, women and minorities remain underutilized in many roles, and particularly in management.

Beyond these initial strides for women in the workplace, we are also witnessing more dual-career couples and working parents, whether married or not, with young children (Allen, 2001; Greenhaus & Kossek, 2014). According to the Employment Characteristics of Family Survey, the 2017 labor participation rate of mothers with children under 18 years (71.1%) increased ever so slightly from 2013 (70.5%). A similar trend was found for mothers with children under 6 years, with the 2017 estimate at 65.5% compared to the 2013 estimate of 64.8% (U.S. Bureau of Labor Statistics, 2018). Dual-career couples and working parents, both male and female, certainly have a balancing act between work, home, and familial responsibilities (Allen, 2001). Although not discussed here in depth, this is also true for those caring for their aging or sick elders (Greenhaus & Kossek, 2014).

A final note with respect to socio-demographic changes is increasingly diverse nature of the workforce, both in terms of surface (demographic) and deep (attitudinal) factors (Harrison, Price, & Bell, 1998). As noted by Harrison and colleagues (1998), roughly 80% of entrants into the U.S. workforce today are women or ethnic minorities. There is not a "one size fits all" approach to managing diversity, and there is not a place for "monoculturalism" in the workplace (Lynch, 2017). Rather, human resource professionals should take care to identify the differing needs of varying employees, taking care to revisit and modify standards set by past generations in a predominantly white, male workforce. The future is promising in this regard, as Millennials tend to hold more egalitarian attitudes towards women and minority groups and are more likely to have been exposed to racial and cultural diversity from a young age (Ng & Johnson, 2015)

Technological Advancements

Organizations have rapidly gained access to highly sophisticated information technology with major implications for work design and job definition more broadly (Fenner & Renn, 2004; Morris & Venkatesh, 2000). As summarized by Guest (2004), "advances in technology are primarily responsible for an apparent speeding up of the world of work; and speed and flexibility of response is an important basis for competitive advantage (p. 543). Staying up to date with technology will only become more important for companies, as technological progress may very well restructure the labor market as we know it (Baruch, 2004).

Technological developments such as increased affordability, computer portability, and Internet availability made work readily available to employees in and out of the office (Parker et al., 2001). In this way, technology is blurring the boundaries of a "normal" work day, increasing the ease with which employees can extend their working hours outside their traditional workspace (Fenner & Renn, 2004). Technology has further changed the way in which work is organized and communicated. Large quantities of data are easily shareable across the globe in a nearly instantaneous fashion (Burke & Ng, 2006; Greenhaus & Kossek, 2014), contributing largely to the recent push for added flexibility through unconventional work arrangements.

Challenges for Contemporary Human Resource Management

Given the diverse organizational landscape in contemporary workplaces, it is clear that companies benefit from the effective management of diversity (Baruch, 2006). This notwithstanding, there are several corresponding challenges for human resource professionals including (1) a perceived mismatch in employee needs and workplace policies, (2) reluctance of technology innovations, and (3) pressure for enhanced work-life balance and workplace flexibility. Below, we provide a brief overview of each potential challenge and offer suggestions as to how those challenges may be addressed within human resources.

HR Challenge 1: Aligning Employee Needs and Workplace Policies. Employees may express concern about a mismatch between their needs and preferences with workplace policy. This is a valid concern, as Johnson (2004) reports that both workplace policies and employment structures have remained largely unchanged over time. In this regard, there appears to be a "structural lag" due in part to the multigenerational makeup of today's workforce, such that old policies remain intact despite becoming outdated and/or growing obsolete with time (Matz-Costa & Pitt-Catsouphes, 2010). To address this challenge, human resource professionals are encouraged to revisit existing psychological contracts with respective organizational members. A psychological contract is defined as a set of "individual beliefs, shaped by the organization, regarding terms of an exchange agreement between individuals and their organizations" (Rousseau, 1995, p. 9). As noted previously, employees are increasingly balancing multiple roles and commitments (Baruch, 2004; Halpern, 2005). Accordingly, granting employees voice and agency in discussing psychological contract terms, albeit informal, would signal that human resources is a true partner and alliance. HR professionals could further strengthen this partnership by offering support to employees and consulting them, rather than telling them, about impending policy changes (Baruch, 2003, 2004).

HR Challenge 2: Encouraging Technological Advancements and Use. Companies often face backlash from employees when undergoing change, which means that evolving technologies may be met with recoil. Although technology has clear advantages from an organizational perspective by way of attracting and retaining younger employees (McDonald, 2006), older workers in particular may be wary of technological advancements out of a concern for becoming obsolete (e.g., Noe, 2017). Interestingly, evidence indicates that the extent to which one responds positively or negatively toward adopting a new form of technology is the extent to which he or she views the technology as useful or instrumental to successful job performance (Morris & Venkatesh, 2000). Accordingly, HR professionals are advised to offer regular training and development programs to ensure all employees remain relevant and up to date on available technologies and to communicate the respective utility of newly introduced forms of technology.

HR Challenge 3: Adopting Work-Life Initiatives and Workplace Flexibility. Younger generations are increasingly identifying work-life balance as a key contributor to their job satisfaction (Lyons & Kuron, 2014). The Society for Human Resource Management's 2016 Employee Job Satisfaction and Engagement Survey, for example, indicated that more than half (53%) of respondents indicated that work-life balance was "Very Important" to their job satisfaction. Perhaps more notable, however, is that work-life balance was reported as equally important to base pay in determining job satisfaction (SHRM, 2016). Working parents, in particular, tend to express work-life and work-family tensions stemming from demanding jobs and blurred boundaries between work and home (Greenhaus & Kossek, 2014). Older workers comprise another group expressing concern regarding rigid work schedules (Pitt-Catsouphes & Matz-Costa, 2008). For example, the Taskforce on the Aging of the American Workforce (2008) indicated that workplace flexibility, or the lack thereof, is a main reason for retirement among older workers. Likewise, the Taskforce described a lack of flexible working arrangements as a barrier to employment for older workers wishing to remain in the workforce.

As with HR Challenge 1, we advise HR professionals to give up control, to the extent possible, through implementation of family friendly policies and increased workplace flexibility. Employees are regularly experiencing escalating commitments to multiple, distinct roles resulting in growing expectations and felt pressure for work-life balance (Allen, et al., 2013; Greenhaus & Kossek, 2014). Such initiatives would further serve to keep older generations involved in the workforce. In fact, evidence suggests that many Baby Boomers would remain in the workforce if flexible or alternate work arrangements were made available (Beinhocker et al., 2008). This is not surprising, as Kossek (2006) indicated work-family tensions have continued to rise for all demographic groups and occupations across the nation. Taken together, it would behoove human resource departments to empower and invest in their workers through the adoption of family-friendly policies made possible through increased flexibility and alternative work arrangements (Baruch, 2004).

MAKING THE CASE FOR HUMAN RESOURCE FLEXIBILITY

Workplace flexibility is broadly defined as "the ability of workers to make choices influencing when, where, and for how long they engage in work-related tasks" (Hill et al., 2008, p. 152). Central to this definition is that flexibility provides an opportunity for employees to exercise agency (Seeck & Parzefall, 2008). Employees are granted the freedom to determine how best to arrange their core work responsibilities so long as they attend to the broader organizational context, culture, and structure in doing so (Hill et al., 2008). In this way, human resource flexibility can reframe the employment relationship as a true partnership as opposed to top-down policies based on control and command (Baruch, 2004). According to the Society for Human Resource Management (2014), this partnership contributes to a mutually beneficial agreement between employees and employers regarding the manner in which the work will be completed, and how it will meet organizational needs.

The growing preference for flexibility among employees is a trend witnessed across geographical location and business sector (Baruch, 2006; Matz-Costa & Pitt-Catsouphes, 2010). Indeed, workplace flexibility is typically framed as an employee benefit. Yet, organizations have much to gain from using flexibility as a management tool as well (SHRM, 2014, 2016). Flexible work arrangements have been met with a great deal of success at multiple levels. The following discussion makes the case for the broad classification of flexible work arrangements by highlighting benefits to employees, organizations, and local communities.

Individual Benefits

One of the primary areas in which flexible work arrangements have been shown to benefit employees is through reduced work-family conflict (Masuda et al., 2011; McNall, Masuda, & Nicklin, 2010). Work-family conflict occurs when role demands at work interfere with one's role demands at home, or vice versa (Boswell & Olson-Buchanan, 2007; Greenhaus & Beutell, 1985). This is not surprising, as workplace flexibility has been specifically touted as a method to help employees manage their work and family roles (Allen et al., 2013; Hill et al., 2010). Because employees may adjust job features to meet personal needs and goals (Putnam, Myers, & Gailliard, 2014), flexible work arrangements enable workers to better "juggle" their work and life commitments (Matz-Costa & Pitt-Catsouphes, 2010). Beyond work-life enrichment, workplace flexibility has also been linked to enhanced personal vitality (Hill et al., 2008), improved health and well-being (SHRM, 2014), higher life satisfaction, and fewer mental health problems (Pitt-Catsouphes & Matz-Costa, 2008).

In the work domain, flexible work practices have been shown to bolster job satisfaction, employee engagement, and commitment (e.g., Bal & De Lange, 2015; Golden, 2006; Kelliher & Anderson, 2010; Masuda et al., 2011; McNall, Masuda, & Nicklin, 2010), while reducing job stress (Halpern, 2005). In fact, according to the Society for Human Resource Management's 2016 Job Satisfaction Report, 53 percent of employees rate the flexibility to balance home and work responsibilities as a key aspect of their job satisfaction, a seven percent increase from the 2010 survey (SHRM, 2010, 2016). Moreover, although there are mixed views, prior research has indicated that flexible work practices may lead to "career premiums," or greater success in terms of salary and job level (Gariety & Shaffer, 2001; Weeden, 2005), particularly for employees who are viewed as committed and productive by their direct supervisors (Leslie, Manchester, Park, & Mehng, 2012). Taken together, employees have much to gain from flexible work options.

Organizational Benefits

From an organizational perspective, flexible work arrangements can provide a strong competitive advantage and support towards strategic business objectives (Allen, 2001; SHRM, 2014). For example, advertising a firm's workplace flexibility may help human resource departments attract and retain top talent (Beauregard & Henry, 2009; Blair-Loy & Wharton, 2002). Scholars have pointed to the utility of flexibility in reducing absenteeism and turnover (Golden, 2006; Masuda et al., 2011; McNall, Masuda, & Nicklin, 2010), and have highlighted the corresponding cost savings (SHRM, 2014). Flexible work has been further linked to improvements in productivity, performance, profits, and customer service (Baltes, Briggs, Huff, Wright, & Neuman, 1999; Cascio, 2000; Hill et al., 2008). Drawing from social exchange theory, Kelliher and Anderson (2010) highlighted that flexible arrangements may result in work intensification due to the perception that employees should trade flexibility for effort.

In addition to these beneficial outcomes, flexible work options should further promote employee extra-role behavior. Flexible HR practices communicates to employees that their organization cares and wants to invest in them, constructs that have long been known to predict organizational citizenship behavior (e.g., Organ & Ryan, 1995). Similarly, as noted by Jiang, Lepak, Hu, and Baer (2012), increased flexibility may trigger employees' intrinsic motivation, which in turn should lead such employees to seek out challenges. The increased flexibility afforded by FWA may accommodate such endeavors, allowing for added creativity in when and how employees engage in extra-role behavior.

Community Benefits

Beyond advantages of flexible work practices on employees and employers, local communities may benefit as well. For example, given that flexibility affords employees greater work-life balance (e.g., McNall, Masuda, & Nicklin, 2010), employees may find themselves engaging more freely in volunteer initiatives with the community. Likewise, time spent with family and friends may in turn enrich the local community through increased visibility at local schools and events (e.g., SHRM, 2014). Moreover, when employees are able to cut back on their driving due to flexible work arrangements such as telework or compressed workweeks, they are helping to reduce commuting mileage and corresponding carbon dioxide emissions (Cascio, 2000), supporting a more sustainable environment.

Summary

Workplace flexibility is gaining traction as a human resource strategy due to its mutually beneficial outcomes for employees and employers, alike (Allen et al., 2013). Management scholars have referred to flexibility as "a necessity in the contemporary workplace" (Halpern, 2004, as cited by Hill et al., 2008), forecasting its impending adoption across organizations. Employers will soon be evaluated on whether or how they implement flexible work practices, and these evaluations will signal the extent to which companies are aware of and responsive to workforce needs (Matz-Costa & Pitt-Catsouphes, 2010). Yet, many U.S. companies have been slow to move towards greater flexibility, due in part to a general lack of awareness or availability of established policies to easily incorporate across industry (SHRM, 2014). Accordingly, we turn next to a more detailed discussion of specific types of flexible work arrangements.

AN OVERVIEW OF PROMINENT FLEXIBLE WORK ARRANGEMENTS

Flexible work covers a range of "working patterns," or options for employees seeking nontraditional means for work completion (Kelliher & Anderson, 2010). As there are multiple dimensions to workplace flexibility (Pitt-Catsouphes & Matz-Costa, 2008), the following section provides an introduction to four specific arrangements including (1) flextime, (2) compressed workweek, (3) telecommuting, and (4) job sharing. Each flexible work arrangement is first defined and then discussed with respect to corresponding benefits for employees and organizations, respectively, and may be referenced human resource professionals wishing to provide employees with enhanced flexibility.

Flextime

Flextime (Flexible Working Hours) Defined. "With a flextime work arrangement, employees may choose the starting and ending time of their workday as long as they work the appropriate number of hours per day or week" (Lepak & Gowan, 2016, p. 127). Although employees are given considerable leeway in scheduling their work, generally, flextime scheduling is built around special *core hours*, such as 11 A.M. to 2 P.M., during which employees are required to be present (Dessler, 2015; Snell, Morris, & Bohlander, 2016). Therefore, with these particular core hours, workers may choose to work from 7 A.M. until 3 P.M., or from 11 A.M. until 7 P.M., all the while ensuring that they are in attendance during the specified core hours. It is important to understand that flextime work arrangements do not shorten work time but simply rearrange them to accommodate workers' needs (Hochschild, 1997).

Benefits of Flextime. Allowing for alternative work scheduling by means of flextime arrangement has been touted by organizations to be beneficial to both employees and employers alike. At the individual level, flextime allows employees to accommodate their specific lifestyles, resulting in decreased work-family conflict (Boswell & Olson-Buchanan, 2007; Greenhaus & Beutell, 1985). Work-family conflict has been consistently associated with various destructive personal and professional outcomes such as decreased job satisfaction, life satisfaction, organizational commitment, organizational citizenship behavior (OCB), marital satisfaction, family satisfaction, as well as a slew of stress-related outcomes (e.g., Allen, Herst, Bruck, & Sutton, 2000; Kossek & Ozeki, 1998). Thus, managing this inter-role conflict should be of paramount importance for organizations in order to maintain a healthy and productive workforce.

In addition to improved work-family balance, deviations from commuting during peak hours due to some latitude in departure times not only mitigates heavy traffic congestion caused by employees forced to adhere to fixed work schedules (Mun & Yonekawa, 2006), but also allows employees to spend less time on the road. Moreover, work by Lucas and Heady (2002) has indicated that commuters on flextime schedules reported less driver stress and decreased feelings of time pressure compared to workers with fixed work hours. Consequently, improved commuting and decreased driver stress are yet additional individual-level advantages of flextime cited by employees in extant literature (Ralston, 1989).

Finally, flextime arrangements have also been associated with various improvements in employee attitudes (Hicks & Klimoski, 1981). A number of studies to date have investigated the relationship between flextime and job satisfaction. Majority of this work corroborates the notion that flextime scheduling leads to increased job satisfaction for employees. In fact, Baltes, Briggs, Huff, Wright, and Neuman (1999) conducted a meta-analysis examining this specific relationship and concluded that, in general, flexible work hours had a positive impact on job satisfaction. Following this meta-analysis, others have confirmed the positive association between these two variables across diverse samples and settings (e.g., Allen, 2001; McNall, Masuda, & Nicklin, 2010). More recently, a quantitative review of 43 studies and 22,882 employees revealed that flexible work arrangements—among them flextime—were positively associated with job satisfaction and psychological health (Kröll, Doebler, & Nüesch, 2017).

At the organizational level, granting employees flextime has been associated with a reduction in tardiness and general absenteeism (Zeidner, 2008). Early longitudinal work by Ralston and Flanagan (1985) compared female and male employees on and off flextime, postulating a decrease in absenteeism and turnover for employees with flextime arrangements. Although no significant differences were found for turnover, significant decreases in absenteeism were found for both female and male worker on flextime. The authors concluded that flextime reduced employees' need for absenteeism and thus ultimately positively contributed to work-life balance, as well. Similarly, Rainer and Wolf (1981) conducted an experiment at the U.S. Social Security Administration and found that along with generally favorable appraisals of flextime by employees, they saw a significant decline in tardiness. On top of these organizationally-relevant benefits, many employers name flextime as a strong recruitment and retention tool (Snell et al., 2016). Mitchell, Brooks, Holtom, and Lee (2001), for instance, argue that allowing employees to craft their own work hours by deciding when to start and quit each day, can aid in creating a solid fit between employees and their off-the-job environments, permitting employees to maintain their recreational and interpersonal lives. Flextime has even been hyped as an important retention tool in non-profit organizations—often discussed in terms of a coveted nonfinancial benefit (Ban, Drahnak-Faller, & Towers, 2003).

Finally, and perhaps of greatest significance to most organizations, flextime has been linked to improved productivity and overall performance. For one, productivity can improve simply because employees can arrange to work during hours they believe to be their most alert and productive (Snell et al., 2016). Others have found that, consistent with tenets of Hackman and Oldham's (1976) job characteristics theory, flextime contributes to employees' job autonomy, resulting in increased job performance. For example, Eaton (2003) demonstrated the positive association between workplace flexibility policies, among them flextime, with self-reported productivity. On a larger scale, in their quantitative review of flexible work arrangements literature, Baltes et al. (1999) upheld that flextime had a positive effect on employee productivity.

Compressed Workweek

Compressed Workweek Defined. In this particular work arrangement, the number of days in the workweek is reduced (compressed) as a result of increasing the number of hours worked per day (Snell et al., 2016). Specifically, employees may choose to work only four days (Monday–Thursday), but be required to put in 10 hours a day in order to maintain their 40-hour workweek. This particular arrangement is commonly referred to as 4/10 or 4/40. Other variations of the compressed workweek exist. A much less common variant consists of working a 12-hour shift (Venne, 1997), while others may involve working 80 hours spread over nine days (9/80), allowing for a day off every other week (Snell et al., 2016).

Benefits of compressed workweek. At the individual level, one of the most obvious benefits of the compressed workweek arrangement is the acquisition of one business day a week away from work. Having a day off during a workweek allows employees to schedule and attend to personal business—medical, dental, financial—as well as accommodate recreational activities and time with family and friends (Pierce & Dunham, 1992; Ronen & Primps). Akin to the benefits of flextime, compressed workweek schedules have also been touted as useful transportation demand management (TDM) strategies. Ho and Steward (1992), for example, examined travel logs completed by employees before and after implementation of the 4/40 compressed workweek arrangement in a busy metropolitan city and found a significant reduction in the average number of vehicle miles traveled over the course of a week, leading to an inevitable reduced carbon footprint. Additional individual-level benefits include improvements in employee job satisfaction, morale, and satisfaction with work schedules (Baltes et al., 1999; Breaugh & Frye, 2007). Even an early review of literature on behavioral and attitudinal consequences of compressed workweeks indicated improvements in employees' satisfaction with their jobs (Ronen & Primps, 1981).

When it comes to organizationally-relevant outcomes, most managers cite improvements in recruitment and retention of employees (Gurchiek, 2006), although surprisingly, no reduction in absenteeism was observed in a review of flexible work arrangements literature (Baltes et al., 1999). With respect to performance, summaries of research on compressed workweeks have revealed mixed results (Baltes & Sirabian, 2017). Although several studies have indicated an improvement in performance and productivity following the implementation of a compressed workweek schedule (Ronen & Primps, 1981), meta-analytic evidence on this relationship is more ambiguous. Specifically, the review of literature showed that compressed workweeks improved supervisory ratings of performance, yet had no positive effects on objective measures of productivity. Of studies that indicate a decrease in productivity, fatigue acquired due to long work shifts is assumed to be the culprit for the negative relationship (Baltes & Sirabian, 2017).

Telecommuting

Telecommuting Defined. According to Gajendran and Harrison (2007) "Telecommuting is an alternative work arrangement in which employees perform tasks elsewhere that are normally done in a primary or central workplace, for at least some portion of their work schedule, using electronic media to interact with others inside and outside the organization" (p. 1525). Although telecommuters commonly work from home, there are other variations of this arrangement to note. Some telecommuters may be found working from satellite offices—located outside the home and the organization—while other telecommuters may work from neighborhood offices—occupied by employees from various organizations (Blanchard, 2017). Yet another variation of this involves working entirely on the go, the so-called *mobile workers*—conducting business from planes, vehicles, and hotel rooms. All four types of telecommuters are still considered to be performing *distributed work,* or work being done away from the organization's physical location (Gajendran & Harrison, 2007), so all four are types of telecommuters. This widespread practice is just one outcome of drastic advancement in technology and its impact on how today's organizations conduct business.

Benefits of Telecommuting. As with other flexible work arrangements, telecommuting bears both individual- and organizational-level benefits. At the individual level, telecommuting promotes a better work-life balance (Snell et al.,

2016). This positive effect is facilitated mainly by the improved flexibility for employees, leading to reduced work-family conflict (Gajendran & Harrison, 2007; Golden, Veiga, & Simsek, 2006). Additional advantages include increased job satisfaction, lower turnover intent, and reduced role stress (Gajendran & Harrison, 2007). Some work on these relationships indicates that job satisfaction associated with telecommuting was due to fewer interruptions and less time spent on office politics (Snell et al., 2016). Beyond these, employees also find the reduction in stress due to minimal commuting and control over one's work environment to be added benefits (Piskurich, 1996).

Organizationally, meta-analytic evidence regarding the link between job performance and telecommuting indicates that this work arrangement is associated with higher supervisory ratings or archival records of performance (Gajendran & Harrison, 2007). Interestingly, no relationship between telecommuting and self-rated performance was observed. Additional work in this domain suggests that telecommuting also reduces absenteeism, overtime, and sick time on the part of the employee (Piskurich, 1996). Resembling flextime and compressed workweeks, telecommuting helps attract and retain valued employees—serving as a vital recruitment and retention tool for companies (Piskurich, 1996). Telecommuting has also been found to impact the physical space of the organization, with managers and HR professionals citing reduced office space (Snell et al., 2016) and maximization of office space (Piskurich, 1996) as two important advantages for the company. Cascio (2000) highlights the potential cost savings associated with reduced office space and corresponding real-estate expenses, and notes additional opportunities for cost savings as a result of decreased travel and lodging needs

Job Sharing

Job sharing defined. Job sharing refers to an arrangement whereby one full-time job is performed by two part-time employees (Olmsted, 1979). The success of this particular type of flexible work arrangement depends highly on consistent and effective interaction and collaboration between the two part-time employees in order to get the work done (Thomas, Spitzmueller, & Sady, 2017). Job sharers must work as a team and pick up where the other leaves off mainly because both employees are responsible for the same job (Thakur, Bansal, & Maini, 2018). According to Snell et al. (2016), job sharers commonly work three days a week, overlapping one day in order to facilitate effective communication. Given this scheduling, job sharers are paid three-fifth of a normal, full-time salary.

Benefits of Job Sharing. Although literature on job sharing discusses fewer overall advantages than that of flextime, compressed workweeks, and telecommuting, the benefits are nonetheless there and are not trivial. Most of those who opt for this arrangement do so because they either do not want to work full-time (as in the case of older workers wishing to phase into retirement) or they cannot work full-time (as in the case of parents of young children needing to work part-time in order to be mindful of their family responsibilities). Thus, one of the biggest pros to job sharing is the achievement of a better work-life balance (Stables & Watton, 2017). Employees engaged in job sharing often cite the ability to balance work and family demands, raise children, conduct personal business, advance their education, and attend to other interests and goals as the main benefits of this work arrangement (Thomas et al., 2017).

Managers, on the other hand, tout having a second trained employee who can always fill in for the first if one is on vacation or out sick (Thomas et al., 2017), minimizing the inevitable disruption to productivity associated with illness and vacation. Employers also relish job sharing because they can schedule the part-time employees to work during peak hours of workload, maximizing productivity (Snell et al., 2016). And, if hard times arise, employers can institute job sharing in order to keep both workers employed, reducing the need for layoffs (Snell et al., 2016).

GENERAL DISCUSSION

It is our hope that the current effort helps reframe the way businesses think about flexible work options. Rather than viewing flexible work as solely an employee or employer benefit, organizations should highlight the utility of flexible work practices as both a management tool (via enhanced efficiency and productivity) and a means to meet employee interests (via work-life enrichment) (Reilly, 1998; SHRM, 2014). Through this lens, workplace flexibility is best viewed as a mutually beneficial employment arrangement.

The current effort delved into workplace flexibility through discussion of four flexible work arrangements including (1) flextime, (2) compressed workweek, (3) telecommuting, and (4) job sharing. Although important in and of themselves, these arrangements only constitute part of what it means to enact a flexible workplace. For example, Pitt-Catsouphes and Matz-Costa (2008) deconstructed the flexibility construct into multiple key dimensions including formal versus informal policies, attitudes and values characterizing the broader organizational climate and culture, work design and employment structure, and interpersonal interactions. Kossek, Lewis, and Hammer (2010) condensed these dimensions into two factors. According to the authors, structural components entail the actual flexible job design and corresponding HR policies, whereas cultural components are comprised of supportive supervisors and climates. Inherent in both of the above conceptualizations of workplace flexibility is the need for social support in addition to structural changes, and we certainly echo this sentiment.

Before concluding, several practical implications of this chapter are worth noting. First, managers seeking to integrate flexible work arrangements should first decide whether they will do so in a standardized or individualized fashion. Companies may opt to include alternate work arrangements within benefits packages made available to all employees, thereby ensuring equal access to such programs. Others may choose to accept "I-Deals," or idiosyncratic terms in employment (Hornung, Rosseau, & Glaser, 2008). I-Deals allow employees to customize, or negotiate, for employment conditions that best align with their personal needs and preferences. Often, I-Deals take place at the time of hire, although some organizations are willing to accept them on an ongoing basis. Determining whether standardized or individualized approaches to flexible work arrangements is likely to depend on the nature of the job as well as the organization as a whole.

Second, human resource professionals should be cognizant of how best to manage employees on flexible work arrangements, inclusive of regular communications to incentivizing and measuring performance. Prior to the start of a new flexible work arrangement, managers are encouraged to meet with employees to jointly determine (1) how best to communicate with one another, (2) how work will get done, and (3) how performance will be evaluated (see SHRM, 2014 for a detailed list of support activities for flexible workers). Moreover, flexible work arrangements should not come with an "out of sight, out of mind" mentality. Rather, managers should be equipped with regular check-in questions focused on the work (task completion, time management) as well as the worker (general well-being, level of comfort working alone) (SHRM, 2014).

Lastly, it is important to note that workplace flexibility may not be appropriate for all people or contexts (Cascio, 2000). Not all workers will prefer flexible work to traditional work, as individual differences may impact whether an employee chooses to opt into such arrangements (Lambert, Marler, & Gueutal, 2008). For example, individuals who exhibit personal innovativeness, or a tendency to explore new and unfamiliar forms of technology (Fenner & Renn, 2004), may respond very well to flexible arrangements. Employees who exhibit openness to experience, known for their intellectual curiosity, creative thought, and willingness to accept change (Judge, Piccolo, & Kosalka, 2009) are likely to respond in a similar fashion. Not everyone exhibits such characteristics, however, and many employees may be reluctant to transition into such novel working conditions. In this regard, it is important to consider "flexibility fit," or the extent to which employees perceive that their employer is offering a flexible arrangement that meets their needs (Pitt-Catsouphes & Matz-Costa, 2000). Although work-family tensions are on the rise across all demographic groups (Kossek, 2006), the types of flexibility needed by older workers may very well differ from those preferred by younger generations.

CONCLUDING REMARKS

The 21st century workforce bears little resemblance to the workforce of the past, and continued change, whether radical or incremental, is certain to contribute to an ever-changing organizational landscape. A company's willingness to remain flexible and adapt to changing times not only signals its responsiveness to workforce needs, but moreover, its long-term viability (Matz-Costa & Pitt-Catsouphes, 2010). Human resource departments are often the first stop in heeding and addressing employee concerns. Staying abreast of changing values and preferences among new generations can thus contribute to favorable HR policies and practices that facilitate a positive organizational environment for all (Westerman & Yamamura, 2007). Accordingly, the current effort made a case for increased flexibility within human resource departments as a mutually beneficial arrangement for employers and employees. It is our hope that the evidence provided herein will encourage HR professionals to implement flexible work arrangements, granting employees agency in determining how to perform their work, and in turn facilitating enhanced work-life balance.

REFERENCES

Allen, T. D. (2001). Family-supportive work environments: The role of organizational perceptions. *Journal of Vocational Behavior, 58*(3), 414–435.

Allen, T. D., Herst, D. E., Bruck, C. S., & Sutton, M. (2000). Consequences associated with work-to-family conflict: A review and agenda for future research. *Journal of Occupational Health Psychology, 5*(2), 278–308. doi:10.1037//1076-8998.5.2.278

Allen, T. D., Johnson, R. C., Kiburz, K. M., & Shockley, K. M. (2013). Work-family conflict and flexible work arrangements: Deconstructing flexibility. *Personnel Psychology, 66*(2), 345–376.

Arthur, M. B., & Rousseau, D. M. (1006). *The boundaryless career.* New York, NY: Oxford University Press.

Bal, P. M., & De Lange, A. H. (2015). From flexibility human resource management to employee engagement and perceived job performance across the lifespan: A multisample study. *Journal of Occupational and Organizational Psychology, 88*(1), 126–154.

Baltes, B. B., Briggs, T. E., Huff, J. W., Wright, J. A., & Neuman, G. A. (1999). Flexible and compressed workweek schedules: A meta-analysis of their effects on work-related criteria. *Journal of Applied Psychology, 84*(4), 496–513.

Baltes, B. B., & Sirabian, M. A. (2017). Compressed workweek. In S. G. Rogelberg (Ed.), *The SAGE encyclopedia of industrial and organizational psychology* (2nd ed.). SAGE Publications, Inc.

Ban, C., Drahnak-Faller, A., & Towers, M. (2003). Human resource challenges in human service and community development organizations: Recruitment and retention of professional staff. *Review of Public Personnel Administration, 23*(2), 133–153.

Baruch, Y. (2003). Career systems in transition: A normative model for organizational career practices. *Personnel Review, 32*(1), 231–251.

Baruch, Y. (2004). Transforming careers - from linear to multidirectional career paths: Organizational and individual perspective. *Career Development International, 9*(1), 58–73.

Baruch, Y. (2006). Career development in organizations and beyond: Balancing traditional and contemporary viewpoints. *Human Resource Management Review, 16*(2), 125–138.

Beauregard, T. A., & Henry, L. C. (2009). Making the link between work-life balance practices and organizational performance. *Human Resource Management Review, 19(1),* 9–22.

Beinhocker, E. D., Farrell, D., & Greenberg, E. (2008). Why baby boomers will need to work longer. *The McKinsey Quarterly.* Retrieved from *https://www.incomesolver. com/wp-content/uploads/2014/08/why_baby_boomers_will_need_to_work_longer. pdf*

Blair-Loy, M., & Wharton, A. S. (2002). Employee's use of work-family policies and the workplace social context. *Social Forces, 80*(3), 813–845.

Blanchard, A. (2017). Telecommuting. In S. G. Rogelberg (Ed.), *The SAGE encyclopedia of industrial and organizational psychology* (2nd ed.). SAGE Publications, Inc.

Boswell, W. R., & Olson-Buchanan, J. B. (2007). The use of communication technologies after hours: The role of work attitudes and work-life conflict. *Journal of Management, 33*(4), 592–610. doi: 10.1177/0149206307302552

Breaugh, J. A., & Frye, N. K. (2007). An examination of the antecedents and consequences of the use of family-friendly benefits. *Journal of Managerial Issues, 19*(1), 35–52.

Burke, R. J., & Ng, E. (2006). The changing nature of work and organizations: Implications for human resource management. *Human Resource Management Review, 16*(2), 86–94.

Cascio, W. F. (2000). Managing a virtual workplace. *The Academy of Management Executive, 14*(3), 81–90.

Dessler, G. (2015). *Human resource management* (14th ed.). Pearson Education.

Doverspike, D., Taylor, M. A., Shultz, K. S., & McKay, P. F. (2000). Responding to the challenge of a changing workforce: Recruiting nontraditional demographic groups. *Public Personnel Management, 29*(4), 445–459.

Eaton, S. C. (2003). If you can use them: Flexibility policies, organizational commitment, and perceived performance. *Industrial Relations: A Journal of Economy and Society, 42*(2), 145–167.

Ely, R. J., & Thomas, D. A. (2001). Cultural diversity at work: The effects of diversity perspectives on work group processes and outcomes. *Administrative Science Quarterly, 46*(2), 229–273.

Fenner, G. H., & Renn, R. W. (2004). Technology-assisted supplemental work: Construct definition and a research framework. *Human Resource Management, 43*(2–3), 179–200.

Festing, M., & Schäfer, L. (2014). Generational challenges to talent management: A framework for talent retention based on the psychological-contract perspective. *Journal of World Business, 49*(2), 262–271.

Gajendran, R. S., & Harrison, D. A. (2007). The good, the bad, and the unknown about telecommuting: Meta-analysis of psychological mediators and individual consequences. *Journal of Applied Psychology, 92*(6), 1524–1541. doi:10.1037/00219010.92.6.1524

Gariety, B. S., & Shaffer, S. (2001). Wage differentials associated with flextime. *Monthly Labor Review, 124*(3), 68–75.

Golden, T. D. (2006). Avoiding depletion in virtual work: Telework and the intervening impact of work exhaustion on commitment and turnover intentions. *Journal of Vocational Behavior, 69*(1), 176–187.

Golden, T. D., Veiga, J. F., & Simsek, Z. (2006). Telecommuting's differential impact on work-family conflict: Is there no place like home? *Journal of Applied Psychology, 91*(6), 1340–1350. doi:10.1037/0021-9010.91.6.1340

Greenhaus, J. H., & Beutell, N. J. (1985). Sources of conflict between work and family roles. *Academy of Management Review, 10*(1), 76–88.

Greenhaus, J. H., & Kossek, E. E. (2014). The contemporary career: A work-home perspective. *Annual Review of Organizational Psychology and Organizational Behavior, 1,* 361–388.

Gurchiek, K. (2006). Good news for moms reconsidering work. *HR Magazine, 51*(7), 39.

Hackman, J. R., & Oldham, G. R. (1976). Motivation through the design of work: Test of a theory. *Organizational Behavior and Human Performance*, *16*(2), 250–279.

Halpern, D. F. (2005). How time-flexible work policies can reduce stress, improve health, and save money. *Stress and Health*, *21*(3), 157–168.

Harel, G., Tzafrir, S., & Baruch, Y. (2003). Achieving organizational effectiveness through promotion of women into managerial positions: HRM practice focus. *International Journal of Human Resource Management*, *14*(2), 247–263.

Harrison, D. A., Price, K. H., & Bell, M. P. (1998). Beyond relational demography: Time and the effects of surface- and deep-level diversity on work group cohesion. *Academy of Management Journal, 41*(1), 96–107.

Hicks, W. D., & Klimoski, R. J. (1981). The impact of flexitime on employee attitudes. *Academy of Management Journal, 24*(2), 333–341.

Hill, E. J., Erickson, J. J., Holmes, E. K., & Ferris, M. (2010). Workplace flexibility, work hours, and work-life conflict: Finding an extra day or two. *Journal of Family Psychology, 24*(3), 349–358.

Hill, E. J., Grzywacz, J. G., Allen, S., Blanchard, V. L., Matz-Costa, C., Shulkin, S., & Pitt-Catsouphes, M. (2008). Defining and conceptualizing workplace flexibility. *Community, Work, & Family, 11*(2), 149–163.

Ho, A., & Stewart, J. (1992). Case study on impact of 4/40 compressed workweek program on trip reduction. *Transportation Research Record*, *1346*, 25–32.

Hochschild, A. (1997). The time bind. *Journal of Labor and Society*, *1*(2), 21–29.

Hornung, S., Rousseau, D. M., & Glaser, J. (2008). Creating flexible work arrangements through idiosyncratic deals. *Journal of Applied Psychology*, *93*(3), 655.

Jackson, S. E., & Schuler, R. S. (1995). Understanding human resource management in the context of organizations and their environments. *Annual Review of Psychology, 46*, 237–264.

Jiang, K., Lepak, D. P., Hu, J., & Baer, J. (2012). How does human resource management influence organizational outcomes? A meta-analytic investigation of mediating mechanisms. *Academy of Management Journal, 55*(6), 1264–1294.

Johnson, R. W. (2004). Trends in job demands among older workers, 1992–2002. *Monthly Labor Review*, *127*, 48–56.

Joice, W. (2007). Implementing telework: the technology issue. *Public Manager*, *36*(2), 64–68.

Judge, T. A., Piccolo, R. F., & Kosalka, T. (2009). The bright and dark sides of leader traits: A review and theoretical extension of the leader trait paradigm. *The Leadership Quarterly, 20*(6), 855–875.

Kelliher, C., & Anderson, D. (2010). Doing more with less? Flexible working practices and the intensification of work. *Human Relations, 63*(1), 83–106.

Kossek, E. E. (2006). Work and family in America: Growing tensions between employment policy and a change workforce. In E. Lawler & J. O'Toole (Eds.), *America at Work: Choices and Challenges* (pp. 53–72). New York, NY: Palgrave Macmillan.

Kossek, E. E., Lewis, S., & Hammer, L. B. (2010). Work-life initiatives and organizational change: Overcoming mixed messages to move from the margin to the mainstream. *Human Relations, 63*(1), 3–19.

Kossek, E. E., Lobel, S. A., & Brown, J. (2005). Human resource strategies to manage workforce diversity. In A. M. Konrad, P. Prasad, & J. M. Pringle (Eds.), *Handbook of workplace diversity* (pp. 53–74). Thousand Oaks, CA: Sage.

Kossek, E. E., & Ozeki, C. (1998). Work–family conflict, policies, and the job–life satisfaction relationship: A review and directions for organizational behavior–human resources research. *Journal of Applied Psychology, 83*(2), 139–149.

Kröll, C., Doebler, P., & Nüesch, S. (2017). Meta-analytic evidence of the effectiveness of stress management at work. *European Journal of Work and Organizational Psychology, 26*(5), 677–693. doi:10.1080/1359432X.2017.1347157

Lambert, A. D., Marler, J. H., & Gueutal, H. G. (2008). Individual differences: Factors affecting employee utilization of flexible work arrangements. *Journal of Vocational Behavior, 73*(1), 107–117.

Lepak, D., & Gowan, M. (2016). *Human resource management: Managing employees for competitive advantage* (2nd ed.). Chicago Business Press.

Leslie, L. M., Park, T-Y., & Mehng, S. A. (2012). Flexible work practices: A source of career premiums or penalties? *Academy of Management Journal, 55*(6), 1407–1428.

Lucas, J. L., & Heady, R. B. (2002). Flextime commuters and their driver stress, feelings of time urgency, and commute satisfaction. *Journal of Business and Psychology, 16*(4), 565–571.

Lynch, F. R. (2017). *The Diversity Machine: The drive to change the "White Male Workplace."* New York, NY: Routledge.

Lyons, S., & Kuron, L. (2014). Generational differences in the workplace: A review of the evidence and directions for future research. *Journal of Organizational Behavior, 35,* S139–S157.

Lyons, S. T., Schweitzer, L., & Ng, E. S. W. (2015). How have careers changed? An investigation of changing career patterns across four generations. *Journal of Managerial Psychology, 30*(1), 8–21.

Masuda, A. D., Poelmans, S. A. Y., Allen, T. D., Spector, P. E., Lapierre, L. M., Cooper, C. L., . . . Moreno-Velazquez, I. (2011). Flexible work arrangements availability and their relationship with work-to-family conflict, job satisfaction, and turnover intentions: A comparison of three country clusters. *Applied Psychology: An International Review, 61,* 1–29.

Matz-Costa, C., & Pitt-Catsouphes, M. (2009). Workplace flexibility as an organizational response to the aging of the workforce: A comparison of nonprofit and for-profit organizations. *Journal of Social Service Research, 36*(1), 68–80.

McDonald, P. (2006). The quest for talent. *Internal Auditor, 63*(3), 72–77.

McNall, L. A., Masuda, A. D., & Nicklin, J. M. (2010). Flexible work arrangements, job satisfaction, and turnover intentions: The mediating role of work-to-family enrichment. *The Journal of Psychology, 144*(1), 61–81. doi:10.1080/00223980903356073

Mitchell, T., Holtom, B., Lee, T., & Ted Graske. (2001). How to keep your best employees: Developing an effective retention policy. *The Academy of Management Executive, 15*(4), 96–109. Retrieved from http://www.jstor.org/stable/4165789

Morris, M. G., & Venkatesh, V. (2000). Age differences in technology adoption decisions: Implications for a changing work force. *Personnel Psychology, 53*(2), 375–403.

Mun, S. I., & Yonekawa, M. (2006). Flextime, traffic congestion and urban productivity. *Journal of Transport Economics and Policy (JTEP), 40*(3), 329–358.

Ng, E. S., & Johnson, J. M. (2015). Millennials: Who are they, how are they different, and why should we care? In R. J. Burke, C. B. Cooper, & A. G. Antoniou (Eds.), *The mutigenerational workforce: Challenges and opportunities for organizations* (pp. 121–137). Northampton, MA: Edward Elgar Publishing.

Ng, E. S., & Parry, E. (2016). Multigenerational research in human resource management. In M. R. Buckley, J. Halbesleben, & A. R. Wheeler (Eds.), *Research in personnel and human resource management* (Vol. 33, pp. 1–41). Emerald Group Publishing.

Noe, R. (2017). *Employee training and development* (7th ed.). New York, NY: McGraw Hill Irwin.

Olmsted, B. (1979). Job sharing: An emerging work-style. *International Labour Review, 118*(3), 283–297.

Organ, D. W., & Ryan, K. (1995). A meta-analytic review of attitudinal and dispositional predictors of organizational citizenship behavior. *Personnel Psychology, 48*(4), 775–802.

Parker, S. K., Wall, T. D., & Cordery, J. L. (2001). Future work design research and practice: Towards an elaborated model of work design. *Journal of Occupational and Organizational Psychology, 74*(4), 413–440.

Pierce, J. L., & Dunham, R. B. (1992). The 12-hour work day: A 48-hour, eight-day week. *Academy of Management Journal, 35*(5), 1086–1098.

Piskurich, G. M. (1996). Making telecommuting work. *Training & Development, 50*(2), 20–28.

Pitt-Catsouphes, M., & Matz-Costa, C. (2008). The multi-generational workforce: Workplace flexibility and engagement. *Community, Work and Family, 11*(2), 215–229.

Putnam, L. L., Myers, K. K., & Gailliard, B. M. (2014). Examining the tensions in workplace flexibility and exploring options for new directions. *Human Relations, 67*(4), 413–440.

Rainey, G., & Wolf, L. (1981). Flex-time: Short-term benefits; long-term...? *Public Administration Review, 41*(1), 52–63. doi:10.2307/975724

Ralston, D. A. (1989). The benefits of flextime: Real or imagined? *Journal of Organizational Behavior, 10*(4), 369–373.

Ralston, D. A., & Flanagan, M. F. (1985). The effect of flextime on absenteeism and turnover for male and female employees. *Journal of Vocational Behavior, 26*(2), 206–217.

Reilly, P. A. (1998). Balancing flexibility—Meeting the interests of employer and employee. *European Journal of Work and Organizational Psychology, 7*(1), 7–22.

Ronen, S., & Primps, S. B. (1981). The compressed work week as organizational change: Behavioral and attitudinal outcomes. *The Academy of Management Review, 6*(1), 61–74.

Rousseau, D. M. (1995). *Psychological contracts in organizations*. Thousand Oaks, CA: Sage.

Seeck, H., & Parzefall, M. R. (2008). Employee agency: challenges and opportunities for psychological contract theory. *Personnel Review, 37*(5), 473–489.

Shen, J., Chanda, A., D'Netto, B., & Monga, M. (2009). Managing diversity through human resource management: An international perspective and conceptual framework. *The International Journal of Human Resource Management, 20*(2), 235–251.

Smola, K. W., & Sutton, C. D. (2002). Generational differences: Revisiting generational work values for the new millennium. *Journal of Organizational Behavior*, *23*(4), 363–382.

Snell, S. A., Morris, S. S., & Bohlander, G. W. (2016). *Managing human resources* (17th ed.). Boston, MA: Cengage Learning.

Society for Human Resource Management. (2010). *2010 Employee job satisfaction: Examining employee benefits in the midst of a recovering economy.* Alexandria, VA: SHRM.

Society for Human Resource Management (2014). *Leveraging workplace flexibility for engagement and productivity*. Alexandria, VA: SHRM.

Society for Human Resource Management (2016). *2016 Employee job satisfaction and engagement: Revitalizing a changing workforce.* Alexandria, VA: SHRM.

Stables, S., & Watton, E. (2017). The benefits of job sharing: A practice-based case study. In *Overcoming challenges to gender equality in the workplace* (pp. 67–77). Routledge.

Thakur, M., Bansal, A., & Maini, R. (2018). Job sharing as a tool for flexible work systems: Creating opportunities for housewives in the Indian labor market. *Gender in Management: An International Journal.* doi:10.1108/GM-08-2016-0149

Thomas, C. L., Spitzmueller, C., & Sady, K. (2017). Job sharing. In S. G. Rogelberg (Ed.), *The SAGE encyclopedia of industrial and organizational psychology* (2nd ed.). SAGE Publications, Inc.

U.S. Bureau of Labor Statistics. (2018). *Employment characteristics of families summary.* Economic News Release, Apr. 19. Retrieved from https://www.bls.gov/news.release/famee.nr0.htm

Venne, R. (1997). The impact of compressed workweek on absenteeism: The case of Ontario prison guards on a twelve-hour shift. *Relations Industrielles/Industrial Relations*, *52*(2), 382–400.

Weeden, K. A. (2005). Is there a flexiglass ceiling? Flexible work arrangements and wages in the United States. *Social Science Research*, *34*(2), 454–482.

Zeidner, R. (2008). Bending with the times. *HR Magazine, 53*(7), 10.

CHAPTER 5

EQUAL RIGHTS FOR WOMEN: NOT YET

William J. Woska

INTRODUCTION

Women in Rwanda, Iceland, Vietnam, and 131 other nations have constitutionally guaranteed equal rights, but American women do not. Polls show that a majority of Americans believe that the United States Constitution already guarantees equal rights (Przybyla, 2017). Adoption of an Equal Rights Amendment (ERA) to the Constitution is more than symbolic. "It has implications for how gender-based violence and workplace sex discrimination are addressed and litigated, for corporate standards involving accommodations for pregnant women, and for guaranteed access to prenatal care and contraception." Furthermore, "it could force a narrowing of the gender-based imbalance in top leadership roles" (Spier, 2017).

Just like African Americans, women started from the back of the pack when the United States was founded. For more than a century, they could not vote. In most states, they could not serve on juries. Into the 1970s, they could be barred from getting a credit card without a male co-signer. It was only recently that the barrier keeping them from military combat fell.

Human Resources Management Issues, Challenges and Trends:
"Now and Around the Corner", pages 103–118.
Copyright © 2019 by Information Age Publishing

There is a sordid underpinning of societal discrimination behind the thousand indignities, little and big, that women have to deal with to this day. Examples include the shortage of women in executive positions in corporate America, the pay inequities, the unequal distribution of child-raising responsibility, and the historical abuse endured by individuals in positions of authority.

Expectations about attributes and behaviors appropriate to women and men are shaped by culture. Gender identities and gender relations are critical aspects of culture because they shape the way daily life is lived in the family and also in the workforce. The cultural meanings given to being a man or a woman is apparent in the division of labor. History has provided clear patterns of "women's work" and "men's work" that must be overcome in addressing gender equality issues in the workplace.

The inequality that exists in the workforce is apparent irrespective of arguments that may be used to justify the underrepresentation of women. For example, the extreme work demands of corporate environments, inexperience, not being "tough" enough, and family responsibilities, are perceptions that impact executive level opportunities for women. Other questions impacting women seeking top management positions include:

- Are men and women different to the extent that women require different treatment?
- Are women's values and approaches to workplace issues so different that when entering the work force women find that the male culture is not to their likening and driven off?
- Do women need to become more like men to become corporate executives?
- Are women who take time away from work for family caregiving responsibilities subject to questions concerning their work ethic?
- Do women have a problem in communicating with men in the C-suite?
- Is there an assumption that assertive/aggressive women lack leadership potential?

When it comes to the barriers holding women back from achieving greater representation in leadership positions, the fact that there are small numbers of women in many fields point to social and environmental factors contributing to the underrepresentation of women. The striking disparity between men and women in the C-suite, irrespective of their preparation through education and experience, may lead to the conclusion that women are being held to a higher standard and need to do more to prove themselves.

THE ABSENCE OF WOMEN IN C-SUITE

Only 18 percent of C-suite positions are held by women even though women have been more prepared than men when entering the workforce in a professional capacity for many years (Pham, 2016). Almost 47 percent of the workforce are women (DeWolf, 2017). Women earned 52 percent of doctoral degrees for the eighth straight year and 57 percent of master's degrees in 2016 (Perry, 2017). Women received more law degrees (Olson, 2016). More women than men are enrolled in medical schools (Chandler, 2018). Women earn 60 percent of undergraduate degrees (Warner, 2014). However, women continue to be underrepresented not only in the professions but at all levels in executive, administrative, and professional positions, in addition to elected positions in Congress and at the state and local levels.

As of January 2017, there were 27 female Chief Executive Officers (CEOs) of Fortune 500 companies. By April 2017 there were 24 women leading three major corporations have announced that they will be stepping down (Fortune, 2017). The following is a listing of the number of women CEOs of Fortune 500 companies during the last 10 years (Suh, 2015).

Women CEOs in Fortune 500 companies (2008–2017)

Year	No. CEOs	% Women
2008	12	2.4
2009	15	3.0
2010	15	3.0
2011	12	2.4
2012	18	3.6
2013	20	4.0
2014	24	4.8
2015	24	4.8
2016	21	4.2
2017	27	5.4

Women are leading some of the largest companies in the United States including General Motors, IBM, PepsiCo, and Lockheed Martin. Although Fortune Magazine recently released its most recent Fortune 500 list reporting 32 women (6.4%) in CEO positions for 2018, an all-time high, the numbers of female CEOs are so small that one new posting can noticeably alter the statistics.

Women are also absent in other C-suite positions including Chief Financial Officer (CFO). On a global basis, only 11 percent of the positions are filled with women. Only 19 percent of women serve in Board of Director positions. Since it is not unusual that board positions are often filled by experienced CEOs and CFOs, and with so few women in those positions, the shortage of female executives, results in minimal competition against their male counterparts (Soledad, 2017).

Fortune Magazine annually publishes a listing of their ranking of most powerful women (MPW). There are 126 women who fell off Fortune's MPW list between 2000 and 2015. Of those, 30 retired purposely or are over 65 and not otherwise interested in another executive position at another company. Four women had health problems or passed away. Sixteen were replaced by higher-ranked women. Others went to small startups, private equity, and nonprofits or work part-time as directors on boards. Only 12 went on to another major operating role in a large company, and only eight hold the CEO title at a private or public company of any size. Only 17 (13%) of the women once on the MPW list had another major role at a large public company (Reingold, 2016).

There are a limited number of CEO positions, and as companies pursue internal succession, becoming an external chief executive is difficult. In 2015 ten percent of new CEOs were outside hires. That means that a person of either gender who doesn't get the job at his or her own company may find difficulty getting one elsewhere. Even though there are a limited number of CEO positions, scarcity does not explain the fact that there are only 32 women in chief executive positions in Fortune 500 companies in 2018.

BACKGROUND

When the Declaration of Independence proclaims that all men are created equal, it means that all human beings, regardless of religion, sex, or skin color, possess the same natural rights. The Founders were well aware that different people are unequal in physical and mental capacities. But however noticeable the differences between people may be, they are never so great as to deprive them of their rights. Since all men and women share a common human nature, they are all therefore equally entitled to the same natural rights such as life, liberty, and the pursuit of happiness.

There will always be inequalities with respect to skill, ability, income, or educational attainment. These should not be confused with the purpose of equal rights as set forth in the Declaration of Independence. Whether through luck, skill, or determination, some people will always succeed more than others, and others will fail. As long as no one's rights are being denied, inequalities are perfectly normal and desirable expressions of natural diversity (Shaw, 2012).

Civil rights ensure equality and include protection from unlawful discrimination for both men and women. Many civil rights in the United States stem from action in response to the Civil Rights Movement. The Civil Rights Movement was a struggle for social justice that took place primarily during the 1950s and 1960s for blacks to gain equal rights under the law in the United States. However, there were many significant occurrences affecting civil rights that preceded that era going back an entire century to the United States Supreme Court decision denying citizenship and basic rights to blacks (*Dred Scott v. Sanford,* 1857). The attempt to provide equal rights through the Civil Rights Movement has addressed de-segregation issues including schools (*Brown v. Board of Education of Topeka, Kansas,* 1954), public transportation (*Bailey v. Patterson,* 1962), inter-racial marriage (*Loving v. Virginia,* 1967), and the right of same sex couples (*Lawrence v. Texas,* 2003).

The concept of civil rights is an outgrowth of historical situations in which rights have been denied to members of certain groups. Since the adoption of the Constitution, groups whose members have been denied rights have been defined mainly by race, sex, age, and sexual orientation. Especially pervasive examples have included denial of the right to vote to African Americans living in the South in the century following the Civil War and the denial of the right to vote for women until the passage of the 19th Amendment in 1920 (Salem Press, 1999).

The Equal Pay Act (EPA) was passed by Congress in 1963 requiring that employers pay all employees equally for equal work, regardless of whether the employees are male or female. Women, on average, earn less than men in nearly every single occupation for which there is sufficient earnings data for both men and women to calculate an earnings ratio. The earnings of women workers in each state ranges from a low of 70 percent to a high of 89 percent compared to a man's earnings (see Appendix A). Even in the professions, women earn considerably less than men. In 2015 women lawyers earned less than 90 percent of their male counterpart's salary (see Appendix B). It is now 2018, more than a half century since the enactment of the EPA, and women earn 79 cents for every dollar earned by a man (Sheth & Gould, 2017).

The only specific written guarantee of women's rights in the Constitution is the 19th Amendment, which declared, "The right of citizens of the United States to vote shall not be denied or abridged by the United States or by any state on account of sex." (U.S. Const. amend XIX). A question still in need of being resolved in the 21st century is what are the rights of women with respect to gender equality?

The History Behind the Equal Rights Amendment

Alice Paul was one of the most prominent members of the 20th century women's rights movement. She led the change for women's suffrage and equal rights in the United States. In 1916 she founded the National Woman's Party (NWP). The NWP was a small, radical group that not only lobbied but conducted marches, political boycotts, picketing of the White House, and civil disobedience. As a result, they were attacked, arrested, imprisoned, and force-fed. But the country's conscience was stirred, and support for woman suffrage grew.

In 1920, the 19th Amendment was ratified, giving women the right to vote. Paul believed that the right to vote was the first step in the quest for full equality. In 1922 she reorganized the NWP with the goal of eliminating all discrimination against women. "The work of the NWP is to take sex out of law to give women the equality in law they have won at the polls" (Paul, 1922).

In 1923, in Seneca Falls, New York, for the 75th anniversary of the 1848 Woman's Rights Convention, she introduced the "Lucretia Mott Amendment," (an early civil rights activist) which read:

Men and women shall have equal rights throughout the United States and every place subject to its jurisdiction.

In 1943, Paul adapted the ERA to reflect the language of the 15th (right to vote not denied on account of race, color, or previous condition of servitude) and 19th Amendments (right to vote not denied on account of sex) (Langford, A., n.d.). The revised "Alice Paul Amendment" reads:

The Equal Rights Amendment

Section 1. Equality of Rights under the law shall not be denied or abridged by the United States or by any state on account of sex.

Section 2. The Congress shall have the power to enforce, by appropriate legislation, the provisions of this article.

Section 3. This amendment shall take effect two years after the date of ratification.

Between 1923 and 1970, the ERA was introduced in every session of Congress, but buried in committee. In 1971 the women's liberation movement demanded a gender-neutral society in which men and women would be treated exactly the same, no matter how reason-able it might be to respect differences between them. The ERA was the chosen vehicle to achieve this goal.

A radical feminist organization called the National Organization for Women stormed the halls of Congress and forced a vote on the ERA. Only 24 members of the House and eight in the Senate voted against it. On March 22, 1972, Congress sent the amendment to the states to ratify it (Schlafly, 2007). Congress placed a seven-year time limit on the ratification process.

A proposed amendment becomes part of the Constitution as soon as it is ratified by three-fourths (38 of 50) of the states. The seven-year deadline expired on March 22, 1979. Only 35 of the necessary 38 states had ratified the amendment. The ratification process was subsequently extended by Congress an additional three years to June 30, 1982. There were no additional ratifications prior to the deadline on the extension approved by Congress.

The ERA has been introduced into every session of Congress since 1982 but has not made it to the floor for a vote. Nevertheless, the ERA may still have a lifeline to passage. On March 21, 2017, the State of Nevada became the 36th state to approve the amendment to the Constitution (Chereb, 2017). Considering the women's movement following the 2016 presidential election, if two additional states ratify the amendment satisfying the requirement of approval by three-fourths of the states, the decision would be up to Congress as to the ERA becoming the 28th Amendment to the Constitution of the United States.

OPPOSITION TO THE ERA

Rose Schneiderman, an emigrant from Poland, was a labor activist in the early 1900s who supported women's rights including a living wage, housing, and other basic rights along-side the need for education, community, and self-development. She served as president of the Women's Trade Union League (WTUL) from 1926 to 1950. In 1933 President Franklin D. Roosevelt (FDR) appointed her to the Labor Advisory Board of the National Recovery Administration. She was a key architect of FDR's New Deal and the Social Security Act.

Schneiderman was a life-long opponent of the ERA. She and other activists, many of whom were Jewish and Italian women from immigrant backgrounds, did not consider themselves "feminists," since they believed that the term applied more specifically to middle class women activists who had focused specifically on gender issues. Schneiderman believed that the idea of absolute equality between men and women was a "meaningless distraction" when working women experienced such an extreme measure of workplace discrimination (Young, 2016).

Schneiderman's opposition to the ERA was that protective legislation for women proposed by the WTUL would no longer apply if the amendment was ratified. In 1950 Arizona's Senator Carl Hayden introduced the "Hayden Amendment" proposing that a new section to the ERA be added protecting any rights, benefits, or exemptions previously conferred by law upon women. Although Schneiderman supported the amendment, other ERA activists, including the NWP, refused to support the change. Schneiderman passed away in 1972, the same year that Congress sent the ERA to the states for ratification.

Phyllis Schlafly, a longtime conservative activist, led the fight against the ERA in the 1970s. Her argument was that even though most people would not find the proposed language objectionable, the courts would use it to push through policies that many of those same people would dislike. Furthermore, she claimed that a gender-neutral society would deprive a woman of the fundamental right to stay home and care for her family. It would mark the end of the traditional family.

Congress sent the ERA to the states in 1972. A year later 30 states had ratified the amendment. Schlafly launched the STOP-ERA anti-feminist organization formed to prevent ratification of the gender-equality amendment. She took to the lecture circuit to urge state legislatures to reject the constitutional change. She echoed Schneiderman's argument about destroying labor legislation protecting working women in addition to arguing that an ERA would force women into military service and would lead to laws that would make gay marriage and abortion legal. There was a considerable slowing of state ratifications following the STOP-ERA movement with only five additional states providing approval (Haberman, 2016).

Schlafly's arguments against changes contained in the ERA subsequently happened over time as a result of legislation and/or court decisions. Schlafly passed away in 2016.

The Continuing Struggle for Equality

When it comes to equality in the workplace, women see it as a work in progress where men view it as mission accomplished. Significantly more men than women say their companies are level playing fields and have plenty of women leaders, even in places where less than ten percent of top executives are female. This disconnect between the opinions of men and women matters given that a large percentage of middle and senior managers are men. A woman's daily interaction with her immediate supervisor often sets the course with respect to her opportunity for career advancement (Fuhrmans, 2017).

During the civil rights movement, there came a time when it was no longer OK just to frown on George Wallace standing in the schoolhouse door or Bull Connor aiming his fire hoses at black people. There had to be institutional change and a societal mind shift.

On January 21, 2017, hundreds of thousands of women gathered in what is known as the Women's March on Washington. More than one million people gathered in Washington and in cities around the country and the world to protest the inauguration of President Donald Trump. What started as a Facebook post by a Hawaiian retiree became an unprecedented international rebuke of a new president that packed cities large and small from London to Los Angeles, Paris to Park City, Utah, Miami to Melbourne, Australia. Many in the nation's capital and other cities said they were inspired to join because of Trump's divisive campaign and his disparagement of women, minorities and immigrants (Stein, Hendrix, & Hauslohner, 2017). Participants feared that the new administration and the Republican-led Congress would roll back reproductive, civil and human rights.

As the year progressed, millions of women energized by the Women's March on Washington and frustrated by the continuing abuse and sexual harassment by men in positions of authority, came together in the #MeToo Movement. The purpose of the #MeToo Movement was to encourage women who have experienced sexual assault or harassment to share their experience irrespective of the costs that may go with it. Sexual harassment is not about sex. It's about work and power. It is a means of policing gender roles and maintaining hierarchies. Sexual harassment undermines a woman's work performance and calls her competency into question. It pressures her to conform to stereotypes and penalizes deviation. It subordinates her to men in power and reminds her of who ultimately controls her career (Arnow-Richmond, 2018). #MeToo provided an opportunity to get people to understand the prevalence of sexual harassment and assault in society.

As the New Year (2018) began more than 300 women in Hollywood—executives, actors, agents, writers, directors, and producers—announced the formation of Time's Up, an effort to counter systemic sexual harassment in industries across the country. It is different than the #MeToo movement in that it aims to address workplace sexism through legal recourse, improved representation in board rooms, and placement of women in chief executive positions. The initiative includes efforts to create legislation that will penalize companies that tolerate harassment and will discourage the use of nondisclosure agreements that have helped silence victims of abuse. Time's Up also includes a legal defense fund that will connect victims of sexual harassment, assault, or abuse, with legal representation (Garber, 2018).

Times Up, like #MeToo, is an effort to counter systemic sexual harassment throughout the workplace - to call out abuse of women, especially by men in positions of authority. "For too long, women have not been heard or believed if they dared to speak their truth to the power of those men. But their time is up" (Russonello, 2018).

The #MeToo and Times Up movements have again surfaced the issue of the need for an ERA and constitutional equality. There is broad support for an ERA with more than 90 percent of Americans supporting equal rights for women. In fact, more than 80 percent believe women already have equal rights (Neuwirth, 2018).

The #MeToo and Times Up movements may be a beginning whereby men make a mind shift away from the attitude that women can be accommodated only to the extent that it doesn't inconvenience other men (Brown, 2017). Nevertheless, the process of providing equal rights for women cannot be accomplished until the United States Constitution is amended providing equal rights for women.

The absence of equal rights for women may be read into a 2000 United States Supreme Court case. In a 5–4 decision, *United States v. Morrison,* the Court invalidated the section of the 1994 Violence Against Women Act (VAWA) that gave victims of gender-motivated violence the right to sue their attackers in federal court. Chief Justice Rehnquist, writing for the majority, held that Congress lacked authority, under either the Commerce Clause or the Fourteen Amendment, to enact this section. If an ERA had been a part of the Constitution, it is likely that VAWA would have been validated by the Court.

TITLE VII – IMPACT ON SEXUAL HARASSMENT LAW

Title VII of the Civil Rights Act of 1964 (Title VII) makes it "an unlawful employment practice for an employer . . . to discriminate against any individual with respect to compensation, terms, conditions, or privileges of employment, because of such individual's race, color, religion, sex, or national origin" (Civil Rights Act of 1964). The use of the term "sex" was not included in Title VII legislation first proposed to Congress. It was not until the legislation was debated on the House floor that "sex" was added to prevent discrimination against another minority group—women (Freeman, 2008). Initially only intended to provide protection for women from discrimination, the prohibition of sex discrimination applied to both males and females.

The term "sexual harassment" did not originate until several years later. The term was used by women's groups in Massachusetts in the early 1970s. The term was further used in a report to the president and chancellor of the Massachusetts

Institute of Technology in 1973 addressing various forms of gender issues (Rowe, 1990).

In the years immediately following passage of Title VII, sexual harassment claims were rarely brought under the statute, and when they were, courts dismissed them, reasoning that Title VII was not applicable. Finally, in the mid-1970s, courts began to accept sexual harassment as a form of gender discrimination under Title VII.

In 1986 the United States Supreme Court accepted its first sexual harassment case, *Meritor Savings Bank v. Vinson.* The primary question before the court was whether a hostile working environment created by unwelcome sexual behavior is a form of employment discrimination prohibited by Title VII when no economic loss or quid pro quo harassment exists. In a unanimous decision, the court found that the Vinson's charges were sufficient to claim hostile environment sexual harassment. This case became the cornerstone of answering sexual harassment questions under Title VII (Woska, 2015).

Five additional cases were accepted by the Court following *Meritor* which have clarified and established sexual harassment law. Nevertheless, sexual assault and/or harassment incidences are all too common and continue to be brought forward on an individual basis. In August 2017 a well-known and powerful Hollywood producer was accused of sexual harassment which was followed by similar accusations by many other women not only in the entertainment industry, but throughout the workforce against men in positions of authority. The #MeToo movement was born.

ERA—A CHALLENGE FOR HUMAN RESOURCES

The Equal Pay Act (EPA) was approved by Congress in 1963. The EPA prohibits pay dis-crimination based on sex and states that men and women must be paid equally for substantially equal work performed in the same establishment (Equal Pay Act of 1963). In 1963, women who worked full-time, year-round, made 59 cents on average for every dollar earned by men (Cho & Kramer, 2016). In 1964 Title VII of the Civil Rights Act was passed to prohibit discrimination in employment on the basis of race, color, religion, national origin, and sex. The scope of Title VII is much broader than the EPA and makes it illegal to discriminate based on sex in pay and benefits (Civil Rights Act of 1964).

It is now more than a half century later and women earn 79 cents for every dollar earned by a man. Compensation policies are administered by human resource (HR) departments throughout the United States. The fact that the pay disparity between men and women continues 55 years after enactment of the EPA is significant with respect to what appears to be HR's limited role in contributing to and/or establishing pay policy within an organization.

Evolving technology is having a direct impact on HR. Although many of the basic functions and responsibilities remain the same including recruitment, managing employee benefit programs, providing advice on HR issues, regulations, and policies, and handling staff issues and disciplinary procedures, the role of HR is not only evolving, but expanding. It is important that HR be looked upon as a team of experts who can work hand-in-hand with top management to influence and direct employee engagement, company culture, and other change within an organization.

Equal rights for women will require HR to address issues including paid parental leave, pay equity policies, gender diversity, subsidized on-site child care, and improving the culture around flexible work policies. Flexible work options such as telecommuting, flexible work schedules, freelance work, job sharing, and professional part-time opportunities are critical issues for women who are disproportionately impacted by burdens imposed by family caregiving responsibilities. Women are more likely than men to take time out of the work force for family reasons, and these interruptions hurt the advancement of their careers and earnings. Offering more flexible workplaces can help attract and retain more women and move toward gender equity at all levels within an organization (Onley, 2016). HR must take the initiative to make flexibility and work-life balance a part of the wider company culture.

The fact that the private sector provides limited information with respect to salary ranges for work that requires the same knowledges, skills, and abilities, continues to be a factor as to why women earn considerably less than men for the same or similar work. Greater transparency in pay systems is associated with a smaller pay gap between men and women. By making salary ranges for job categories available, like the public sector, employers provide women with information that depicts a fair and equitable comparison with men.

HR is a key agent of change in an organization. HR's role as a change agent is to replace resistance with resolve, planning with results, and fear of change with excitement about its possibilities (Ulrich, 1998). HR is unique from other services in that it provides assistance to employees irrespective of where they work within a company. Business plans and strategies and implementation of these plans are dependent on how HR develops innovative approaches to resolve employee-related issues. With respect to equal rights for women, for HR to be an effective change agent, it's critical that they have the ability to influence the decisions made by top management to address gender diversity initiatives necessary to attain equal rights.

Some of these employment policies such as parenting and child care assistance have been available with a few employers, most notably in high technology companies. However, it will be necessary for flexible workplace practices to become as common as paid vacation benefits throughout the workforce before women can feel that they have equal rights. HR must be at the forefront as an agent of continuous transformation, shaping the processes and culture that together improve an organization's capacity for change.

CONCLUSION

History may eventually reveal that the 2017 Women's March on Washington was the beginning of a new political landscape with respect to women's rights. The Women's March was not a one and done event. Women have become more engaged and involved as disparate groups of females have come together recognizing the inequality that has festered since the beginning of our democracy. The feeling of feminist solidarity born of the Women's March brought power that has swelled well beyond politics (Wildermuth, 2018).

State and federal legislation is beginning to address pay equity issues instrumental to bridging the pay gap between men and women. Pay equity laws have been adopted in several states including California, New York, Maryland, and Massachusetts (Seyfarth, 2016).

Effective January 1, 2018, the State of California banned an employer from inquiries into an individual's salary history (California Labor Code §432.3). The new law applies to all employers, including state and local government. California joins a growing list of jurisdictions across the country that have prohibited salary history inquiries including the states of Delaware, Massachusetts, and Oregon. Legislation has been introduced in other states including Texas, Florida, Montana, Virginia, and Wisconsin. In addition, many other cities and local jurisdictions have either adopted or are considering similar legislation including New York City, Pittsburgh, San Francisco, and New Orleans (Hartman, 2017). The elimination of an individual's past salary on job applications prevents gender discrimination from being passed from one workplace to another by basing an employee's pay on his or her past salary.

Gender equality in the workplace is about everyone having an equal chance. It is not about favoritism, granting privileges, or offering special assistance to overcome an obstacle. The purpose of gender equality is simply to remove barriers to create a level playing field irrespective of sex. Perhaps, with a political landscape that appears to be in the process of change, equal rights for women will become a reality with the passage of the ERA as the 28th Amendment to the Constitution.

APPENDIX A: THE SIMPLE TRUTH ABOUT THE GENDER PAY GAP: AAUW STATE MEDIAN ANNUAL EARNINGS AND EARNING RATIO FOR FULL-TIME, YEAR-ROUND WORKERS, BY STATE AND GENDER, 2016

		Male	Female	Earnings Ratio
1	New York	$53,124	$47,358	89%
2	California	$51,417	$45,489	88%
3	Florida	$41,586	$36,112	87%
4	District of Columbia	$75,343	$64,908	86%
5	Vermont	$47,840	$41,122	86%
6	Colorado	$51,264	$43,206	84%
7	Alaska	$56,422	$47,518	84%
8	Maine	$47,890	$4,024	84%
9	Maryland	$61,321	$51,247	84%
10	Hawaii	$48,373	$41,224	83%
11	New Hampshire	$53,581	$44,550	83%

		Male	Female	Earnings Ratio
12	Minnesota	$53,200	$44,132	83%
13	Tennessee	$73,661	$35,916	82%
14	Massachusetts	$62,868	$51,666	82%
15	Delaware	$50,924	$41,771	82%
16	New Mexico	$72,297	$34,668	82%
17	Georgia	$46,712	$38,278	82%
18	North Carolina	$45,180	$36,987	82%
19	Arizona	$46,386	$37,966	82%
20	Rhode Island	$53,400	$43,541	82%
21	New Jersey	$62,311	$5,574	81%
22	Nevada	$45,326	$36,681	81%
	United States	$51,640	$41,554	80%
23	Virginia	$55,817	$44,798	80%
24	Kentucky	$45,521	$36,259	80%
25	Connecticut	$64,220	$50,991	79%
26	Texas	$47,351	$37,576	79%
27	Oregon	$50,676	$40,193	79%
28	Illinois	$53,111	$42,108	79%
29	Pennsylvania	$51,780	$41,047	79%
30	Missouri	$46,543	$36,514	78%
31	Arkansas	$41,156	$32,242	78%
32	Michigan	$50,869	$39,825	78%
33	Wisconsin	$50,399	$39,440	78%
34	South Dakota	$54,384	$35,436	78%
35	South Carolina	$45,038	$35,043	78%
36	Nebraska	$47,352	$36,699	78%
37	Kansas	$47,891	$37,091	77%
38	Ohio	$50,227	$38,750	77%
39	Wyoming	$51,234	$39,338	77%
40	Washington	$58,864	$45,056	77%
41	Iowa	$49,385	$37,791	77%
42	Idaho	$45,305	$34,403	76%
43	Mississippi	$42,146	$31,757	75%
44	Alabamas	$47,034	$35,012	74%
45	North Dakota	$51,789	$38,407	74%
46	Indiana	$49,157	$36,440	74%
47	Oklahoma	$46,027	$33,972	74%
48	Montana	$46,545	$34,028	73%
49	West Virginia	$46,029	$33,228	72%
50	Utah	$51,099	$36,022	70%
51	Louisana	$50,031	$34,793	70%

APPENDIX B

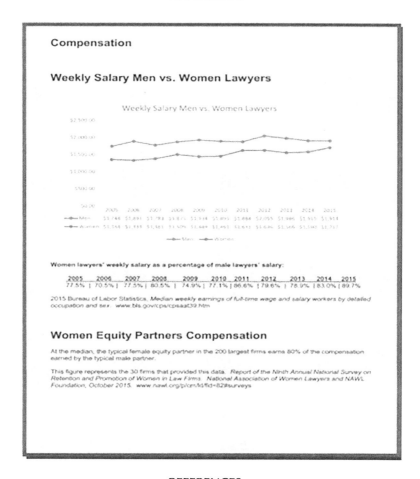

REFERENCES

Arnow-Richmond, R. (2018, January 28). Why we must separate sex from sexual harassment. *San Francisco Chronicle*, p. E5.

Bailey v. Patterson. (1962). 369 U.S. 31.

Brown v. Board of Education of Topeka, Kansas. (1954). 347 U.S. 483.

Brown, W. (2017, November 26). Chronic inequality fosters mistreatment of women. *San Francisco Chronicle*, p. B1.

California Labor Code. § 432.3.

Chandler, M. (2018). Women are now a majority of entering medical students nationwide. *The Washington Post.* Retrieved from https://washingtonpost.com/local/social-issues/women-are-now-a-majority-of-entering-medical-students-nationwide/2018/1/22.html

Chereb, S. (2017). Nevada ratifies equal rights amendment on 45th anniversary of passage by congress. *Las Vegas Review Journal.* Retrieved from https://www.reviewjournal.

com/news/politics-and-government/nevada/nevada-ratifies-equal-rights-amendment-on-45th-anniversary-of-passage-by-congress

Cho, R., & Kramer, A., (2016). Everything you need to know about the Equal Pay Act. *ICRW.* Retrieved from https://www.icrw.org/wp-content/uploads/2016/11/Everything-You-Need-to-know-about-the-Equal-Pay-Act.pdf

Civil Rights Act of 1964. (1964). §7, 42 U.S.C. §2000e et seq.

DeWolf, M., (2017). 12 stats about working women. *U.S. Department of Labor blog.* Retrieved from https://blog.dol.gov/2017/03/01/12-stats-about-working-women

Dred Scott v. Sanford. (1857). 60 U.S. 393.

Equal Pay Act of 1963, 29 U.S. Code Chapter 8 § 206(d).

Fortune Editors. (2017). These are the women leading fortune 500 companies. *Fortune.* Retrieved from http://fortune.com/2017/06/07/fortune-500-women-ceos/

Freeman, J. (2008). *We will be heard: Women's struggles for political power in the United States.* Lanham, MD: Rowan & Littlefield.

Furhmans, V. (2017, October 10). The hidden battle of the sexes at work. *The Wall Street Journal,* R1, R2.

Garber, M. (2018). Is this the next step for the #MeToo movement? *The Atlantic.* Retrieved from https://www.theatlantic.com/entertainment/archive/2018/01beyond-metoo-can-times-up-effect-real-change/549482/

Haberman, C. (2016). Phyllis Schlafly's lasting legacy in defeating the era. *The New York Times.* Retrieved from https://www.nytimes.com/2016/09/12/us/phyllis-schlaflys-lasting legacy-in-defeating-the-era.html

Hartman, M. (2017). The old salary history question could be on its way out for good. *Marketplace.* Retrieved from https://www.marketplace.org/2017/10/25/world/new-laws-ban-employers-using-salary-history-hiring

Langford, A. (n.d.). The equal rights amendment: a debate. *National Woman's Party.* Retrieved from http://nationalwomansparty.org/the-equal-rights-amendment-a-debate/

Lawrence v. Texas. (2003). 539 U.S. 558.

Loving v. Virginia. (1967). 388 U.S. 1,.

Neuwirth, J. (2018). Unbelievably, women still don't have equal rights in the Constitution. *Los Angeles Times.* Retrieved from http://latimes.com/opinion/op-ed/la-oe-neuwirth-equal-rights-amendment-for-women-metoo-2018105-story.html

Olson, E. (2016). More law degrees for women, but fewer good jobs. *The New York Times.* Retrieved from https://www.nytimes.com/2016/11/30/business/dealbook/more-law-degrees-for-women-but-fewer-good-jobs.html

Onley, D. (2016). HR key in helping employers achieve gender equity. *SHRM.* Retrieved from https://www.shrm.org/hr-today/news/hr-magazine/1116/pages/hr-key-in-helping-organizations-achieve-gender-equality.aspx

Paul, A. (1922). Who is Alice Paul? *National Women's Party*. Retrieved from http://national-womensparty.org/learn/who-is-alice-paul/

Perry, M. (2017). Women earned majority of doctoral degrees in 2016 for 8th straight year and outnumber men in grad school 135 to 100. *AEI.* Retrieved from http://www.aei.org/publication/women-earned-majority-of-doctoral-degrees-in-2016-for-8th-straight-year-and-outnumber-men-in-grad-school-135-to-100/

Pham, T. (2016). Think you're not biased against women at work? Read this. *Forbes.* Retrieved from https://www.forbesw.com/sites/break-the-future/2016/12/20/think-youre-not-biased-against-women-at-work-read-this#3d72579b7e5a

Przybyla, H. (2017, March 15). ERA fight gets new life from California democrat. *USA Today,* 1A, 2A.

Reingold, J. (2016). Why top women are disappearing from corporate America. *Fortune. com.* Retrieved from http://fortune.com/women-corporate-america/

Rowe, M. (1990). Barriers to equality: The power of subtle discrimination to maintain unequal opportunity. *Employee Responsibility and Rights Journal, 3*(2)*,* 153–163.

Russonello, G. (2018). Read Oprah Winfrey's golden globes speech. The *New York Times.* Retrieved from https://www.nytimes.com/2018/01/07/movies/oprah-winfrey-gold-en-globes- speech-transcript.html

Salem Press. (1999). The civil rights movement. Retrieved from https://www.salempress. com/press_titles.html?book=104

Schlafly, P. (2007). Equal rights for women: wrong then, wrong now. *Los Angeles Times.* Retrieved from http://www.latimes.com/la-op-schalfly8apr08-story.html

Seyfarth, S. (2016). *The New U.S. Pay Equity Laws: Answering the biggest questions.* Retrieved from www.seyfarth.com/dir_docs/publications/PayEquityBrochurd.pdf

Shaw, J. (2012). Not all equality is equal: What does equality mean? *Daily Signal.* Retrieved from http://dailysignal.com/2012/01/30/not-all-equality-is-equal-what-does-equality-mean/

Sheth, S., & Gould, S. (2017). 5 charts show how much more men make than women. *Business Insider*. Retrieved from http://www.businessinsider.com/gender-wage-pay-gap-charts-2017-3/#women-with-children-are-penalized-while-men-with-children-are-rewarded-4

Soledad, C. (2017). Why are women set up to fail in the c-suite? *Fortune.* Retrieved from http://fortune.com/2017/09/28/women-c-suite-leadership-ceos/

Spier, J. (2017, May 15). ERA fight gets new life from California democrat. *USA Today.* Retrieved from https://www.pressreader.com/usa/usa-today-us-edi-tion/20170315/281565175570209

Stein, P., Hendrix, S., & Hauslohner, A. (2017). Women's marches: more than one million protesters vow to resist President Trump. *The Washington Post.* Retrieved from https://www.washingtonpost.com/.../womens...washington...protesters-vow-to-resistt...

Suh, M. (2015). Women CEOs in fortune 500 companies, 1995–2017. *Pew Research Center.* Retrieved from http://www.pewsocialtrends.org/chart/women-ceos-in-fortune-500-companies-1995-2014/

Ulrich, D. (1998). A new mandate for human resources. *Harvard Business Review.* Retrieved from https://hbr.org/1998/01/a-new-mandate-for-human-resources

United States v. Morrison. (2000). 529 U.S. 598.

U.S. Const. amend. XIX.

Warner, J. (2014). Fact sheet: the women's leadership gap. *Center for American Progress.* Retrieved from https://www.americanprogress.org/issues/women/reports/2014/03/07/85457/fact-sheet-the-womens-leadership-gap/

Wildermuth, J. (2018, January 19). Women's marches get serious about a new political landscape. *San Francisco Chronicle*, A1, A10.

Woska, W. (2015). *Legal and regulatory issues in human resources management.* Charlotte, NC: Information Age Publishing.

Young, J. (2016). It wasn't just Phyllis Schlafly who opposed the equal rights amendment. *History News Network.* Retrieved from http://historynewsnetwork.org/article/163815

CHAPTER 6

WEARABLES IN THE WORKPLACE

An Analysis of Ethical Issues

James S. Bowman and Jonathan P. West

Wearables are mini-computers and sensors near, on, or in the body (e.g., smart phones, watches, implants), enabling mobility, connectivity, and applications that can encourage or compromise engagement and collaboration (Vaze, 2014).[1] Many of these devices offer anytime-anywhere access and have the ability to record, track, interpret, report, and store a wide array of behavioral, medical, and cognitive data. The expanding use of wearables is attributed to technical advances in data analytics, micro-electro-mechanical systems, robotics, biometrics, neuroscience, nanotechnology, and integrated optics (Ajunwa, Crawford, & Schultz, 2017).[2]

One in five people in the United States own a personal wearable and one in ten use it on a daily basis (Ubiq Team, 2015). With fitness devices leading the way, over ten percent of American organizations issue them, and eight percent are con-

---

[1] "Consumers want to lump smart phones into the wearable category," because they are already "wearing" them everywhere (PricewaterhouseCoopers, 2014, p. 6).

[2] Selected portions of this chapter are adapted from West & Bowman, 2016a; 2016b)

Human Resources Management Issues, Challenges and Trends:
"Now and Around the Corner", pages 119–143.

sidering adoption (Brin, 2016). Employers can now outfit employees with body-worn instruments that measure brain activity, document moods and movements, and analyze voice, facial expressions, and posture. The objective is to optimize performance and productivity in personnel and organizations by integrating smart technology with work. Some three-fourths of workers around the world say they are willing to try wearable tools if they help them do their jobs (Kronos, Inc., 2014). By 2018, two million employees worldwide likely will be required to wear such equipment as a condition of employment (Gartner, Inc., 2015; Manokha, 2017).

While products like Google Glass and Apple Watch are not yet widely adopted, as the technology evolves high performance, light-weight wearables may impact daily life like personal computers did near the end of the last century. The global market for the technology is projected to balloon to $70 billion by 2025 (Aubrey, 2016). The research firm Tractica estimates that more than 75 million smart instruments will be deployed in the workplace by 2020 (Bell, 2016). Many of these devices were originally cobbled together from mobile phone parts not designed as wearables, but rapid miniaturization, extended battery life, growing sophistication, and falling costs suggest that they could become the next multi-billion unit and transformational market (Hsieh, Komisar, Jazayeri, &Yeh, 2016).

Fort, Raymond, and Shackelford (2016, p. 146) capture the promise and prospects of the "wearable revolution" in America:

> Seventy-nine percent of [organization] adopters agree that wearables are or will be strategic to their company's future success. Seventy-six percent report improvements in business performance … And early adopters such as construction, manufacturing, energy, oilfield services, and medical industries have now developed short, yet supportable, improvement in efficiency with fewer job-related mistakes.

The advent of this technology suggests the need to shift from what such smart-wear can do to the effects that may accompany its proliferation. With nearly every aspect of work now quantifiable, the issue is not whether wearable engineering will expand, but rather how it will affect employer-employee dynamics in all workplaces regardless of economic sector.

The purpose of this study, then, is to address the question, "What are the ethical issues that need attention when wearable technology is used in public, private, and non-profit organizations? Body-worn computer devices will be common at work, transforming the way daily operations are conducted. Value conflicts will develop as managers seek to capitalize on these new technologies for efficiency gains while raising cost-effectiveness, fairness, privacy, security and integrity problems. How will values be managed and balanced against each other? Although professional publications and practitioner magazines discuss smartware and sometimes the ethical cautions associated with it, curiously these concerns have not yet surfaced in the academic literature.

This scholarly oversight is addressed by considering how smartware will affect organizations. The background section reviews the ubiquity of the attire and its accoutrements. The core of the inquiry examines arguments for and against these tools, using classical philosophical and modern behavioral approaches to ethics. Although the goal is primarily descriptive and analytical, the conclusion discusses guidelines and future use of this innovation at work and lessons for human resource professionals.

BACKGROUND

Organizations have long sought ways to maximize employee efficiency, most famously in Fredrick Winslow Taylor's time-motion studies a century ago. Facilitated by wearable devices, present-day efficiency initiatives go beyond classical studies to directly scrutinize individual physiological heart and brain functions that underlie behavior. The focus has changed from analyzing the job by breaking down its components to studying the individual to improve efficiency (Ajunwa et al., 2017). Wearables provide data that were not previously easy to gather, as the technology can (a) surveil physical and environmental changes, (b) process information, perform calculations, assign tasks, give instructions, and (c) identify training needs (Gale, 2016). In so doing, organizations can monitor, track and understand employee activities, speeding access to information, interpreting policy, and allowing hands-free use of data.

The industry believes that there could be 130 million wearable devices on wrists, heads, and bodies at home and the office worldwide by 2018, an adoption rate comparable to tablet computers (Clancy, 2014). IDTECHEX found the global market to be worth more than $30 billion in 2016, reaching over $150 billion by 2026 (Hayward, Chansin, & Zervos, 2016). The overall consensus of market research is that the technology will continue to develop, permeate the workplace, and change the way work is done. Public sector adoption is expected to be slower than the private sphere due to costs, but analysts agree that it is a matter of when, not if (Infiniti, 2015).

Although still in a nascent stage, engineering advances have combined to produce a remarkable differentiation in digitally enabled clothing and accessories: backpacks, anklets, shoes, badges, caps, hoods, lanyards, gloves, jewelry, patches, glasses, contact lenses, "hearables," medallions, tattoos, implants, and skin-grown electronics. Scientists are developing brain chips that may improve cognitive tasks, including intelligence and memory. The expanding presence of these instruments is driven by: the promise of data-driven efficiencies (to reduce waste), the power of convenience (to make tasks easier), and the "selfie culture" desire to be connected and entertained (to belong and socialize in new ways).

The data provided by wearables, and the algorithms that drive them, are a critical component of the Internet of Things—the infrastructure of the Information Society. It connects "everything": anything with an on-off switch that can be connected will be connected (people-people, people-things, and things-things) by getting them on to one network. Network connectivity automatically collects and exchanges data and generates insights into the use and explanation of data (International Institute for Analytics, 2015). Everything and everyone will become a node on the network with increasing fusion and crossover between wearables and the Internet of Things. According to one projection, a trillion networked devices will be hooked up worldwide by 2028 (Corsello, 2013).

Internet of Things encompasses not only smart wearables, but also smart enterprises and smart government (Perera, Liu, & Jayawardena, 2015). At the individual level, smart devices will merge seamlessly into daily life as activity trackers, for example, record pulse, connect to medical records, alert medical staff, and identify the nearest health care facility. At the organizational level, among the many applications, employers can promote healthy lifestyles and leverage the data to negotiate insurance premiums as well as gather environmental data to optimize office energy consumption. At the municipal level, Barcelona is "the most wired city in the world" as the application of digital principles has improved water management, street lighting, parking, and public transportation.[3] Smart cities promise enhancements in disaster response, sustainability, security, education, administrative efficiency, and convenience. A firefighter outfitted with smart glasses, for instance, can listen to instructions, see the floorplan of a burning building, and call for support as she looks for residents.

Yet, greater processing power, diminishing costs, and robust post-9/11 legal authorities permit the wholesale acquisition of largely unprotected data. The US Equal Employment Opportunity Commission (EEOC) has proposed limitations on the types and use of information that can be collected from personnel with wearables (Ubiq Team, 2016). Indeed, implementation of this new technology is not immune to discrimination, privacy, security, data storage, self-incrimination, and harassment issues and allegations. Since many concerns arising from wearables are not clearly addressed in existing legislation, EEOC regulations may offer needed job-related guidelines on how programs can be compliant with relevant health and labor relations legislation.[4]

However, the asymmetrical relationship between employers and employees, exemplified by the at-will employment doctrine, generally means that an employer's legitimate management interests are accorded paramount importance over employee rights (self-identifying reference removed). American employment contracts, in fact, often require agreement with administrative practices, includ-

---

[3] Smart cities are also underdevelopment in South Korea, China, and the United States and will integrate wearable devices into the environment embedded with sensors (Taylor, 2014).

[4] This body of law includes the: Americans with Disabilities Act (generally forbids inquiries about health), Genetic Information Nondiscrimination Act (prohibits asking about genetic information), Health Insurance Portability and Accountability Act (establishes standards to protect personal health information), National Labor Relations Act (permits employees to discuss terms of employment, including personal data collection and surveillance which could chill free speech), and Stored Communication Act (creates Fourth Amendment-like privacy protection for digital communications stored on the internet) and their state and local analogues.

ing the waiver of legal protections (Ajunwa et al., 2017). Further, organizations may need to update their communication, confidentiality, and dress code policies to clearly state that wearables are employer-issued, and their use is expected.

The growth of smartwear, in summary, potentially will have a widespread effect by 2025 in reducing inefficiencies in the movement of goods, people and information; improving decisions as data overtakes intuition; and avoiding errors in planning and assumptions (J.P. Rangaswami in Anderson, 2014). In fact, the remarkable nature of smartwear has received attention in trade magazines, the business press, nonprofit and consulting firm reports, blogs, newspapers, and law reviews. Yet it has garnered very little coverage in scholarly policy and management journals, and even less consideration has been devoted to emerging ethical questions.[5] It is prudent, therefore, to examine conflicting claims because ethical ramifications are often overlooked or subsumed into other topic areas. Wearables and the Internet of Things hold possibilities that were science fiction a generation ago. Management models and the nature of the work may profoundly change, resulting in a wearable utopia, dystopia, or something in between. Given that technology often out paces policy, it is critical that stakeholders confront difficult questions, avoid hurried judgements, and employ reliable decision-making processes when adopting wearables at work.

METHODOLOGY

A variety of decision-making strategies could illuminate whether or not wearable deployment is ethical, but two are particularly helpful because their comprehensive scope reduces the chances of an incomplete assessment: the ethics triad and behavioral ethics (Table 6.1).

The ethics triad or triangle (Svara, 2014) recognizes the complementarity and interdependence of the imperatives in three schools of thought based on: results of an action (consequentialism or teleology), pertinent rules (duty ethics or deontology), and personal integrity or character (virtue ethics).

When considering results the question is, "Which policy produces the greatest good for the greatest number?" (e.g., "Would I want my decision to be in the newspapers tomorrow?"). In contemplating rules, the issue is, "Would I want everyone else to make the same decision that I did?" (e.g., do no harm). From the virtue ethics vantage point, one might ask, "What would a person of integrity do?" (e.g., seek the "golden mean" between the extremes of excess and deficiency). This inclusive, yet succinct, tool can provide a defensible evaluation by teasing out the underlying logic by which decisions are justified (for further discussion, see self-identifying

---

[5] Although employee surveillance and privacy issues are long-standing research topics (see, e.g., self-identifying reference removed), wearables—with the partial exception of police body-worn cameras—have not been explored in academic periodicals. The "pre-wearable" technology surveillance literature (most of the references below published prior to 2013) was consulted when it shed light on smartwear.

TABLE 6.1.   Philosophical and Behavioral Methodologies: Complementary Approaches

(A) The *philosophical approach* recognizes three schools of thought based on:

	Consequentialism or Teleology Expected results of an action	**Duty Ethics or Deontology** Application of moral rules	**Virtue Ethics** Personal character
Consideration of results, rules, and virtues, this "ethics triad" can enable a balanced, defensible decision (Svara, 2015).			
Employing "Ockham's Razor"* to cut to the essence of an argument, three queries can be posed:	Which decision produces the greatest good for the greatest numbers?	Would I want everyone else to come to the same conclusion that I did?	Does the decision improve my character and that of my community?
An over emphasis on one school of thought, at the expense of the others, risks:	Expediency	Rigid rule application	Self-justification

*Use the simplest possible explanation of a problem, and only make it more complex when absolutely necessary. Adding qualifications, explanations may make a position less elegant, less convincing—and less correct.

(B) *Behavioral ethicists* believe that to improve policy-making, psychological tendencies leading to unethical decisions should be taken into account. To explain human actions, insights like the following are germane:

(1) Bounded rationality Human rationality is constrained by the situation and cognitive limitations	**(2) Decision framing** The manner in which a situation is defined can affect the outcome	**(3) Confirmation bias** Gathering information that conforms to pre-existing beliefs without objectively evaluating all evidence
(4) Herd behavior In cases of uncertainty, people tend to follow the crowd and/or experts because they seem know more	**(5) Action bias** The felt pressure to do something	**(6) Unconscious incompetence** Lack of awareness about one's own ignorance
(7) Overconfidence Over-estimating the ability to make sound decisions	**(8) Ethical fading** Visceral responses (e.g., denial) or situational factors (e.g., incrementalism) become dominant	**(9) Naïve idealism** The belief that one's own view reflects reality and is shared by others

reference removed). However, an overreaching application of a single perspective, at the expense of the others, holds considerable dangers—expediency (results-based ethics), rigid rule application (rule-based ethics), and self-justification (virtue-based ethics). In light of the shortcomings of the individual perspectives, it is evident that this eclectic, amalgamated technique can be helpful.

Nonetheless the philosophical method has been criticized for its failure to link moral theorizing and ethical action (Gazzaniga, 2008). This suggests that other factors—unconscious biases, moral emotions, unintentional blindness—are likely to influence conduct (Shao, Aquino, & Freedman, 2008) as shown in Table 6.1 (panel B). Behavioral ethicists believe that to improve policy-making, psychological tendencies leading to unethical decisions should be taken into account. Subliminal cognitive tendencies, feelings, intuition, and perceptions are at least as important in affecting conduct as logic, reason, and calculation.

Thus, for example, bounded rationality and decision framing—as well as action bias, herd behavior, and ethical fading—can lead to unintentional minimization of genuine moral concerns. Similarly, naïve idealism (like confirmation and over confidence biases) could mean a failure to involve important stakeholders in policymaking and implementation decisions. Behavioral ethics ideas are not necessarily new, but what is new is the growing evidence that behavior is less under conscious control than previously believed.

The heroic assumptions of the philosophical approach–that individuals are universally rational, possess full information, and have the willpower to use it–often do not hold in real life. For Bazerman and Tenbrunsel (2011), the goal is to be prepared for the unconscious psychological forces that routinely impact decisions. In short, while the philosophical approach focuses on what constitutes a balanced, ethical decision, behavioral ethics helps predict and explain why a decision may be deficient. It does not replace traditional methods, but supplements them to better describe how choices are made. The philosophical and behavioral ethics analyses may not produce definitive answers; they do, however, provide direction by probing the reasoning used to explain conduct. Individual ethical theories may lead to different assessments, but these differences must be assessed, not passed over. Not necessarily good or bad, wearables can be problematic.

The nascent wearables era makes it difficult—and crucial—to scrutinize the promise and problems of this technology. To take into account contending interests, body-worn computers will be investigated using the classical philosophical perspective, followed by a behavioral ethics analysis. The study, which intended to provide equal space to competing claims, reflects the nature of the literature: much of it is promotional with limited discussion of risks. Accordingly, possible advantages are counterbalanced here by an examination of drawbacks. Given space limitations, the authors attempt to use Ockham's Razor to cut to the essence of arguments: use the simplest possible explanation of a problem, and only make it more complex when absolutely necessary, as adding qualifications may make a position less elegant, less convincing, and less correct.

FINDINGS

Technology is often seen as neutral, but each technology has embedded values, and the decision to deploy it is to adopt those values (cf., Verbeek, 2011). Data-generating wearables can be regarded either as a justifiable, impartial practice serving the interests of all or an oppressive technique catering to the interests of some at the expense of others. The discussion here weighs the ethical issues in the use of these devices.

The focus is on general arguments and generic management concepts that can be applied to particular national circumstances to test their relevance in diverse types of organizations. It refrains from examining either the highly technical aspects of wearables or precise policy provisions. Case-specific details—the host institution and the environmental context within which the technology operates—are important, but fundamental principles are at least as compelling. As will be seen, the inquiry is necessarily speculative and anticipatory, because little empirical work is available. While affirmative and negative contentions raise significant concerns, few are conclusive.

RESULTS-BASED ANALYSIS

In consequentialism, the best policy results in "the greatest good for the greatest number." What is right is that which creates the largest amount of human happiness with the least harm. This utilitarian approach is helpful in seeking the common good. As a key indicator of this criterion, the advantages and disadvantages of wearables are examined on the grounds of *cost-effectiveness*—i.e., the time, effort, and money to achieve the greater good is clearly worth it.

In Support of Wearables. Advocates contend that these devices, by transcending the practical restraints of earlier technology and enhancing *cost-effectiveness*, facilitate maximization of resources. Cheaper, smaller, with greater data capacity and allowing continuous operation, their use in the workplace increases productivity (Frankel, 2016; Newman, 2015; Wilson, 2013). Administrators, in a data-driven approach to managing people, will have dashboards to monitor and track performance indicators that, in turn, can be predicted and incentivized.

Wearables also aid in promoting efficiency by collecting consistent, moment-to-moment personal information (e.g., alerting personnel to hazardous conditions or a dangerously high heart rate) and enabling Big Data analytics (e.g., sending drivers safety warnings or recommending rest breaks). As noted, the technology can document activity, enable access to real-time information, serve as a training tool, improve data accuracy, streamline procedures, furnish on-going performance feedback, and provide improved service. Manual processes such as logging in and completing reports could be simplified; a census taker, for instance, could send data directly to a central data base.

Assuming a healthy workforce is a productive workforce, organizational effectiveness also can be achieved by offering smartwear as part of a wellness program: employees are given fitness devices as an incentive to participate and to receive reduced health insurance premiums (Lavalliere, Burstein, Arezes, & Coughlin., 2016). Overall and if early experiences hold, knowing that they are being monitored, personnel will act in a more productive manner. An effectively performing workforce believes it is contributing to the common good. When judiciously implemented, wearables foster cost-effectiveness.

In Opposition. The very features that attract managers to smart technology concern skeptics, as the positive uses can distract attention from the dangers they pose. It should be evident, opponents argue, that this technology is more than merely one more innovation. Wearable attire and applications have the capacity to record, store, analyze, and report more personal data than any other workplace device.[6]

Ethical risks associated with these body-worn computers that impact *cost-effectiveness* include: (a) manipulation, (b) utility, (c) security, (d) tracking, and (e) data quality (Fort, Raymond, & Schackelford, 2015, p. 21; Sunstein, 2015, p. 25). Concerning manipulation, consider the employer who extracts data from a wearable device that shows an employee with a serious disease, and then finds a pretext to terminate them to avoid an insurance liability. Another risk may occur under the Americans with Disability Act if fitness data identify "less active" employees who are then denied promotions based on such reports.

The utility of wearables to enhance performance, second, are not as problem-free as proponents suggest. Tools like Google Glass allow the real world to be overlaid with data enabling multi-tasking. Yet, the volume, velocity, and variety of information supplied can be overwhelming, producing "data fatigue." The goggles can be distracting when displaying information (e.g., e-mail, web searches), diverting attention and diminishing work quality, as employees become disengaged from actual work and concentrate on material appearing on the lens (Haberman, 2013). Indeed, it is well-established when two relatively complex tasks are done at the same time, performance deteriorates substantially (Norman, 2013).

Additionally, incentivizing behavior by offering extrinsic financial rewards often backfires when internal motivation is crowded out at the expense of the public interest (Drevitch, 2017).[7] Rutkin (2014) concludes that there is little research to show that employees with wearable tech actually are more productive. This may help explain why people are generally uncomfortable with others knowing their productivity (PricewaterhouseCoopers, 2014, p. 41). Further, organizational liability can be created when devices like smart glasses allow individuals to covertly make video and audio recordings.

Third, as the technology races ahead of security measures, data hacking, as well as breaches from human error, have plagued public, private and nonprofit organizations (Identity Theft Resource Center, 2015). Given widespread system vulnerabilities, security researcher Rob Graham states that security is "laughably bad" (Porup, 2016), a problem that could clearly undermine confidence in the employer. Fourth, tracking worker movements can be stressful; even though aggregated data may be anonymized, employee trust can be put at risk. Relatedly,

---

[6] It is not unreasonable, in light of the 2013 National Security Agency expose, to suggest that employers might take undue advantage of these new tools.

[7] When the Boston fire department reacted to an increase in sick leave on Mondays and Fridays, it imposed a limit of 15 sick leave days. Over the next year, the total number of days taken more than doubled—i.e., when the department treated the firefighter as a self-interested economic man, they responded accordingly. Both the department's and employees' sense of duty was crowded out, as the new policy implied that workers were not professionally motivated (Drevitch, 2017).

there are difficulties of gaining real performance benefits from anonymized data sets (Gray, 2015).

A final dimension of cost-effectiveness is wearable-derived productivity data can be mistake-prone and invalid. Fibit, for instance, states that it "does not represent, warrant or guarantee that its trackers can deliver the accuracy…of medical devices" (Chauriye, 2016, p. 501). Even with sound information, imperfect proxies are typically used when performance cannot be measured directly. Because current sensor technology is "notoriously unreliable" (Senemar, 2015), deciding how information will be interpreted to justify personnel actions could give rise to charges of discrimination and lawsuits. In addition, smartwear can easily be taken off, worn by others, or used to falsify data. In a time of dissemination of inaccurate information, that dismisses or confuses facts with "alternative facts," it is critical that measures be in place to safeguard data. When records, in short, are misused, a work environment can be created that damages morale and performance. A single-minded emphasis on quantitative measurements, then, can erode personal dignity and high quality work, give rise to feelings of mistrust and resentment, and foster a divisive mentality in the workplace (Blakemore, 2005).

From a results-oriented perspective, in sum, what is ethically correct is the consequences of an action on the greatest good. Dependency asymmetry between institutions and individuals can suggest that smart technology is cost-effective. It, however, can be problematic due to potential: data-gaming, performance, recording, security, tracking, and data error or misuse concerns. Paternalistic and manipulative use of wearables, as well as the technology's vulnerability, can endanger the ethical rights of the workforce (Michael, 2014).

Yet, an over-emphasis on any single part of the ethics triad may produce an inadequate decision. Advocates might think that the greatest benefit is found, but perhaps the decision is simply expedient. Opponents, in seeking the most good, may be susceptible to opportunistic, self-serving behavior. In the discussion of the effects of smartwear both sides rely on prediction, the accuracy of which is a well-known weakness in human behavior. In light of these concerns, attention now shifts to the second school of thought.

PRINCIPLE-BASED ANALYSIS

In principle-based decision-making certain actions are inherently right (e.g., promise keeping) or wrong (e.g., inflicting harm), irrespective of predicted consequences. This approach is useful because officials are expected to follow the principles found in the Constitution, court cases, laws and regulations, and organizational codes and policies. In deciding what rule to apply, the person asks, "Would I want everyone else to do what I did?" (stated differently, "what is good for one is good for all"). In examining competing positions, the emphasis here is on *fairness* and *privacy*.

In Support. Advocates hope to foster *fair* treatment of individuals, and avoid capricious actions; public and private institutions have responsibility to use technology appropriately by gathering and using accurate, consistent, and impartial personal information. Properly implemented, wearables promise sound policies and objective administration, thereby fostering procedural and distributive justice and promoting social welfare. Adherence to best practice policies (e.g., transparency, consent, notice) can mitigate objections so that what is good for one is good for all should naturally develop.

Regarding *privacy*, during the last decade video monitoring of daily life has become the "new normal." It follows, wearables can be seen as just one more manifestation of the use of technology for the social well-being. Federal agencies are required by the 2002 E-Government Act to prepare privacy impact assessments before authorizing programs that collect data; these statements must stipulate the purpose for, use of, and access to the information gathered. Further, the 1986 Electronic Communications Privacy Act (ECPA) provides some limits on electronic communications (self-identifying reference removed). While administrators have wide discretion in deploying wearables, awareness of ECPA provisions, consultation with IT professionals, and employee agreement is prudent. Nonetheless, to the extent that the technology includes increased security or safety at the expense of privacy, many may find the trade-off acceptable (PricewaterhouseCoopers, 2014). Collection of personal data, moreover, can have a deterrent effect—if someone has nothing to hide, then there is nothing to fear.

Finally, the Fourth Amendment of the US constitution (unreasonable search and seizure) includes a reasonable expectation of privacy for public servants and may furnish a benchmark for private sector decision making. State constitutions often contain privacy protections, but determinations regarding whether an individual's rights have been violated depend on an expectation of privacy that does not diminish the employer property rights. Employers may have a valid interest in collecting information on employees, but should be sure that it is an impartial management practice (Abril, Levin, & Del Riego, 2012; self-identifying reference removed). The upshot is that privacy can be safeguarded by law-abiding behavior and by the constitution. Generally, the use of new technologies has been seen as extension of traditional management prerogatives.

In Opposition. Data gathering often over-reaches, and when this occurs it is neither *fair* nor necessary. Over 80 per cent of citizens indicate concern that wearables, by making them more visible and vulnerable, invade their privacy (PricewaterhouseCoopers, 2014, p. 31). Adding to this apprehension is that there are reduced expectations for privacy on the job: employee work spaces, as well as electronic devices owned by the employer, can be searched without permission.

Organizations, in fact, may condition employment upon workers acquiescing to such restrictions. It is arguable whether valid consent exists under these asymmetrical, coercive conditions. Indeed, at least in America, standard notice-and-consent provisions in employment contracts serve as a seal of approval for surveillance (Ajunwa et al., 2017, p. 42). As Ball and Margulis (2011, p. 115) point out, consent is "rarely, if ever, freely given [as it] serves to perpetuate existing inequities and creates new ones." Use of wearable data under these circumstances violates both the categorical imperative ("what is good for one is good for all") and the "golden rule" ("do unto others as you would have them do unto you"). Employers would be reluctant, for example, to accept employee tracking of their behaviors.

Further, few individuals operating behind the Rawlsian "veil of ignorance" would, *a priori*, approve of tracking (Rawls, 2005). Not only is there a concern for creating panoptic effects (e.g., not knowing when one is watched, resulting in acting as if always being watched), but who monitors the monitors? Management, critics believe, regards employee monitoring to be their prerogative (Michael, 2014): whether it should be introduced is seldom up for debate (Sarpong & Rees, 2014). Detrimental effects occur when data are used to intimidate and punish; it can also take the form of voyeurism, identifying whistleblowers, and creating pretenses to investigate workers (Ciochetti 2011). Body-worn computer applications may promote a climate of distrust, and can violate human rights by harming the quality of life, demeaning the individual, and treating people like property. Resistance could be anticipated if the use of smartwear impacts the employer-employee relationship by giving more power to institutions. The failure of many organizations to have their IT policies manage the effect of wearables only exacerbates the situation (Influx of Wearable Technology in the Workplace, 2015).

In addition, smart technology holds potential to usurp individual *privacy*: if a device is employer-issued, is used for job-related purposes, and notice is provided, then the employee has little expectation of privacy.[8] The privacy issues above (technical capacity, the "nothing-to-hide" argument, and Fourth Amendment protections), therefore, warrant further discussion. First, although in some respects wearables represent just another step in technological progress, they magnify the risk to privacy due to the very personal nature of the information collected. Ball and her colleagues (2016) express caution that "harvesting" data from employees raises problematic ethical questions given .".the expansion of big data into public interest settings such as energy consumption, education and health" (p. 62). For example, these authors cite organizations that gather individuals' Fitbit-derived health information, and then sell it to health care providers for marketing purposes. Other third parties (e.g., an insurance agent, loan officer, criminal prosecutor, or potential employer) could be interested in such material as well. Extracting, analyzing, and sharing records may help institutions to maximize returns and minimize risks (see Smith, 2016), while compromising individual privacy.

Second, the nothing-to-hide concern is misplaced; the issue is not about what people want to conceal, but about the power of institutions. Even if an individual has done nothing wrong, organizations can cause harm. The unequal relationship between business or government and employees, for instance, is exacerbated when critical components of privacy—the command persons have over their

---

[8] The increasing use of bringing your own device (BYOD) to the job does not necessarily create an expectation of worker privacy, because the organization's "policy can define the scope of any expectation" (Mehta, 2014, p. 633).

confidential information and their control over the access others have to it—are subsumed by the organization (Knapp & Soylu, 2013). The nothing-to-hide argument, it should be evident, can justify nearly any level of intrusion.

Some organizations sensitive to legal and privacy concerns have taken action. To illustrate, USAA insurance company prohibits employees from wearing Google Glass fearing that the device might compromise privacy by secretly recording video or audio of people near them at work (Olson, 2015). The problem is not simply about secrecy, but also "accumulation" (compiling and interpreting small bits of data) and "exclusion" (being barred from learning how information is used) (Solove, 2011). Stated differently, are the right kinds of data collected for the right reasons—and how is that known? Some polls suggest that respondents support wearables or are remarkably unconcerned about the impact of the devices. Yet these same surveys find that employees may doubt that benefits outweigh the risks to privacy (e.g., PricewaterhouseCoopers, 2014). For instance, the deterrent effect on illegal behavior claimed by advocates of police body cameras may be less likely than the chilling effect on lawful activity.

Personal privacy, additionally, does more than protect information: it "is so integral to our identity and autonomy that it (is) a social good fundamental to our society" (Martin & Freeman, 2003, p. 357). Privacy is not only an individual right, but also a political and social good: the presumption of freedom from being constantly watched and the ability to create one's persona in an authentic manner. Vital to the functioning of democracy, critics believe that omnipresent technologies are a weapon to control and spy on people (Lee, 2007). Intrusions on privacy, especially when publicized, can compromise personal autonomy, freedom, identity, and/or place a person in a false light. The National Security Agency's routine and indiscriminate collection of information on millions of people demonstrates the risks involved.

Furthermore, sources of individual privacy—the Fourth Amendment, common law, statutory law—provide limited rights (Knapp & Soylu, 2013), as there is no comprehensive federal privacy law. A Congressional Research Service examination of Fourth Amendment jurisprudence—which regulates how, when, and where government may conduct searches and seizures—reveals that it may provide very little protection against wearable abuse (Thompson, 2013). The US Supreme Court has not yet ruled on wearables and privacy, and there are few relevant case law precedents. For now, it will be difficult to find a reasonable expectation of privacy. Indeed, authorities have begun deploying smartwear for routine operations. It should be noted that pervasive use of the technology also impacts First Amendment freedoms, especially free speech and assembly. As for state legislation, lawmakers have attempted to regulate the general use of technology (e.g., employee notice and consent) under privacy legislation (e.g., mini-ECPAs).[9]

---

[9] Provisions vary by state, but include employee notice and consent, prohibitions in areas where employees remove their clothing, prohibitions on employer adverse actions for employee off-duty activities, restrictions on information-gathering about people's non job-related communications, and prohibitions on organizations embedding radio frequency identification chips in workers.

To summarize, advocates recognize an ethical duty to run well-managed organizations in the name of social fairness and personal privacy; Kantians seek to treat individuals as ends, not means to some supposed good. Without clear rules, skeptics fear that employers will exercise too much power. However, if wearable policy is a product of labor-management relations necessity and the result of open, participatory, informed decisions, then such concerns may be overcome. The obligation is to ensure fairness and protect privacy; broad, deep personal data collection can create unnecessary harm. Yet relying exclusively on principle-based analysis could provide inadequate guidance and induce rigidity.

VIRTUE-BASED ANALYSIS

In virtue ethics, answers to the question of "What to do?" have little to do with results or rules and everything to do with the kind of person one is. Character, then, offers a third perspective when assessing the advisability of body-worn computer devices. It asks, "What would a person of integrity decide?" and "Does a proposed policy improve individual and community character?" This philosophy is compelling because it is a personal approach to ethics—i.e., decisions are not so much informed by consequences and duties, but by the quality of one's moral fiber.

While no definitive list of virtues exists (the theory avoids formulaic thinking and emphasizes moral identity instead), a virtue is an excellence or trait. It is found between the extremes of excess and deficiency, Aristotle's "golden mean" (e.g., friendliness is the mean between grouchiness and promiscuity). In every situation, the person will determine the mean—neither excessive nor deficient—based on reason and experience appropriate to the circumstance. A pre-eminent virtue—*integrity* (a product or synthesis of virtues such as honesty, moderation, justice, and the prudence to recognize ethical challenges and respond)—is integral to moral nobility.

In Support. What constitutes good practice includes regard for personal *integrity.* In their discussion of surveillance, Iedema and Rhodes (2010) suggest that it makes for better employees as they may become more accountable and disciplined. Respect for the moral agency of a person can also serve to mitigate the asymmetry in employer-employee relations. In fact, when coupled with transparency and responsibility, employees are regarded more as partners in management than as subjects; if so wearable attire can promote honesty, moderation, and prudence. Intrusive programs, however, are difficult to justify.

In Opposition. Absolute power can corrupt absolutely: it heightens the probability that corruption will occur, and that the individual and the public interest will be compromised (self-identifying reference removed). Ethics requires a sound policy, but even when accomplished, Rosenberg (2005) argues that action contrary to policy often prevails because executives are reluctant to empower their workforce. If wearables are deployed in a command-and-control manner, it indicates that leaders believe that the employees lack *integrity* to perform their duties, an approach not likely to contribute to human flourishing.

Moreover, when subjected to observation, Palm (2009, p. 55) believes that individuals fail to act in concert with their true selves and at the expense of personal integrity. Rather than behave in accordance with their values and convictions, they engage in adaptive behaviors such as a "manufactured" self, anticipatory conformity and self-subordination, unworthy of ethical treatment (Brown, 2000; Rosenberg 2005, pp. 142, 148). Individual behavior becomes rationalized and people are objectified, manipulated and devalued, denying them not only voice, but also the necessity to regard them as moral agents.

Further, the asymmetrical advantage of centralized power offers temptations and alters the relationship between employers and employees. The seeming science fiction nature of wearable technology—especially when enabled by secret algorithms—gives employers a potent, invasive tool to entice them to do things that otherwise they could not or would not do. When this happens, wearables are prone to improper use of discretion at the expense of personal integrity and well-being of the community.

From a virtue ethics perspective, in brief, integrity focuses on supporting individual and collective character. Responsible policymakers will ensure that wearable programs have measures to avoid and correct abusive practices. Yet, virtue theory's strength—subjective judgments inferred from personal character—is also its shortcoming: if advocates and opponents of smartwear perceive they are right, they can be convinced that what they do is good.

BEHAVIORAL ETHICS EFFECTS ON DECISION-MAKING

While rational decision making models like the ethics triad are valuable, behavioral ethics identifies significant shortcomings. It aims to make traditional rational models more practical by adding insights from psychology, sociology, and neuroscience. Based on the actual behaviors, decision makers are not expected to have perfect information and to act rationally; they are expected to be influenced by intellectual limitations and non-economic, emotional factors, both conscious and unconscious. Accordingly, decisions are characterized by cognitive illusions as they are frequently error-prone and biased as a consequence of seemingly irrelevant or unknown factors.

In light of the unrealistic assumptions about rationality found in philosophical decision models, they cannot adequately describe, explain, or predict how humans behave. People prefer to believe that they are like judges, conscientiously deliberating over the issues and arriving at reasoned conclusions after examining all the evidence; instead, they are more like lawyers, looking for anything that might help make their case. Rationality is very much bounded by the situation and human cognition. Individuals do not have complete information; even if they did, they have less-than-perfect capacity for information processing to reach an optimal solution. Bounded ethicality, stated differently, may result in an otherwise ethical policy maker making questionable decisions whether in support of, or opposition to, smart technology.

In a world of bounded rationality, choices are embedded in psyches and social norms, and behavioral tendencies matter (Table 6.1). It is not surprising, then, that judgements may be flawed. Thus, the definition of the situation (decision framing) may be affected by:

- What other organizations are doing (herd behavior),
- The desire to take action (action bias),
- Unacknowledged bias in collection of evidence to coincide with pre-existing views (confirmation bias),
- Unjustified conviction in their talent for good decisions (over-confidence and unconscious incompetence),
- Emotional responses, denial, and rationalizations (ethical fading), and
- Beliefs that others share their views (naïve idealism).

As Elder Shafir observes, "People do not respond to objective experience; rather, stimuli are mentally construed, interpreted, and understood or misunderstood" and "Things that ought not to matter…often do, and things that ought to matter often fail to have an impact" (cited in self-identifying reference removed). When it is known why personnel make mistakes, steps can be taken to minimize them (Prentice, 2015, p. 84). Poor decisions may be made the result of an unawareness of significant psychological, organizational, and social influences that affect behavior.

Behavioral ethics introduces considerations like those noted above that can provide insight into decision making and offer an alternative view of the individual as a moral agent. Understanding bounded ethicality is crucial: if unethical behavior occurs unintentionally, then encouraging right conduct must not merely focus on the dishonesty of dishonest people, but also on the dishonesty of honest people. Such awareness does not mean that mistakes will always be avoided, but it should reduce their probability.

Wearables supporters may use motivated reasoning, confirmation bias, and action desire to profit from commercialization, and their focus on technical advances tends to down play drawbacks. Bennett (2011), for instance, argues that anytime a tool exists that makes management easier (e.g., body cameras), police will do more of it. Decision framing, as well as ethical fading, can cause unintentional minimization of moral objections. Indeed, ethicality bias exacerbates these tendencies: people predict that they will make an ethical decision, but when faced with a dilemma, they make an unethical decision—yet they still think of themselves as being honorable and just. "Their own blind spots prevent them from meeting their own ethical standards" (Bazerman & Tenbrunsel, 2011, p. 22). Claims that they are not affected by bias may be sincere, even as self-serving decisions are made.

It may be that an initial introduction of smartwear raises few objections, but as usage spreads more legal and ethical concerns will emerge. Naïve idealism and over confidence biases can mean the failure to involve employees in designing the policy, developing guidelines for its use, and keeping personnel informed. While such predispositions challenge the functioning of moral conscience, wearables may also assist in ethical decision making. Thus, for example, smart glasses can nudge officials to consult the organization's code of ethics and use a decision matrix to identify alternative behaviors (Fort et al., 2016, p. 152). Overall, although the rational approach embodied in the ethics triad suggests a link between sound ethical reasoning and upright conduct, behavioral ethics provides a caution to decision makers, maintaining that interpersonal relations and situational forces are crucial in understanding moral judgments.

DISCUSSION

Responsible decision makers, by definition, are obligated to develop virtues, respect rules, examine results, and heed behavioral insights. Doing so, nevertheless, cannot produce a final, perfect decision. Instead, an attempt to reconcile conflicting values highlights a key function of policy making: generating alternative viewpoints, systematically evaluating them, and crafting a considered judgment that accounts for behavioral constraints. The result of such an analysis would be to apply, using contingency theory, the findings to specific organizational circumstances as the optimal strategy is dependent upon the situation.

The approach used here, thus, enables the management of ethical ambiguity and provides help in making the inevitable compromises. An integrated strategy that includes both philosophical rationalism and behavioral realism can facilitate achievement of that goal. The prescriptions found in the former and the descriptions of conduct in the latter contain contending arguments for and against wearables. Taken separately, a single position may appear ethical at some points and unethical at others. The approach, accordingly, offers choices, not formula; it informs, but does not eliminate, the need for judgment.

Looking at each part of the triad in sequence (Table 6.2), what then is the greatest good for the greatest number? As indicated, it may be realized when cost-effectiveness is enhanced to serve both institutions and individuals. This implies that the use of wearables, initiated for legitimate reasons, produces the promised results, and is not arbitrary or invasive. While courts tend to defer to management, neither the organization nor the individual has absolute rights. The right to manage can be a seductive rationale for finding the greatest good, exceeding what is reasonable at the expense of important rights; if so, the technology can be counterproductive.

The second component of the triad, principle-based ethics, focuses on what is good for one is good for all. Carefully designed, data gathering by body-worn computer tools promises fair and impartial administration of employer-employee relations, thus mitigating objections. Opponents, however, believe that this function often overreaches; genuine consent is seldom given thereby violating the Golden Rule and the categorical imperative, creating unnecessary harm, and placing privacy at-risk. Because few officials would agree to be monitored, the burden of proof falls on those who would watch others.

TABLE 6.2.   Arguments For and Against Wearables Using the Ethic Triad

Smartwear Advocates	Smartwear Opponents
Question: What is the greatest good for the greatest number?	
Cost-effectiveness: Maximizes resources and minimizes loss, thereby enhancing cost efficiencies; wearables are cheaper, smaller with greater capacity, thereby transcending political restraints of earlier technology; promotes efficiency by collecting real-time personal information and enabling Big Data Analytics; advances organizational effectiveness by offering smartware as part of a wellness program; to promote a healthy productive workforce.	Allows individuals to covertly make video and audio recordings; organizational vulnerability to data hacking could undermine confidence; tools like Google Glass enable multi-tasking, but can distract from actual work; rewards crowd out internal motivation at the expense of public interest; tracking worker movements can be stressful and risk loss of trust; wearable-derived data can be mistake-prone and invalid; detrimental effects occur when data are used to intimidate and punish workers.
Question: Would I want everyone to make the same decision that I did?	
Principles Fairness: Properly implemented, wearables promise sound policies and objective administration, thereby fostering procedural and distributive justice and promoting social welfare; following best practices and mitigate objections so that what is good for one is good for all should naturally develop	Data gathering often over-reaches, which is neither fair nor necessary; asymmetric power of employers vis-à-vis employees can create conditions where workers consent to restrictions on privacy is not freely given; use of wearable data violates both the categorical imperative and the golden rule as employers would be reluctant to accept tracking of their behaviors.
Privacy: Federal agencies are required to prepare privacy impact statements stipulating the purpose for, and use of the information gathered; the Electronic Communications Privacy Act provides some limits on electronic communication; when technology includes increased security or safety at the expense of the privacy, many may fine the trade-off acceptable; the Fourth Amendment includes an expectation of privacy for public servants; collection of data can have a deterrent effect—if someone has nothing to hide, then there is nothing to fear	Wearables magnify the risk to privacy due to the personal nature of the information collected; extracting, analyzing, and sharing records violate individual privacy; the nothing-to-hide contention can justify nearly any invasion of privacy; instructions can compromise personal autonomy, freedom, identity and/or place a person in a false light; sources of individual privacy—the Fourth Amendment, common law, statutory law—provide only limited rights.
Question: Does the decision improve my character and that of the community?	
Virtue Integrity: Data-driven smartware makes for better employees as the may become more accountable and disciplined; when coupled with transparency and responsibility, they are regarded more as partners in management than as subjects—if so, wearable attire can promote honesty, moderation, and prudence.	Integrity: If wearables are deployed in a command-and-control manner, it indicates that the employees lack integrity to perform their duties, an approach not likely to contribute to human flourishing; when subjected to observation, individual fail to act in concert with their true selves and at the expense of personal integrity.

Finally, virtue ethics seeks individual excellence and collective well-being. Wearables proponents argue that the data generated can reinforce the autonomy of individuals by emphasizing personal empowerment and the imperative to better one's self. Alternatively, the technology can erode these same characteristics according to critics. In the end, virtue ethics demands a thoughtful decision—neither excessive nor deficient—based on the situation and experience; the choice to use wearables must enrich the quality of the individual and the community. Yet virtue theory's strength—subjective judgments derived from personal character—is also its limitation: if supporters and opponents of smartwear believe they are laudable, they are likely to regard what they do as praiseworthy.

The drawbacks of each component of the ethics triad (results: prediction mistakes; principles: rule rigidity; virtue: self-righteousness) highlight the significant biases and errors revealed by behavioral ethics. In ethical fading, for instance, employers using wearable-derived data to monitor employee union organizing in the workplace and then singling out the organizers for adverse personnel action on the pretense of poor work performance. For employees, detailed, complex codes of conduct can be rationalized, having the opposite effect—any wrongdoing not covered is acceptable (Prentice, 2015, p. 81).

By anticipating such forces and deliberately considering their influence, officials may ensure that they do not override personal integrity, the categorical imperative, and the greatest good. The prescriptions of the philosophical decision-making model and the descriptions of conduct in the behavioral model, when seen as complementary approaches, furnish a more complete understanding of social dynamics. Both ask decision-makers to think about thinking: the first emphasizes intentional judgments and the second focuses on cognitive illusions and unconscious biases in a decision context. Policies that incorporate a synthesis of these two models should enhance the quality of decision-making.

CONCLUSION

Although there is a tendency to overestimate dramatic change in the short run and underestimate it in the long run, the transformative potential of the wearable industry suggests a new frontier in workplace dynamics. Accordingly, its promises and perils warrant inspection in the name of the greatest good, duty and character, particularly when tempered by behavioral ethics insights. This is especially true, as noted above, given the lack of comprehensive wearable policies in many government, business, and nonprofit organizations. What, then, are some guidelines for effective use? The summary below offers 10 Lessons for Human Resource Professionals).

10 Take-Away Excerpts and Lessons for Human Resource Professionals

1. Miniature wearable devices, seamlessly integrated into daily work routines, are likely to be mainstreamed in the next decade.

2. Wearables provide data that were not previously easy to gather, as the technology can (a) surveil physical and environmental changes, (b) process information, perform calculations, assign tasks, give instructions, and (c) identify training needs.
3. Data-generating wearables can be regarded either as a justifiable, impartial practice serving the interests of all or an oppressive technique catering to the interests of some at the expense of others.
4. Given that technology often out paces policy, it is critical that stakeholders confront difficult questions, avoid hurried judgments, and employ reliable decision-making processes when adopting wearables at work.
5. Value conflicts will develop as managers seek to capitalize on these new technologies for efficiency gains while raising cost-effectiveness, fairness, privacy, security and integrity problems.
6. Smart technology is cost-effective. It, however, can be problematic due to potential: data-gaming, performance, recording, security, tracking, and data error or misuse concerns.
7. If wearable policy is a product of labor-management relations necessity and the result of open, participatory, informed decisions, then such concerns may be overcome.
8. Wearable technology can empower people by augmenting their capacities, but without meaningful rules it can also menace individual rights.
9. Organizations may need to update their communication, confidentiality, and dress code policies to clearly state that wearables are employer-issued and their use is expected.
10. A model policy would contain principles for device deployment, data collection and retention, and reporting.

It is challenging to make recommendations without knowing what types of body-worn computer devices will be used and the kinds of policies that will survive legal review. Generally, policies should avoid adding to unequal employer-employee power relations. An imbalance exists because employees have few rights, at least in the US, "law currently provides feeble protections" and offers "a meager right to privacy" (Abril et al., 2012, pp. 95, 121). Wearables, it follows, should be evaluated for mutual institutional-individual advantage. Relying solely on the goodwill of employers is not sufficient.

As discussed here, the unique utility of smartwear can be in the public interest, while simultaneously creating ethical risks. As the analysis of competing ethical arguments above showed, wearable technology can empower people by augmenting their capacities, but without meaningful rules it can also menace individual rights. Accordingly, decision-makers could consider these guidelines to gauge their suitability to their situation:

- Ethical impact statements for proposed policies (Finn & Wright, 2012),
- Policy transparency and accountability legislation,
- An independent body to assess the effect of wearables on privacy,

- Limitations on what data is collected and why, how data is processed, and how long it is stored (Desai & von der Embse, 2008);
- Restrictions on the kinds of technologies on smartwear platforms,
- Further development of an "ethical governor" enabling wearable technology to do the right thing (Arkin, 2009); and
- A digital bill of rights (Hundt, 2014).[10]

A model policy, then, would contain principles for device deployment, data collection and retention, and reporting in the name of the greater good, what is good for one is good for all, and virtuous character. It would include what information is tracked, how it is stored, who has access to it, and how it is used (including that these quantitative data are not the sole basis for personnel decisions). Answers to such questions would be addressed by a pilot program, based on a model policy, and will vary by economic sector, organization, and position. In short, organizations need a clear strategy that accounts for its purpose, how the purpose will be accomplished, and the expected outcome of the policy.

At the public policy level, Clarke and Moses (2014) argue that many of the criteria for an effective regulatory regime—clarity of purpose, transparency, stakeholder participation, parsimony and enforceability—are currently absent. What is needed is robust regulation and oversight to allay concerns that deployment of wearables is based on expediency instead of cost-effectiveness, fairness and privacy, and integrity.

Miniature wearable devices, seamlessly integrated into daily work routines, are likely to be mainstreamed in the next decade. The considerable potential of this technology suggests that decisions to implement smartwear should be considered broadly in terms of how they impact a wide variety of organizational practices in the public, private, and not-for-profit sectors. The ethics triad-behavioral ethics discussion here examined important contentions surrounding the benefits and drawbacks of body-worn computers. The analysis may be helpful when managers apply them to specific circumstances to make informed judgments about the use of wearable technology.

REFERENCES

Abril, P., Avner, L., & Del Riego, A. (2012). Blurred boundaries: Social media privacy and the twenty-first century employee. *American Business Law Journal, 49*(1), 63–124.

Ajunwa, I., Crawford, K., & Schultz, J. (2017). Limitless worker surveillance. *California Law Review, 105*(3), forthcoming.

Anderson, J. (2014, May 14). The internet of things will thrive by 2025. *Pew Research Center: Internet, Science and Technology.* Retrieved from http://www.perinteent. org/2014/05/14/internet-of-things/

---

[10] These proposals are adapted from the authors' earlier work (West & Bowman, 2016a,b; West, Bowman, & Gertz, 2015).

Arkin, R.C. (2009). *Governing lethal behavior in autonomous robots*. Boca Raton, FL: Chapman and Hall/CRC.

Aubrey, S. (2016). How wearable technology and smartwatches will change the workplace. *News.com.au.* February 24. Retrieved from http://www.news.com.au/technology/gadgets/wearables/how-wearable-technology-and-smartwatches-will-change-the-workplace/news-story/01ed2f07153e86fe7a379fca271f4e29

Ball, K. S., & Margulis, S. T. (2011). Electronic monitoring and surveillance in call centres: A framework for investigation. *New Technology, Work, and Employment, 26*, 113–126.

Ball, K., Di Domenico, M. L., & Nunan, D. (2016). Big data surveillance and the body-subject. *Body & Society, 22*(2), 58–81. http://bod.sagepub.com/content/early/2016/02/03/1357034X15624973

Bazerman, M. H., & Tenbrensel, A. E. (2011). *Blind spots: Why we fail to do what's right and what to do about it*. Princeton, NJ: Princeton University Press.

Bell, L (2016, March 16). Working wearables: What's in it for the employees? *Wearable.* . Retrieved from http://www.wareable.com/wearable-tech/working-with-wearables-8796

Bennett, B. (2011, December 10). Police employ predator drone spy planes on home front. *Los Angeles Times*. Retrieved from http://www.articles.latimes.com/2011/dec/10/nation/la-na-drone-arrest-20111211.

Blakemore, M. (2005). Surveillance in the workplace—An overview of issues of privacy, monitoring, and ethics. *Stop The Cyborgs.* Retrieved from http://www.mindfully.org/Technology/2005/Surveillance-Workplace-Blakemore1sep05.htm

Brin, D. (2016, February 16). As wearables become more popular, What is HR's responsibility? *Human Resource Management Magazine*. Retrieved from https://www.shrm.org/resourcesandtools/hr-topics/technology/pages/as-wearables-become-more-popular,-what-is-hr%E2%80%99s-responsibility.aspx

Brown, W.S. (2000). Ontological security, existential anxiety, and workplace privacy, *Journal of Business Ethics, 23*(1), 61–65.

Chauriye, N. (2016). Wearable devices as admissible evidence: Technology is killing our opportunity to lie. *Catholic University Journal of Law and Technology, 24*(2), 495–528.

Ciocchetti, C.A. (2011). The eavesdropping employer: A twenty-first century framework for employee monitoring. *American Business Law Journal, 48*, 285–369.

Clancy, H. (2014). Will the workplace lead wearable technology adoption? *Fortune Magazine.* Retrieved from http://fortune.com/2014/10/29/will-the-workplace-lead-wearable-technology-adoption/?iid=sr-link1

Clarke, R., & Moses, L.B. (2014). The regulation of civilian drones' impacts on public safety. *Computer Law and Security Review, 30*, 263–285.

Corsello, J. (2013). What the Internet of Things will bring to the workplace. *Wired.* Retrieved from http://www.wired.com/insights/2013/11/what-the-internet-of-things-will-bring-to-the-workplace

Desai, M., & von der Embse, T. J. (2008). Managing electronic information: An ethics perspective. *Information Management and Computer Security, 16*, 20–27.

Drevitch, G. (2017). The mystery of motivation. *Psychology Today.* Retrieved from https://www.psychologytoday.com/articles/201701/the-mystery-motivation

Finn, R. L., & Wright, D. (2012). Unmanned aircraft systems: Surveillance, ethics and privacy in civil applications. *Computer Law and Security Review*, *28*, 184–94.

Frankel, S. (2016). Employers are using workplace wearables to find out how happy and productive we are. *Quartz*. Retrieved from http://qz.com/754989/employers-are-using-workplace-wearables-to-find-out-how-happy-and-productive-we-are/

Fort, T. L., Raymond, A. H., & Shackelford, S. J. (2016). Angel on your shoulder: Prompting employees to do the right thing through the use of wearables. *Northwestern University Journal of Technology and Intellectual Property, 14*, 140–170.

Gale, S. (2016, August).. Internet of things could be the next talent management thing. *Workforce,* 10.

Gartner, Inc. (2015). *Gartner reveals top predictions for IT organizations and users for 2016 and beyond*. Press Release. Retrieved from http://www.gartner.com/newsroom/id/3143718

Gazzaniga, M.S. (2008). *Human: The science behind what makes us unique*. New York, NY: Harper Collins Publishers.

Gray, R. (2015). Wearable technology for health and wellbeing. *HR Magazine*. Retrieved from http://www.hrmagazine.co.uk/article-details/how-to-use-wearable-technology-for-health-and-wellbeing

Haberman, M. (2013). The impact of wearable technologies on HR. *Blogging4Jobs.* Retrieved from http://www.blogging4jobs.com/hr/the-impact-of-wearable-technologies-on-hr/#5wHVmIrOzSscpHyY.97

Hayward, J., Chansin, G., & Zervos, H. (2016). Wearable technology 2016–2026. *IDTechEx.* Retrieved from http://www.idtechex.com/research/reports/wearable-technology-2016-2026-000483.asp

Hodson, T. J., Englander, F., & Englander, V. (1999). Ethical, legal and economic aspects of employer monitoring of employee electronic mail. *Journal of Business Ethics*, *19*(1), 99–108.

Hsieh, W., Komisar, R. , Jazayeri, R., & Yeh, P. (2016, March 29.). The future of wearable technology is bright, here are some reasons why. *Blog.* Retrieved from http://www.kpcb.com/blog/the-future-of-wearable-technology-is-bright-here-are-some-reasons-why

Hundt, R. (2014). Saving privacy. *Boston Review*. Retrieved from http://bostonreview.net/forum/reed-hundt-saving-privacy

Iedema, R., & Rhodes, C. (2010). The undecided space of ethics in organizational surveillance. *Organizational Studies*, *31*(2), 199–217.

Infiniti. (2015, May 11). Wearable technology promises greater efficiency in cities, industry, and life. *Washington Post*. Retrieved from http://www.washingtonpost.com/sf/brand-connect/wp/tag/infiniti/

Influx of Wearable Technology in the Workplace. (2015, October 15). *Business Wire*. Retrieved from http://www.businesswire.com/news/home/20151007005173/en/Influx-Wearable-Technology-Workplace-Security-Support-Bandwidth

International Institute for Analytics. (2015). *The Internet of Things: Opportunities and applications across industries.* Portland, OR: Enterprise Research Service.

Identity Theft Resource Center. (2015). Identity theft resource center breach report hits near record high in 2015. *ITRC*. Retrieved from http://www.idtheftcenter.org/ITRC-Surveys-Studies/2015 databreaches.html

Knapp, K. R., & Soylu, A. (2013). Technology: The good, the bad, and the ugly: How technology is affecting employee privacy, work life balance, and workplace relationships. *Mustang Journal of Management and Marketing, 2,* 69–81.

Kronos, Inc. (2014, October 27). Survey indicate workers around the world are poised to embrace wearable technology. *Kronos.* Retrieved from http://www.kronos.com/pr/kronos-survey-indicates-workers-around-the-world-are-poised-to-embrace-wearable-technology

Lavalliere, M., Burstein, A., Arezes, P., & Coughlin, J. (2016). Tackling the challenges of an aging workforce with the use of wearable technologies and the quantified self. *DYNA, 83*(197), 38–43.

Lee, J. (2007, April 28). *There is big brother: Workplace control and workforce surveillance.* Paper presented at the Labor's Voices 2007 Conference, New York, NY. Retrieved from http://www.laborfest.net/2007/Korean%20hi-tech%20doc.htm

Manokha, I. (2017, January 3). Why the rise of wearable technology to monitor employees is worrying. *The Conversation,* Retrieved from http://theconversation.com/why-the-rise-of-wearable-tech-to-monitor-employees-is-worrying-70719

Martin, K., & Freeman, R. E. (2003). Some problems with employee monitoring. *Journal of Business Ethics, 43*(4), 353–361.

Mehta, A. (2014). 'Bring your own glass': The privacy implications of Google Glass in the workplace. *John Marshall Journal of Information Technology and Privacy Law, 30*(3), 607–638.

Michael, K. (2014). Redefining surveillance: Implications for privacy, security, trust, and law. *Issues, 109,* 36–39.

Newman, D. (2015). Improving productivity by better utilizing wearables. *Converge.* Retrieved from http://converge.xyz/improving-productivity-by-better-utilizing-wearables/

Norman, D. (2013). The paradox of wearable technologies. *MIT Technology Review.* Retrieved from https://www.technologyreview.com/s/517346/the-paradox-of-wearable-technologies/

Olson, P. (2015, June 1). More bosses expected to track their staff through wearables in the next five years. *Forbes.* Retrieved from http://www.forbes.com/sites/parmyolson/2015/06/01/wearables-employee-tracking/#5bbdcbf3eec9

Palm, E. (2009). Securing privacy at work: The importance of contextualized consent. *Ethics of Information Technology, 11,* 233–41.

Perera, C., Liu, C. H., & Jayawardena, S. (2015). The emerging Internet of Things marketplace of an industrial perspective: A survey. *IEEE Transactions on Emerging Topics in Computing, 3*(4), 585–598.

Porup, J. M. (2016, March 20). The Internet of Things is a surveillance nightmare. *The Kernel.* Retrieved from http://kernelmag.dailydot.com/issue-sections/staff-editorials/16196/internet-of-things-surveillance-nightmare/

Prentice, R. A. (2015). Behavioral ethics: Can it help lawyers (and others) be their best selves? *Notre Dame Journal of Law, Ethics, and Public Policy, 29*(1), 36–85.

PricewaterhouseCoopers. (2014). *The wearable future.* New York, NY: Author.

Rawls, J. (2005). *A theory of justice: Original Edition.* Boston: Belknap Press.

Rosenberg, R. S. (2005). The technological assault on ethics in the modern workplace. In J. W. Budd & J. G. Scoville (Eds.), *The ethics of human resources and industrial relations* (pp. 141–172). Champaign, IL: Labor and Employment Relations Association.

Rutkin, A. (2014, October 15). Wearable tech lets boss track your work, rest, and play. *New Scientist.* Retrieved from https://www.newscientist.com/article/mg22429913-000-wearable-tech-lets-boss-track-your-work-rest-and-play/

Sarpong, S., & Rees, D. (2014). Assessing the effects of "Big Brother" in a workplace: The case of WAST. *European Management Journal, 32*(2), 216–222.

Senemar, A K. (2015, July 13). Wearables in court: How your electronic data becomes evidence. *Sherbit Blog.* Retrieved from https://www.linkedin.com/pulse/wearables-court-how-your-electronic-data-becomes-evidence-senemar

Shao, R., Aquino, K., & Freeman, D. (2008). Beyond moral reasoning: A review of moral identity research and its implications for business research. *Business Ethics Quarterly, 18*(4), 513–540.

Smith, G. J. D. (2016). Surveillance, data and embodiment: On the work of being watched. *Body & Society, 22*(2), 108–139.

Solove, D.J. (2011). Why privacy matters even if you have "nothing to hide." *Chronicle of Higher Education, 57*, B11–B13.

Sunstein, C. R. (2015). *Nudging and choice architecture: Ethical considerations.* Harvard John M. Olin Center for Law, Economics, and Business Discussion Paper 809. Retrieved from https://dash.harvard.edu/bitstream/handle/1/17915544/Sunstein_809.pdf?sequence=1

Svara, J. H. (2014). Who are the keepers of the code? Articulating and upholding ethical standards in the field of public administration. *Public Administration Review, 74,* 561–569.

Taylor, D. (2014, March 31). Wearable tech: The surveillance grid of the future. *Old Thinker News.* Retrieved from http://www.oldthinkernews.com/2014/03/30/wearable-tech-the-surveillance-grid-of-the-future/

Thompson, R. M., II. (2013). *Drones in domestic surveillance operations: Fourth amendment implications and legislative responses.* Report no. R42701. Washington, DC: Congressional Research Service. Retrieved from http://fas.org/sgp/crs/natsec/R42701.pdf [accessed November 17, 2015].

Ubiq Team. (2015). *3 Considerations when implementing wearable tech in the workplace.* Retrieved from https://www.goubiq.com/3-considerations-when-implementing-wearable-tech-in-the-workplace/

Vaze, R. (2014). Wearable technology: Feeding our underlying curiosity to know, to be aware. *Slideshare.* Retrieved from http://www.slideshare.net/RohiniVaze/wearable-technology-report

Verbeek, P.P. (2011). *Moralizing technology.* Chicago, IL: University of Chicago Press.

West, J., & Bowman, J. (2016a). The domestic use of drones: An ethical analysis of surveillance issues. *Public Administration Review 76*(4), 649–659.

West, J., & Bowman, J. (2016b). Electronic surveillance at work: An ethical analysis. *Administration & Society 48*(5), 628–651.

West, J., Bowman, J., & Gertz, S. (2015). Electronic surveillance in the workplace: Legal, ethical and management issues. In R. Sims & W. Sauser (Eds.), *Legal and regulatory issues in human resource management.* Charlotte, NC: Information Age Publishing, 285–315.

Wilson, H. J. (2013). Wearables in the workplace. *Harvard Business Review.* Retrieved from https://hbr.org/2013/09/wearables-in-the-workplace

CHAPTER 7

A CONSIDERATION OF SOCIAL MEDIA MOVEMENTS ON GENDER-RELATED HR POLICY

Angela N. Spranger and Brenna Gonsalves

INTRODUCTION

This chapter summarizes a review of the literature and media in our investigation of the impact of social media phenomena on corporate human resource (HR) management policies. The purpose of our efforts is to identify, first, *if* there has been any significant impact on gender-related HR policies attributable to the #MeToo, #TimesUp, or other social media movements. We seek to analyze how current gender-related social media movements encourage changes in business through HR policy. For this preliminary analysis, we seek to indicate what has emerged thus far in the literature, summarize the pilot data from an initial case study, offer implications for research and for practice, and outline next steps for further consideration. In this chapter we assess current literature on the workplace phenomena of harassment (both sexual and psychological), bullying, and gender stereotypes that lead to discrimination. We also examine leadership style, perceptions and expectations in the context of implicit leadership theory.

Human Resources Management Issues, Challenges and Trends:
"Now and Around the Corner", pages 145–162.
Copyright © 2019 by Information Age Publishing
145

Human Resource (HR) Management and Gender-Related Policy: What We Know

In business, HR is the department that deals with all things personnel. That is, HR helps drive, manage, and facilitate the employment life cycle, from recruiting and onboarding to retirement or termination, including strategic HR planning, performance management, training and development, and employee engagement. As the thought leaders and culture monitors of the organization, HR represents the cornerstone of creating change in the workplace. Through effective change management, including organizational unlearning, HR can facilitate more effective team development (even when that means hiring outsiders or terminating noncompliant team members who violate organizational norms) and use employee engagement initiatives that improve sensitivity and inclusiveness, thereby increasing productivity and morale. HR management policies and training on those policies can create cultural changes in a business if used properly.

Why Research This Problem Now?

Renowned leadership author and speaker Barbara Kellerman suggested that the last ten years have ushered in an end to traditional leader-follower roles and dynamics. Instead, grassroots movements and follower-initiated campaigns have changed the geopolitical landscape and may have equal impact in corporate settings (Kellerman, 2012). While there are many articles written about the social impact of contemporary rights movements, there is no body of literature yet that addresses the impact of these movements on business practices. The recent resurgence of gay rights, racial equality, and women's rights movements has gathered formidable momentum. Grassroots movements create roles of influence for their initiators and organizers. Pride Marches, #BlackLivesMatter, and #MeToo are changing the social and cultural landscape of America. Hashtags and trends on social media outlets such as Twitter (also Instagram, Facebook, Reddit and Tumblr) allow people all over the globe to lend their voices to common causes. We seek to engage the human resources community in a dialogue that addresses HR policy concerns in light of these social media phenomena, within a theoretical framework.

Since 2016, several high-profile sexual harassment allegations were revealed in various news outlets and on social media platforms, primarily from the entertainment industry. Issues such as gay rights, racial inequality protests, and women's rights movements are not new to America. But in the last few years, observers have noted a significant shift from complacency to activism, particularly in politics and the entertainment industry. These fields have received particular attention in the media due to the myriad allegations of harassment by high-profile male figures. For example, Donald Trump, Bill O'Reilly, Bill Cosby, Harvey Weinstein, and Matt Lauer are all celebrities in the entertainment industry who have been accused of sexual harassment or assault. Even after such allegations,

Trump successfully crossed over from entertainment into politics. O'Reilly maintained an unrepentant stance and continued to sell books and participate in online and onscreen controversi es. Following the Weinstein allegations, more and more women have publicized similar allegations accusing a multitude of celebrities, from Ed Westwick to James Franco. The common thread is that these were all workplace occurrences, and they did not appear to be stopping.

Even as we prepared this chapter, new reports emerged of major corporations having been forced to address their gender-related harassment policies. Specifically, Nike has "struggled with their efforts to market to women, and they've had a lot of talent leave the organization" (Wallace, 2018). Women in workplaces like Fox News, NBC's Today Show, and Nike's corporate organization have chosen the "exit" option when they finally tired of misogynistic behaviors, examples of which included males who "constantly would berate women, talk down to women, interrupt," demean women's contributions, and perhaps worst and most pervasive, excuse other men's disrespectful actions and behaviors. The unfortunate component to these stories is that, as with Nike's Wallace, often women make the appropriate complaints to management and HR but receive either explicit or implicit messaging from the company that indicates the woman herself is to blame, has given mixed messages or otherwise invited the bad behavior, or is too sensitive. Or, the messaging may be that it is too difficult to execute the organizational unlearning—discipline, retraining, or termination—or the bad actors. Perhaps the accused is a high value executive, top sales performer, or other "untouchable." Until the impact of bad behavior in the workplace affects the company's bottom line, often no change takes place. Certainly, Nike's "in-house problems" have had a significant impact on retail performance; in the United States market, Adidas and Under Armour are "gaining on them" (Wallace, 2018).

In Wallace's (2018) case after leaving Nike, though, there is a positive strain of news emerging from the company:

> Nike is in the midst of a company-wide overhaul. An informal survey of women at the Oregon headquarters revealed complaints of pay inequity, inappropriate workplace behavior and a lack of career advancement for women. The survey was delivered to CEO Mark Parker. He's apologized to people who were excluded and called them brave for speaking out.

In the first half of 2018, the President of the company announced his retirement. The next day, the Vice President announced his departure. Then, five more senior leaders, and then four more, so that the total in May of 2018 is 11 executives who have either chosen to or been required to leave the company. There is a cultural overhaul taking place, and former Nike employee Wallace attributes it to the #MeToo movement.

An additional unifying factor has been the widespread outpouring of support on social media from female (and male) entertainment industry professionals. With stars opening up about their traumas, more women across the country and around the world have felt comfortable adding to the dialogue. Women who have experienced similar workplace hardships use the hashtags and trends to reclaim their confidence and engage in the campaign to "feel seen, safe, and valued" (Spranger, 2015) in the workplace. These women of varying ages are standing up for what they believe and exposing a workplace phenomenon that been, one might say, an open secret for too long. And in some cases, the women raise legal complaints in a timely fashion so that their offenders (and the organizations where they work) may be held legally accountable.

As a result of these cases, some of which resulted in lawsuits and others which negatively impacted the brand of the company, organizations can no longer afford to ignore issues of potential gender discrimination or harassment. The #MeToo, #NastyWoman, and #TimesUp campaigns paved the way for conversations in the workplace. Have these conversations spread to industries other than entertainment and news media? As in those industries, women in other sectors have begun to initiate dialogue and point out the unfortunate statistics surrounding these uncomfortable topics. Implicit leadership theories, stereotypes, and leadership perceptions all create an image of what employees expect from women in leadership roles, but this often unfairly creates a lose-lose scenario for women interested in climbing the corporate ladder. Potential challenges to this moment of incredible cultural shift include women's perceptions of women in leadership roles, as well as increased hesitation from men to engage in the dialogue for fear of being misunderstood or, worse, accused. The findings of our preliminary and follow-on studies may help executives and HR practitioners to craft more effective harassment policies, or to create them where they do not exist. Additionally, our findings may lead to compelling future research opportunities. Recommendations as well as implications for HR practice are provided.

Assumptions

We assume that employees in any organizational context want to "feel seen, safe, and valued" (Spranger, 2015). People want to feel like they are receiving the proper amount of attention and care from their employers. They want to go to work and only worry about work and not their safety. And, finally, they want to feel like what they are doing is appreciated. This chapter is organized around that concept, and will focus primarily on the idea of safety for purposes of clarity. Also, we use the concept of being "seen" interchangeably with being "heard." Since the goal of social media movements is not so much being physically seen, or visible, as with marches, we focus on the expressed concerns that amplify employees' voices and reasoning behind why they are speaking up, even using anonymous identities online, for their voices to be heard. Last, some of the social media movements referenced have been highly politicized or are political in nature (such as the #NastyWoman and #IAmANastyWomanBecause movement). Our goal is not to examine the politics but to state the facts about the social media movements and consider their impact on gender-related HR policy.

PRELIMINARY LITERATURE REVIEW

Well-known psychologist Abraham Maslow (1943), created a hierarchy of needs showcasing the most important needs for humans. Maslow's Hierarchy of Needs (1943) labels safety needs as second only to physiological needs such as food, water, and sleep. Unfortunately for women, these needs have never been met fully. Sexual harassment at work, as well as bullying, create an environment for women where they do not enjoy going to work every day nor do they feel safe.

Seen, but Not Safe. There are two primary forms of sexual harassment discussed in college classes and basic HR compliance workshops. The first, *quid pro quo*, is the one that is usually thought of when considering sexual harassment-"this for that." In legal terms, this means "making sexual favors a condition of any workplace opportunity" like hiring, promotion, a raise, etc. (Williams & Lebsock, 2018, p. 8). The second form is more ambiguous than *quid pro quo*: it is the hostile work environment. Legally, this form of harassment must be unwelcome, the environment created must be one that any reasonable person would consider to be hostile, and it must be severe or pervasive. Recent HR textbooks separate the hostile work environment into two categories; that of the environment created by supervisors and management, and a separate category for a hostile work environment created by peers, colleagues, customers or suppliers. Sexist comments fall under the category of hostile work environment, and 82% of women and 74% of men have reported hearing sexist comments at work (Williams & Lebsock, 2018). Regardless of type, the number of women who have been sexually harassed at some point during their career fluctuates anywhere between 60–80% depending on the study (Williams & Lebsock, 2018).

The prevalence of psychological harassment, or bullying, is equally dismal. Bullying is a category of antisocial workplace behavior (AWB) that is, as yet, lawful under federal and state laws. Even California, the leading edge for employee-friendly law, has yet to pass anything stronger than a mandate for employers to provide training on abusive conduct. And "abusive conduct" is defined differently in different states. New York's definition seems comprehensive:

Abusive conduct means

acts, omissions, or both, that a reasonable person would find abusive, based on the severity, nature and frequency of the conduct, including, but not limited to:

repeated verbal abuse such as the use of derogatory remarks, insults and epithets;

verbal, nonverbal or physical conduct of a threatening, intimidating or humiliating nature;

or the sabotage or undermining of an employee's work performance.

It shall be considered an aggravating factor if the conduct exploited an employee's known psychological or physical illness or disability.

A single act normally shall not constitute abusive conduct, but an especially severe and egregious act may meet this standard. (Segal, 2015, p. 118)

Unfortunately (trust the lawyers to remind us of this), attempting to put too fine a point on what bullying is may create too much of a restrictive work environment, in which poor performers may use the threat of a bullying accusation to prevent managers from holding them accountable for their behavior, attitudes, outcomes and results.

All across the United States, bullying is legal—if the victim is targeted because she is a competitor, of if the bully behaves equally badly towards everyone on his team. If and only if the bullying behavior is rooted in hostility towards an individual's protected class status such as "race, gender, religion, national origin, age, sexual orientation or disability" (Segal, 2015). The best that a complainant can do is document the situation carefully, and then if they feel they must terminate the employment relationship they may be able to file a wrongful constructive discharge claim based on the documented psychological harassment, or bullying.

Women who work in the service sector, or in low-wage jobs, are the most vulnerable. Hotel housekeepers, late night janitorial staff, restaurant workers, etc. are just a few examples of these types of jobs. In 2011, 37% of the Equal Employment Opportunity Commission (EEOC) complaints filed by women came from the restaurant industry alone- and that was seven years ago. In 2014, in a survey conducted about women restaurant workers, 80% had been harassed by colleagues, almost 80% had been harassed by coworkers, 67% had been harassed by managers, and 52% of these women were harassed on a weekly basis (Williams & Lebsock, 2018). Unfortunately, the EEOC has not yet published information regarding statistics on business women being harassed at work. An article from an alternate source claims, that from 2005 to 2015 professional, scientific, technical services, finance and insurance, and management made up 10.36% of all harassment claims made to the EEOC regardless of gender (Stewart, 2017). While it is less likely for people in business to be harassed overall, harassment at work is still an issue that needs addressing.

Harassment is not the only workplace concern regarding safety. Bullying is another continuous trend making women feel unwanted and unsafe at work. Bullying is described by Spranger and Mitchell (2018) as "repeated attempts to torment, wear down, or frustrate another person; it further compromises treatment that provokes pressures intimidates or otherwise causes discomfort" (p. 9). Overall, it is estimated that 54 million Americans have been bullied at some point in their career (Kane, 2018). According to the Workplace Bullying Institute, 58% of all bullying targets were women (Kane, 2018). In general, 68% of bullying is same-gender, meaning women are more likely to bully women; women bullies choose to target other women about 80% of the time (Kane, 2018). A survey from UCLA in 2011 made up of 60,000 people, found that "women—even those who were managers themselves—were more likely to want a male boss than a female one" (Khazan, 2017, n.p.). This concept is reinforced by Spranger and Mitchell

(2018) who reported that "one study showed that 95% of women felt they were undermined at some point in their career by other women (Ludwig, n.d., p. 7). In a roundtable discussion about Sheryl Sandberg's 2013 book *Lean In*, the concept of the "impostor syndrome" was raised. This syndrome reflects women's feelings of being fake, artificial, undeserving or a fraud when they are recognized for their hard work. Roundtable participants suggested that women need to take Sandberg's advice and "[o]wn your skills, ability, and work," (Folz, 2015, p. 103) while acknowledging that this phenomenon is a throwback to previous generations in the workplace. That is, while a woman may be highly qualified and experienced, she still gets evaluated on her looks by men as well as other women. This leads to women questioning what they have to do to simply be recognized for their contributions. And, other women in the dialogue identify more with the fear of being perceived as aggressive or bossy rather than doubting their own skills (Folz, 2015). Spranger and Mitchell (2018) also found that women feel women leaders foster an environment of competition where women subordinates feel they must compete more for promotions as well as both mentorship and development opportunities.

Another way women feel unsafe at work is through sex discrimination. Discrimination based on sex is not new for women in business, regardless of industry. In 2014, 74.4% of all the sex discrimination complaints filed with the EEOC were from women (U.S. Equal Employment Opportunity Commission, 2018). It is important to note that these numbers only come from complaints that have been filed and do not accurately represent all of the instances of sex discrimination at work. In the *Lean In* book, Sheryl Sandberg suggested that women at her company, Facebook, can and should talk openly about their family planning goals. She even stated that she had raised the issue in job interviews (Folz, 2015). Human resource management professionals would cringe at the very suggestion of women being asked about their plans to have children or adopt, as it harkens back to an era when men were paid more because they "legitimately" had families to provide for and women were judged as betraying their feminine duties if they wanted to work full-time. In a roundtable dialogue about Sandberg's book, several reacted strongly. One said, "it scares the heck out of me to think of managers asking that type of question," another raised the specter of "legal repercussions," and a third stated that "as a compliance nerd, I wouldn't recommend it to my managers. Primarily because I don't think that [the information] would be used as intended" (Folz, 2015, p. 104).

In the past, businesses paid settlements for harassment claims and swept any other possible damages under the rug through non-disclosure agreements. Many complaints went unreported because back then, it was the complainants (women) who were fired after a claim was made. According to the *Harvard Business Review*, Harvey Weinstein paid out settlements to eight of the women who filed harassment claims against him (Williams & Lebsock, 2018). Williams and Lebsock state that "quiet settlements are now becoming harder to justify. The unceremonious firings and forced resignations of famous men demonstrate that companies are moving away from that strategy" (2018, p. 6). With the help of movements like #MeToo, silence is no longer afforded to companies and defendants intertwined in harassment claims. Although more women are speaking up, the big difference now is that they are being believed.

With statistics like these, it comes as no surprise that women do not feel safe at work. Chances of being harassed or bullied at work and in life are incredibly high for women. Women do not even feel supported by one another in their workplace-preferring male bosses over female ones (Jonsen, Maznevski, & Schneider, 2010; Spranger & Mitchell, 2018). Movements like #MeToo are forcing companies to make changes to their policies and practices. Since women have not felt safe, and the current environment created has given women an outlet to speak out, they are using it. These trends, hashtags, marches, and movements are allowing women to be both seen and heard.

Seen

Each of these movements has allowed women to speak up for something they have been silenced by in the past.

> Historically, it has been hard to win a sexual harassment suit, but rapidly shifting public perceptions may change that. Seventy-eight percent of women say they are more likely to speak out now if they are treated unfairly because of their gender. About the same percent of men (77%) say they are now more likely to speak out if they see a woman being treated unfairly. It's a new day for a simple reason: Women are being believed (Williams & Lebsock, 2018, p. 5)

The difference between now and then, is that now both the political environment and the media has created the perfect storm for women to rally together and create a change. #MeToo, #NastyWoman, and #TimesUp are all distinct movements focusing on different women's social issues. Social media is giving women an outlet to showcase how many people are being affected by harassment and discrimination.

Few people know about the origins of #MeToo. Ten years ago, an activist named Tarana Burke created a movement to empower young girls of color; this was when #MeToo was created. However, the story behind this hashtag goes back to 1996 when Burke was a youth camp director. A young girl asked to speak with Burke after a bonding session among all girls. The young girl began to tell Burke about her "stepdaddy" (her mother's boyfriend) and the things he was doing to her during such a vulnerable time in her development. Burke was so overwhelmed with emotions, shocked and horrified, that she stopped the young girl in the middle of her story and directed her to another counselor she thought "could help her better" (Santiago & Criss, 2017). Burke could not bring herself to even whisper the words "me too." Later, Burke decided to help these young survivors of sexual abuse, and sexual assault- to give them an outlet and a voice- she created an organization dedicated to letting others know they were not alone (Santiago & Criss, 2017).

The reason #MeToo has become so well-known is because on October 15th, 2017, actress Alyssa Milano encouraged users to use the hashtag. In light of the Harvey Weinstein allegations, she tweeted this:

Alyssa Milano via Twitter

Later, Milano tweeted out #MeToo with a link to Burke's organization, to further spread knowledge of how to help. The hashtag took off, and people all over the world were using the hashtag as a way to acknowledge that they were not alone and they were no longer ashamed. An immediate bond was created among these (mostly) women, and people could no longer ignore the growing number of people who could relate to being sexually harassed, assaulted, or abused.

Within two days (from the Sunday Milano tweeted, to the Tuesday this article was created), the hashtag was used 825,000 times on Twitter and over 4.7 million times on Facebook (Santiago & Criss, 2017). "According to Facebook, more than 45% of people in the United States are friends with someone who's posted a message with the words 'Me too'" (Santiago & Criss, 2017). Burke was amazed by this viral movement, but hopes that it moves beyond that- "she wants sexual violence or gender-based violence approached as a social justice issue" (Santiago & Criss, 2017). Tarana Burke wants action and change.

#MeToo has inspired marches around the world. For years, Tarana Burke has hosted survivors' marches, leading them with a large sign saying "#MeToo" on the front. Even though Harvey Weinstein was the reason behind Milano tweeting, it is not just celebrities being affected by sexual violence. Women all over the world have used the hashtag as a rallying cry to show other women that they are not alone in this fight and that they are not the only ones being affected. Women are demanding to be seen and heard because they are refusing to be silenced.

The #TimesUp movement is a mostly celebrity response to the Harvey Weinstein allegations. A 'letter in solidarity' was created called "Dear Sisters," to better explain what this movement stands for and what its goals are. One paragraph reads:

> Unfortunately, too many centers of power—from legislatures to boardrooms to executive suites and management to academia—lack gender parity and women do not have equal decision-making authority. This systemic gender-inequality and imbalance of power fosters an environment that is ripe for abuse and harassment against women. Therefore, we call for a significant increase of women in positions of leadership and power across industries. In addition, we seek equal representation, opportunities, benefits and pay for all women workers, not to mention greater representation of women of color, immigrant women, disabled women, and lesbian, bisexual, and transgender women, whose experiences in the workforce are often significantly worse than their white, cisgender, straight peers. The struggle for women to break in, to rise up the ranks and to simply be heard and acknowledge in male-dominated workplaces must end; time's up on this impenetrable monopoly (Time's Up, 2018).

As you can see, this movement has many goals and covers many topics. Overall, it is safe to say they are against discrimination based on gender, sexuality, ability, and race. However, this movement may encounter problems with trying to get more women in positions of power. Since women prefer male bosses over female ones, it may be harder than assumed by this movement to get other women on board with the idea of more women in leadership roles.

One of the most significant ways this movement showcased its solidarity was at the Golden Globe Award ceremony in the winter of 2018, when celebrities dressed in black to show their unity for the #TimesUp movement. At this event, many female celebrities decided to bring women activists as their plus one to use their celebrity for a cause. Actress Michelle Williams brought Tarana Burke; actress Meryl Streep brought Ai-jen Poo, the director of the National Domestic Workers Alliance (White, 2018). The actresses deferred to their 'dates' when asked questions about why they chose to wear all black; to use the opportunity in the spotlight for good and to help instigate conversations around the topic of equality- especially in the entertainment industry (White, 2018).

With the help of these movements, women are now fighting to be seen and heard. Since social media is so wide-spread and anyone can use it from anywhere, women all over the world are coming together. They realize they are not alone and becoming more comfortable speaking up for what they want. Women are refusing to be silenced now and pushing hard for the causes they believe in so deeply. With conversations surrounding harassment, degrading language, and equal pay by both politicians and celebrities, women are making changes to the way they are perceived and valued- especially at work. Many of the allegations brought up through #MeToo occurred in some type of workplace, the "nasty" comment was made to Hilary Clinton in her place of work (so to speak), and the Time's Up movement is focusing on the workplace and equality in pay, numbers, and opportunities.

Valued

It is important to recognize that perception and value are inextricably intertwined. The 'value' one holds is based on other's perceptions of that person, or their perceived value. For women at work, their perceived value has been stifled by stereotypes, perceptions of women leaders, and implicit leadership theories (biases). While there are more women in leadership roles now than ever before- for example, there are now 21 women in the Senate, more than there has ever been- women are still being labeled and devalued at work (Pew Research Center, 2017). Women make up 52% of the United States total population, yet "only 20% of the 'C-suite,' or top executive roles, are women" (Spranger & Mitchell, 2018).

Stereotypes- while not always accurate- can still create obstacles for women to overcome. According to Jonsen, Maznevski, and Schneider (2010) "we stereotype based on familiar women's roles" (p. 551) such as mothers, nurses, and teachers. Implicit leadership theories suggest that we have preconceived notions of a leader that form our expectations of them. We expect women to be motherly, nurturing, and accommodating based on these stereotypes. However, "management jobs have traditionally been understood as being constructed according to male norms and thus creating difficulties for women" (Alewell, 2013; Kyriakidou, 2012, p. 4). The management world is still dominated by men, and many "women have identified stereotypes as an important barrier to the most senior positions in business" (Jonson, Maznevski, & Schneider, 2010, p. 552).

Studies have shown that people- regardless of gender, tend to assume a "leader" has more male associated traits than female ones (Alewell, 2013; Jonson, Maznevski & Schneider, 2010; Kyriakidou, 2012; Mendez & Busenbark, 2015). "These stereotypes create psychological burdens that may contribute to their low rates of self-promotion and concurrent underrepresentation" (p. 6) and make it hard for any women to be successful in a leadership position (Spranger & Mitchell, 2018). Their value as a leader is immediately decreased based on their gender. Also, based on these stereotypes, if women

> adhere to traditional "female" characteristics (e.g. nurturing/communal) they are considered too nice and therefore not capable/competent. If they assume more "male characteristics" (agentic) they are considered to be too harsh. Thus women who attain leadership positions have to make a tradeoff between being liked vs respected. (Jonson, Maznevski, & Schneider, 2010, p. 552)

Sandberg's *Lean In* suggested that women should be more confident and assertive, behaviors and attitudes more traditionally associated with male leaders, but HR managers and executives know that the empirical differences between male and female leadership are negligible. The feminine styles of leadership tends to lead women to be "more willing to admit they don't have all the answers at critical times… more relational… more team-oriented… seeking to understand others… showing the ability to think and then communicate" (Folz, 2015, p. 105).

Being a woman in a leadership role creates a "lose-lose" situation. Not only do women have to compete against stereotypes and inaccurate perceptions, but as mentioned earlier, they also compete against each other for opportunities in the workplace (Spranger & Mitchell, 2018). Overall, it is a commonly-held idea that perceptions of suitable leadership are indeed influenced by gender- and for women, this is not a positive influence.

The effects of these stereotypes on women "include an undermined sense of identity and belonging, and a decrease in motivation to succeed" (Spranger & Mitchell, 2018). #MeToo and other gender-related movements have laid down the groundwork for conversations surrounding these topics to be brought into the workplace. These movements are fighting for stereotypes, perceptions, and implicit theories to stop being barriers to women moving up the corporate ladder. Their goal is to give women the same rights and opportunities as men at work and in life.

IMPLICATIONS FOR HUMAN RESOURCE MANAGEMENT PRACTICE

From a practitioner standpoint, there are many changes businesses can consider in light of these movements to ensure their company is creating a fair and equal workplace where everyone feels seen, safe, and valued. Harassment policies must be carefully thought out, elucidated in an employee handbook that clearly states it is not a contract, and then enforced with explicit complaint policies (Segal, 2015). Additionally, it is important to ensure that everyone is well trained on the harassment policy. Knowledge and training are pertinent for comprehension of the policies already in place. It is important employees already know the steps they are required to take should anything happen while at work. Since it is not unlikely that a woman will be harassed sometime in her career, it may be beneficial to educate everyone on the many types of harassment. It is not just *quid pro quo* harassment; there is also hostile work environment and psychological harassment, or bullying that affect people's working conditions and comfort. Setting the tone right away leaves no room for the excuse "I didn't know." Writing down specific definitions for harassment and bullying will leave no loopholes. For example, Segal (2015) suggests that organizations should lay out a definition for what constitutes bullying *in their company*, and specify what types of behaviors may be considered bullying under that definition:

A policy prohibiting bullying should outline examples of behavior that might constitute bullying, such as:

- Mean-spirited "joking" designed to exploit an employee's perceived weaknesses.
- Discussing an employee's performance problems with the employee's peers or subordinates.
- Yelling at an employee, whether alone or in front of others.

- Encouraging others to avoid an employee.
- Physical intimidation when speaking with an employee.
- Sabotaging an employee's work.
- Insulting an employee's family or friends. (Segal, 2015)

In the current political climate, an unfortunate consequence of the general climate of conversational incivility is that political images (a picture of the current or previous president of the United States with his family, for example) evoke strong feelings in employees, such that

And what about a policy restricting romantic relationships and dating among coworkers? Such a policy may have value should a subordinate and a supervisor become intimate—as with radio and media personality Tavis Smiley, who lost his job at PBS due to "sexual harassment and dalliances with subordinates" (O'Connell, 2018). Indeed, it would not be ideal to encounter a harassment lawsuit at work because an intimate relationship deteriorated (Hunt, Davidson, Fielden & Hoel, 2010; Mainiero & Jones, 2013; Smith, 2018). Cultural changes in business often start with policy changes. Having hiring policies that address equality and accountability will ensure minority groups, like women, are taken into equal consideration. And, taking careful steps to avoid conscious and unconscious bias in hiring decisions will aid greatly in preparing HR generalists and representatives, Talent Acquisition specialists, and hiring managers for following through on equitable, accountable hiring processes. As Segal explains,

> a white male manager may know that gender and race lawfully cannot be considered in a hiring situation. But he, as a white man, may favor a white male candidate over a woman of color based on how 'comfortable' he is with each of them, even though he has no idea that his comfort level may relate to race and/or gender.

> Unconscious bias, often referred to as implicit bias, is bias that we are unaware of. It happens automatically and without any conscious thought process and is triggered by our brain making snap judgments formed, at least in part, as a result of the messages that we received growing up, as well as our own experiences, culture, mass media and other influences. (2017, p. 75)

To prevent the activation of implicit bias and action taken based on stereotypes, HR professionals can encourage their peers and the managers in the organizations they serve to take the Harvard Implicit Awareness Test (IAT), to assess individuals' implicit bias in areas such as gender and sexual orientation, race, religion, and age (Segal, 2017). Segal (2017) urges caution here though, HR professionals should take care with bias testing, as the results of such an instrument are discoverable in case of employment litigation.

Training. While mentioned earlier with regards to policy knowledge and types of harassment, training is a second means by which changes can be made to business culture. Training involving the awareness of implicit leadership theories stereotypes, and perhaps even sensitivity training, might encourage employees to be mindful of how they may play a role in making their women peers, and others feel unseen and under-valued. Many people are unaware of the preconceived notions/biases/stereotypes they bring into a situation. Having trainings to uncover these biases may encourage cultural change in the workplace by holding people accountable for their part. Sensitivity training follows the same idea; it is "training intended to sensitize people to their attitudes and behaviors that may unwittingly cause offense to others, especially members of various minorities" (Google, 2018). Training like this will encourage self-reflection and hopefully start change. A company can only change if the people within it are willing. At the most basic level, businesses are groups of people working toward a common goal; if you can get everyone invested in the same change- change will happen.

With the previously described trends in vocalizing complaints about harassment in the social sphere, reputation management becomes a viable cottage industry. Company executives may wonder about how their organization and its leaders are represented on the social media platforms that matter to their investors, customers, and potential high value employees. Rather than throw good money after bad and escalate a commitment to poor, ineffective policies, executives would do well to address the internal causes (and remedies) of harassment. Bottom line, employees have grown weary of the apologies and public statements. They prefer clearly stated policies, procedural steps, and action.

Procedures. How then can you take effective action to protect your company and reassure employees? Employment lawyer Jonathan Segal (2018) suggests that as a direct result of #MeToo, leaders review their sexual harassment policies and at the same time audit the company's complaint procedure. If the policy is the roar, then the procedure is the teeth that help the organization back up its stated values. One key point to emphasize is that it is not just the target of sexual harassment who can, should, and must report the offensive behavior—immediately!—but also anyone else who witnesses the conduct. Reporting systems should not be "radio-button" restrictive, in that the employee must be able to enter the description of the behavior in his or her own words. It may be that more of your employees than you expect end up reporting "harassing conduct that is not unlawful" (p. 64). That actually benefits your company, because it reveals layers of data about your organizational culture that you might not see otherwise. The policy and the procedure should both cover all protected classes: racial, ethnic, religious, handicap, age, "and other forms of harassing conduct" (p. 64), as well as the sexual and psychological harassment.

A second key point, important to publish widely inside your organization, is that you provide multiple points of contact for employees to report their concerns about harassment policy compliance. An outside consultant can be contracted to receive these complaints and relate directly back to your Chief Executive Officer, Chief Compliance Officer, or other designated responsible party. At the very least, a harassment complaint should be submitted to a chain manager or supervisor and a compliance officer in HR. After all, it may be the supervisor or manager causing the issue that results in the complaint! If your complaint procedure sends the employee right back to them, it offers no safety or protection at all. There are businesses that serve as third-party reporting services for large companies, and consultants who can support small to medium-sized companies in this effort. Such arrangements should require the consultant to provide a report to at least two points of contact, both the executive client and HR. Between them, the accused can be notified and appropriate action taken that incorporates the results and recommendations of the investigation.

A third key point is to define, clarify, and explain. That is, it will help your employees to feel safe if they know what behaviors are unacceptable or prohibited conduct. It may seem like micromanaging to have to specify such behaviors, but employees appreciate having clear guidelines. For example, a corporate policy should specify that customers, vendors, and suppliers may be perpetrators of sexually (or psychologically) harassing behavior. Psychological harassment is known in the research literature and in current employment law as bullying. Unfortunately, while the phenomenon is well documented, no federal or state law stands to make bullying an illegal act, and women, minorities, and members of the LGBTQ community may fall victim to this form of harassment with no legal recourse. Social media and electronic communications, both on and off the job, both professional and "private," may be tools used for harassment, so this should be clarified and explained in your policy as well.

Fourth, an effective complaint procedure must clarify that not only do you have a zero-tolerance policy for sexual harassment, but you must also have a zero tolerance policy for retaliation or reprisal against the complainant. Your procedure should include coverage for the complainant and any witnesses or others "associated with the complainant, such as a spouse" (Segal, 2018, p. 65). In both training programs and in investigations of real complaints, your company policy and complaint procedure must state explicitly that even if it does not qualify as a legal case, the behavior itself and any type of retaliation against the complainant are absolutely forbidden. Segal states that "[t]he courts are flooded with cases where employees' harassment complaints were initially dismissed but the judges later ruled that the ensuing retaliation claims had *sufficient merit to proceed to trial*" (emphasis added) (Segal, 2018, p. 65).

Finally, when faced with a sexual harassment complaint, this is the point at which your organization must "walk its talk," and manifest its values. Actions truly speak louder than words in this kind of situation—either you have a zero tolerance policy for everyone, or you do not. The President of the company, the Chief Financial Officer's nephew, the HR manager, must all be equally susceptible to the company policy, not just the frontline Supervisor, Planner, or Procurement Specialist.

CONCLUSION

Women are now fighting to be seen because they have not felt safe and valued. Using #MeToo, #NastyWoman, and #TimesUP, women are creating a unified voice that can no longer be ignored by the public or by businesses. They want their causes heard and their right to feel seen, safe, and valued back. Due to the environment created by celebrities and politicians bringing topics of workplace harassment, bullying, and stereotyping into the spotlight, women are feeling more comfortable stepping forward and lending their experiences to these causes. Director and entertainment expert Steven Spielberg has shared many opinions surrounding #MeToo and #TimesUp. Spielberg believes there should be a code of conduct at work to eliminate sexual harassment (Blackmon, 2017). He is also quoted saying,

> [Time's Up] is something that is going to change everything for the better... There is always more to come, but the other thing we have to think about is this...Hollywood and celebrity gets a lot of recognition, you can't just think of this as a Hollywood problem, this is a national problem and probably a global problem (Trendell, 2018, n.p.).

This problem goes beyond actors and actresses. While these groups have been instrumental in launching movements into the spotlight, it is now time to take these proposed changes and apply them to the business world. Cultural change in business is possible- you have to start at the very base level- the people. Where better to start encouraging this cultural shift than the people who deal with personnel? Human Resources is an influential change agent in every business- changing the policy, and increasing the training will change the people. With movements like #MeToo in the spotlight, now is the time to start moving forward.

REFERENCES

Alewell, D. (2013). Be successful—Be male and masculine? on the influence of gender roles on objective career success. *Evidence-Based HRM, 1*(2), 147–168. Retrieved from https://0-search-proquest-com.read.cnu.edu/docview/1471843812?accountid=10100

Blackmon, M. (2017). *Steven Spielberg wants a Hollywood code of conduct to eliminate sexual harassment.* Retrieved from: https://www.buzzfeed.com/michaelblackmon/steven-spielberg-dustin-hoffman-hollywood-code-of-conduct?utm_term=.vf27da-3KW#.pdzn3VKBv

Folz, C. (2015, June). Lean In HR: A Roundtable Discussion. *HR Magazine*, 102–105.

Google. (2018). *Search definition: "sensitivity traininhg."* Retrieved from: https://www.google.com/search?q=sensitivity+training&oq=sensiti&aqs=chrome.5.69i57j0l5.4759j1j7&sourceid=chrome&ie=UTF-8

Jonsen, K., Maznevski, M., & Schneider, S. (2010). Gender differences in leadership—believing is seeing: implications for managing diversity, *Equality, Di-*

versity and Inclusion: An International Journal, 29(6), 549–572, https://doi. org/10.1108/02610151011067504

Kane, S. (2018). Who is a workplace bully's target? *The Balance*. Retrieved from: https:// www.thebalance.com/who-is-a-workplace-bully-s-target-2164323

Kellerman, B. (2012). *The end of leadership.* New York, NY: HarperCollins.

Khazan, O. (2017). Why do women bully each other at work? *The Atlantic*. Retrieved from: https://www.theatlantic.com/magazine/archive/2017/09/the-queen-bee-in-the-corner-office/534213/

Kyriakidou, O. (2012). Gender, management and leadership. *Equality, Diversity and Inclusion: An International Journal, 31*(1), 4–9. doi: http://0-dx.doi.org.read.cnu. edu/10.1108/02610151211201296

Hunt, C. M., Davidson, M. J., Fielden, S. L., & Hoel, H. (2010). Reviewing sexual harassment in the workplace—An intervention model, *Personnel Review, 39*(5), 655–673. Retrieved from https://doi.org/10.1108/00483481011064190

Ludwig, R. (n.d.). *Bad female boss? She may have Queen Bee Syndrome.* Retrieved from http://www.today.com/id/42549761/ns/today-today_health/t/bad-female-boss-she-may-have-queen-bee-syndrome/ as cited by Spranger, Angela & Mitchell, Kerry (2018)

Mainiero, L., & Jones, K. (2013). Workplace Romance 2.0: Developing a Communication Ethics Model to Address Potential Sexual Harassment from Inappropriate Social Media Contacts Between Coworkers. *Journal of Business Ethics, 114*(2), 367–379. Retrieved from http://www.jstor.org/stable/23433898

Maslow, A. H. (1943). A theory of human motivation. *Psychological Review, 50*(4), 370–396.

Mendez, M. J., & Busenbark, J. R. (2015). Shared leadership and gender: All members are equal ... but some more than others. *Leadership & Organization Development Journal, 36*(1), 17–34. Retrieved from https://0-search-proquest-com.read.cnu.edu/ docview/1651370090?accountid=10100

O'Connell, M. (2018, March 23). PBS details Tavis Smiley's alleged sexual misconduct in countersuit. *Hollywood Reporter.* Retrieved from https://www.hollywoodreporter.com/news/pbs-details-tavis-smileys-alleged-sexual-misconduct-counter-suit-1096648

Pew Research Center (2017). *The data on women leaders.* Retrieved from http://www. pewsocialtrends.org/2017/03/17/the-data-on-women-leaders/

Sandberg, S. (2013). *Lean in: Women, work, and the will to lead.* New York, NY: Alfred A. Knopf

Santivago, C., & Criss, D. (2017, October 17). An activist, a little girl and the heartbreaking origin of 'Me too.' *CNN*. Retrieved from: https://www.cnn.com/2017/10/17/us/ me-too-tarana-burke-origin-trnd/index.html

Segal, J. A. (2015, June). Attack bullying without being attacked. *HR Magazine*, 116–119.

Segal, J. A. (2017, September). The risks of bias testing. *HR Magazine*, 75–76.

Segal, J. A. (2018, April). Strengthen your harassment complaint process. *HR Magazine*, 64–65.

Smith, A. (2018, January 31). Review your company dating policy in light of #MeToo movement. *Society for Human Resource Management*. Retrieved from: https:// www.shrm.org/resourcesandtools/legal-and-compliance/employment-law/pages/ dating-policy-metoo-movement.aspx

Spranger, A. (2015). *StepOne Consulting*. Retrieved from StepOne Consulting, LLC: www.step1consulting.com

Spranger, A., & Mitchell, K. (2018). *Women's perceptions of working for women: A qualitative study.* Proceedings of the Academy for Human Resource Development Conference in the Americas. Richmond, VA.

Stewart, E. (2017). These are the industries with the most reported sexual harassment claims: Most just don't make the headlines. *Vox*. Retrieved from: https://www.vox.com/identities/2017/11/21/16685942/sexual-harassment-industry-service-retail

Time's Up (2018). Our letter of solidarityp. Retrieved from: https://www.timesupnow.com/

Trendell, A. (2018). Steven Spielberg speaks out on Weinstein scandal and Catherine Deneuve slamming the #MeToo movement. *NME*. Retrieved from: http://www.nme.com/news/music/catherine-deneuve-2218706

U.S. Equal Employment Opportunity Commission (2018), *Women in the American workforce,* Retrieved from: https://www.eeoc.gov/eeoc/statistics/reports/american_experiences/women.cfm

Waitman, H. R. (2014). F*emale HR executives' contributions to firm performance: The effects of gender on decision-making and strategic-planning.* ProQuest Dissertations & Theses Global: Business. (1553437235). Retrieved from https://0-search-proquest-com.read.cnu.edu/docview/1553437235?accountid=10100

Wallace, A. (2018, May 15). *Nike sees executive departures in harassment reckoning.* (E. Morrison, Interviewer) Portland, OR: NPR. Oregon Public Broadcasting, . Retrieved from https://www.npr.org/templates/transcript/transcript.php?storyId=610445057

White, T. (2018). Golden Globes 2018: Why they wore black and why it matters. *Empire*. Retrieved from: https://www.empireonline.com/movies/features/golden-globes-2018-wore-black-matters/

Williams, J. C., & Lebsock, S. (2018). Managing #MeToo. *Harvard Business Review.* Retrieved from https://hbr.org/cover-story/2018/01/now-what

CHAPTER 8

ATTRACTING AND RETAINING MILLENNIALS

Is Servant Leadership the Answer?

Shannon O. Jackson, Pamela Chandler Lee, and Jonathan Shoemaker

According to the Pew Research Census Bureau, more than a third of workers today are millennials, born between 1981–2000 (Fry, 2015). Research shows that this large and growing sector of the workforce expects a different work experience than their predecessors, such as GenXers and baby boomers. Undoubtedly, millennials are the most educated, ethnically diverse, technologically competent and perhaps the most innovative generation in the workforce. Thus, as Mabrey (2015) explains, they want a work environment that is "less formal, less concerned with customs and traditions...honest about [the] view that excessive work demands might not be worth the cost of advancement" (pp. 1, 3). Significant to our discussion is the reporting that millennials also "look for meaningful work in a collaborative environment... [and] a more sustainable work/life balance" (Mabrey, 2015, p. 2). Additionally, since millennials are in constant search of such balance, according to Taylor and Kester (2010), more than 65 percent of millennials plan to switch jobs throughout their careers (p. 48).

Human Resources Management Issues, Challenges and Trends:
"Now and Around the Corner", pages 163–184.
Copyright © 2019 by Information Age Publishing
All rights of reproduction in any form reserved.

So then, the question becomes, how do organizations attract and then retain this ever more important sector of the workforce? As discussed by Reuteman (2015), millennials are comfortable working with teams and having input; they want to feel a part of something bigger than themselves. However, in their desire for work-life balance, participative management, and immediate feedback, they are likely to leave an organization if they become dissatisfied (Ferri-Reed, 2014; Lowe, Levitt, & Wilson, 2008; Malcolm, 2016). As a matter of fact, the number one reason millennials leave their organizations is because they don't feel valued or respected by the people for whom they work (Reuteman, 2015). As Reuteman (2015) explains, "People don't leave companies; they leave managers... they're not mad at the building...they're mad at the people they work with on a day to day basis... they leave managers" (p. 8).

Consequently, this research emphasizes the significance of effective leadership for creating an organizational culture that attracts and retains millennials. In other words, if managers implement a leadership style that is consistent with millennials' perspective of work, these workers will not only be interested in joining the organization, but they may also be more committed to staying with the company for the long-haul. Like the members of other generations, millennials have a desire to contribute and make an impact in their companies; they are motivated by challenging work that allows them to grow and develop, and they especially "want to be part of innovative and energetic organizations that will value their ideas and encourage their creativity" (Lowe, Levitt, & Wilson, 2008, p. 47). However, millennials generally have a different view of loyalty to organizations than other age groups. If the work environment does not meet their needs, they are more likely than other generations to leave the company and seek opportunities elsewhere (Fries, 2018; Lowe, Levitt, & Wilson, 2008; Malcolm, 2016). Additionally, these workers seek confirmation that their work and their contributions are appreciated. If this feedback is not readily provided by their leaders, they are likely to disengage from their work, from their coworkers, and then from the organization.

Thus, this essay proposes that servant leadership is the most appropriate leadership style for engaging millennials and meeting their need for participation, teamwork and serving a vision larger than themselves. Robert Greenleaf's theory of servant leadership, also referred to as "leadership upside down" (Daft, 2010, p. 176), is "based in ethical and caring behavior...[which] enhances the growth of people, while at the same time improving the caring and quality of our many institutions" (Spears, 1996, p. 33). As Barbuto and Gottfredson (2016) insist, "millennials want what servant leaders are suited to provide, which is a leader who focuses on the developmental needs and human capital improvements of its employees, even beyond the needs of the organization or the leader" (p. 2).

In this chapter, we will first discuss the millennial generation and their presence in the workplace. We will then provide a review of leadership research and discuss the relevance of leadership for creating an organizational culture which respects, attracts, and engages millennial workers. This analysis will emphasize the principles of servant leadership and its relevance for the millennial generation. We will then recommend specific strategies for attracting and retaining this expanding sector of the employee population.

THE MILLENNIAL GENERATION: WHO ARE THEY?

For the last few decades, the millennial generation has been the topic of extensive research, discussion and speculation, in popular press as well as academic publications, by managers and practitioners, as well as researchers and scholars. The similarities and differences between millennials and other generations have been lauded, opposed, celebrated, and even denied. Some experts insist that millennials reflect some of the most unique—and possibly the most frustrating—habits in the workplace. There are others who maintain that, other than their age, millennials are not that much different from other generations (Costanza, 2018). In an article for *Entrepreneur* magazine, Christian Brucculeri, CEO of Snaps, a mobile platform that creates branded content, said, "The same basic principles apply to the millennial generation as to any other age group. Some people are inspired, excited, hardworking, humble and curious. Some are entitled, unfocused and political. Not everyone is great!" (McCammon, 2016, para. 18).

Nevertheless, while some of the most sweeping generalizations about millennials may not apply to everyone in the age group, there is a great deal of support for generation theory, which represents generations as social constructs in which sets of ages are defined by historical or social events (Costanza, Badger, Fraser, Severt, & Gade, 2012; Strauss & Howe, 1991; Twenge, 2010). Although the description of each cohort varies widely, prevailing research defines baby boomers as those as born between about 1945 and 1964, GenXers were born between 1965 and 1981, and millennials, also referred to as Generation Y, were born between 1981 and 2000 (Costanza et al., 2012). Millennials are referred to as tech-savvy multi-taskers, who desire instant gratification and recognition, work life balance, flexibility, transparency, career advancement, and team-oriented tasks (Abbot, 2013; Malcolm, 2016).

Millennials also seem to be more comfortable with technology than any other generation in the workforce. As a matter of fact, it is this familiarity with technology which defines the key features that set millennials apart from other generations. Millennials represent the generation that grew up with tablets, laptops, the Internet, and social media as norms in their environment. Thus, immediate access to information and connection with others may inspire the need for teamwork, collaboration, and immediate feedback (Green et al, 2005; PWC, 2011). Along with an appreciation for technology and social media, millennials seek an organizational culture which encourages innovation and creativity, and which provides the resources and support for them to be their best selves. Leadership has the responsibility for establishing and maintaining such a culture in order to attract and retain this growing segment of the workforce.

A REVIEW OF LEADERSHIP

Analyzing the relevance of leadership for engaging millennials in the workplace is a worthwhile endeavor. As this discussion will confirm, leadership influences the culture, climate, and even the performance of an organization more than any other single component. Historical analyses reflect a scholarly interest in the leadership construct since the 1800s. An examination of peer-reviewed articles reveals hundreds of definitions from a variety of perspectives. While there are some distinctions in these viewpoints, there are also some similarities. For example, the most oft-cited definitions of leadership consist of the following components: Power or influence

- Communication
- Inspiration
- Purpose
- Visioning
- Change
- Outcomes
- Objectives
- Process
- People or relationships (Daft, 2010; Rost, 1993; Yukl, 2013)

Some of the most basic functions of leadership, or what leaders do in their organizations include:

- Guiding the activities of the organization to meet a common objective
- Directing and facilitating programs and opportunities for organizational profitability
- Empowering followers to support the mission and vision of the organization
- Training, developing, and supporting followers in their roles
- Influencing the behavior of followers, and
- Establishing and maintaining the organizational culture (Eberly, Johnson, Hernandez, & Avolio, 2013; House & Aditya, 1997; Rost, 1993; Schein, 2010)

Significantly, contemporary research consistently emphasizes the importance of leadership for organizational performance (Center on Leadership, 2009; Yukl, 2008). According to Citigroup (2007), some of the most well publicized corporate failures have pointed to the critical role of leadership in the success or failure of organizations. Kaiser, Hogan, & Craig (2008) concluded that as much as 15–45% of a firm's performance can be attributed to leadership functions. These researchers conducted a meta-analysis of studies investigating managerial succession. Through various methodologies, consistently, the research showed a relationship between leadership and organizational performance. Specifically, changes in leadership were closely followed by changes in the organization's performance.

Studies have also linked organizational performance with organizational or corporate culture (Gordon & DiTomaso, 1992; Kotter & Heskett, 1992). Organizational culture generally refers to the pattern of shared assumptions, beliefs, and values of its members (Schein, 2010; Trice & Beyer, 1993). Schein (2010) further emphasizes that this pattern is then "taught to new members as the correct way to perceive, think, and feel" (p. 18) about organizational problems. Some researchers have postulated that one of the most—if not *the* most—important role of leadership is to establish and maintain the culture of the organization. As a matter of fact, Schein (2010) contends that leadership is manifested "when we are influential in shaping the behavior and values of others…and are creating the conditions for new culture formation" (p. 3).

Scholars assert that leadership has a more significant impact on organizational culture than any other element of a company (Bass & Avolio, 1993; Schein, 2010; Trice & Beyer, 1993). It is important to note that the influence of leadership not only refers to top level leaders, such as the Chief Executive Officer (CEO) of a company, but also mid-level managers and supervisors performing the function of leadership. In his seminal work examining leadership and organizational culture, Schein (1985, 2010) identifies specific mechanisms or tools that leaders use to teach and then reinforce the values, beliefs, and assumptions of the organization. Schein refers to these tools as Primary Embedding Mechanisms and Secondary Articulation and Reinforcement Mechanisms. The Primary Embedding Mechanisms represent "the most powerful daily behavioral things that leaders do" (Schein, 2010, p. 236); the Secondary Mechanisms represent "the more formal mechanisms that come to support and reinforce the primary messages" (Schein, 2010, p. 236). Importantly, the secondary mechanisms are only effective if they are consistent with the primary mechanisms. Schein identifies the following leadership behaviors as the Primary Embedding Mechanisms:

- What leaders pay attention to, measure, and control on a regular basis
- How leaders react to critical incidents and organizational crises
- How leaders allocate resources
- Deliberate role modeling, teaching, and coaching
- How leaders allocate rewards and status
- How leaders recruit, select, promote, and excommunicate

Thus, according to Schein (2010), new employees learn more about the culture of their organizations from the daily behaviors of leadership than they learn from formal training or orientation sessions (p. 250). Significant for this research is the leader's role in recruiting, rewarding, and retaining employees.

Because millennials are assigned to and work in various levels and departments throughout an organization, the organizational culture must reflect an appreciation for millennials and their contributions. In other words, an organizational culture which embraces millennials' perspective of work must permeate the company. The role of leadership for establishing and maintaining organizational culture cannot be ignored. The following subsections will briefly discuss the progression of leadership research from the 19th through the 21st centuries.

Trait Approach

The scholarly and practical appreciation for the relevance of leadership for organizational performance has evolved through more than a century of research. In the early days, scholars presumed that the basis for leadership was found in a set of innate traits such as drive, a desire to lead, honesty, integrity, self-confidence, intelligence, job-relevant knowledge, extraversion and a leaning toward guilt as a way of encouraging a sense of responsibility for others (Kirkpatrick & Locke, 1981). Hundreds of empirical studies investigated the correlation between traits and a propensity for leadership; and traits and leadership effectiveness. The results of these studies "…failed to find any traits that would guarantee leadership success" (Yukl, 2013, p. 12). Scholars concluded that the narrow view of leaders as being ***born*** did not explain the relevance of followers, nor did it acknowledge the importance of the leaders' behaviors for organizational performance.

Behavioral Approach

In the late 1930s and early 1940s, several researchers demonstrated that a person's behaviors are more significant for understanding the function or practice of leadership than his innate traits. The implications of these findings indicated that leadership could be ***learned***. For example, in 1939, Lewin, Lippett and White led a research project commonly known as the Iowa State Studies, published in the *Journal of Social Psychology*. This seminal research found that leaders tended to display one of three leadership styles: (1) a democratic style, in which follower participation was a key element; (2) an autocratic style, in which decision making was centralized rather than participative; or (3) a laissez-faire style, in which the leader relegated responsibility for decision making to followers. Lewin, Lippett and White found that the democratic style, in which followers were empowered and encouraged to participate, was correlated with the most positive organizational outcomes (Lewin, Lippett, & White, 1939).

A decade later, in the 1950s, Stogdill and Coons led the Ohio State Studies, which also examined the behavioral tendencies of leaders. The research showed that there were two dimensions involved in how leaders behaved: (1) they held a high consideration for followers' ideas and feelings, or (2) they were more concerned with the structure through which relationships were oriented toward completing work tasks. Stogdill and Coons discovered that having a high consideration for employee needs and feelings, combined with a high recognition for the importance of a structure in which job completion was paramount, was the most effective leadership style (Stogdill & Coons, 1951).

Research in the 1960s brought us the University of Michigan studies by Kahn and Katz. These studies followed a similar line of thought to the Iowa State and Ohio State studies, in that Kahn and Katz examined the behavior of leaders in terms of whether they were primarily *employee oriented* or *production oriented*. Again, the question of whether followers' needs mattered for effective leadership was the primary research question. Kahn and Katz found that leaders who were primarily concerned with their followers had the highest levels of productivity, and their employees experienced the highest levels of job satisfaction (Kahn & Katz, 1960).

Then in the mid-1980s, Blake and Mouton published their now famous Managerial Grid, once again examining the relationship between productivity and attention to follower needs, wants and desires. Blake and Mouton found that leaders performed best when they demonstrated a high consideration for both people and production (Blake & Mouton, 1984).

Transforming Approach

In 1978, while leadership scholars were proclaiming the significance of relationships between leaders and followers for organizational success, James MacGregor Burns introduced the theory of the "transforming" or transformational leader (Burns, 1978). Distinct from transactional leadership, in which leaders and followers exchange services to meet organizational objectives, Burns suggested that effective leadership is based on trusting and mutual relationships between leaders and followers that evolve over time. He defined transforming leadership as a process through which "leaders and followers raise one another to higher levels of morality and motivation" (p. 20). In many ways, transformational leadership is a motivational theory, in which the leader appeals to followers' moral values, in order to influence followers to transcend their self-interests for the good of the organization (Bass, 1985; Burns, 1978). Thus, while the theory focuses on developing and transforming individuals, the end goal is transformation in the organization to achieve organizational objectives.

Over the last two decades, transformational leadership has become the most popular and most well-regarded theory of leadership in the literature. With hundreds of articles extoling its virtues, transformational leadership has been correlated with constructs such as profitability, job satisfaction, trust, emotional intelligence, charisma, and corporate social responsibility (DuBrin, 2013; Groves & LaRocca, 2011; Rubin, Munz, & Bommer, 2005). Nevertheless, many of the leaders in these organizations are concerned about attracting and engaging millennials, suggesting that there may be some inconsistency between the components of transformational leadership and the needs of the millennial generation.

It could be argued that while transformational leadership appeals to followers' morality and values, the objective of the model is organizational performance, profitability, and success. Conversely, while millennials certainly want to be compensated fairly, they are more concerned about work-life balance and quality of life (Dixon, 2016; Scalco, 2017). Interestingly, some researchers have suggested that the leader's focus—on the organization or on the employee—is what distinguishes transformational leaders from servant leaders (Chaudhuri, Kettunen, Naskar, 2015; Stone, Russell, & Patterson, 2003). According to Stone, Russell, and Patterson (2003), "the transformational leader's focus is directed toward the organization, and his or her behavior builds follower commitment toward organizational objectives, while the servant leader's focus is on the followers...the achievement of organizational objectives is a subordinate outcome" (p. 1).

Thus, leaders who listen to their employees and demonstrate concern for their individual growth and development may be in the best position to establish an organizational culture in which millennials are valued and appreciated. As Fries (2018) asserts:

> Millennials want to work with leaders who value feedback from all employees... millennials are often keenly aware that the further up the corporate food chain leaders are, the more they tend to lose understanding of the challenges other employees face...and tend to dismiss the validity of their experiences. (para. 9, 10)

Based on these findings, this analysis proposes that Servant Leadership is an appropriate model for recruiting, rewarding, and retaining this millennial wave of employees.

SERVANT LEADERSHIP THEORY

In the 1970s, based on an illustrious 40-year career in management at AT&T, and after reading Herman Hesse's short novel entitled *Journey to the East*, Robert Greenleaf began examining the concept of leaders as servants (Spears, 1996). As a result of his research, Greenleaf concluded that "the great leader is first experienced as a servant to others...true leadership emerges from those whose primary motivation is a deep desire to help others" (Spears, 1996, p. 33).

Researchers have noted that the concept of leaders as servants is not original to Greenleaf. This model is seen in ancient, historic, religious and even contemporary leaders such as Jesus Christ, Moses, Confucius, Mother Theresa, and Martin Luther King, Jr. (Keith, 2008). It is important to acknowledge that it is not necessary for one to be a deity or a Saint to be characterized as a servant leader. Many successful contemporary leaders are identified as servant leaders. One of the most notable is C. William Pollard (Sendjaya & Sarros, 2002), a former executive of ServiceMaster who twice served as CEO of the firm (1983–1993 and 1999–2001). Describing himself as a person who leads with a servant's heart:

> Pollard contends that the real leader is not the person with the most distinguished title, the highest pay, or the longest tenure...but the role model, the risk taker, the servant; not the person who promotes himself or herself, but the promoter of others. (Sendjaya & Sarros, 2002, para. 50)

Also, according to the founder and former CEO of Southwest Airlines, Herb Kelleher, Southwest was founded in 1971 based on Kelleher's desire to serve; Kelleher insists that Southwest's success is sustained by people "who have a pre-disposition to serve others" (Leader Network.org, 2007, para. 6). While Kelle-her has not held an active leadership role at Southwest since 2008, the airline is consistently recognized as one of the most admired companies in the world. One of the four core values which creates the foundation for the organization's busi-ness strategy and unique corporate culture encourages employees to demonstrate a "Servant's Heart" (Southwest, 2015).

Servant leadership is becoming widely accepted as an effective model of lead-ership for the 21st century. Servant leaders are more concerned about developing others than promoting themselves; they welcome and appreciate the importance of diversity, empowerment, and collaboration for their organizations' success. Unlike many other leadership theories which are defined by the *actions* of the leader, servant leadership relates to the *character* of the leader who has a heart for serving and ministering to the needs of others (Carter & Baghurst, 2014).

When Greenleaf first introduced the theory in the 1970s, scholars were initially skeptical of its merits and its practicality for contemporary business. However, in the last four decades, some of the most successful leaders in the world have demonstrated a leadership style consistent with this theory. The theory has also received widespread attention in mainstream media outlets such as *Fortune* maga-zine and *Dateline NBC*. Leading scholars in the management and leadership disci-plines—such as Max DePree, Stephen Covey, Peter Block and Peter Senge—have also confirmed the positive impact of servant leadership in organizations.

Based on Greenleaf's work, Spears (1995) identified the following 10 charac-teristics of servant leaders:

- **Listening**: Servant leaders listen intently to others, without prejudging
- **Empathy**: Servant leaders know that people need to be recognized for their unique gifts
- **Healing**: Servant leaders recognize the opportunity to help make whole those they serve
- **Awareness**: Servant leaders have general as well as self-awareness; they view situations from a perspective of ethics, power and values
- **Persuasion**: Servant leaders build consensus rather than coerce compli-ance
- **Conceptualization**: Servant leaders dream great dreams; they stretch tra-ditional thinking and are not consumed with attaining short term goals
- **Foresight**: Servant leaders foresee and forecast the likely outcome of a situation based on the lessons of the past, the realities of the present, and the consequences of decisions for the future
- **Stewardship**: Servant leaders assume a commitment to serving the needs of others, such as employees, shareholders and the wider community

- **Commitment to the Growth of People**: Servant leaders believe people have an intrinsic value that is more than their value as employees or workers
- **Building Community**: Servant leaders believe true community is created among those who work in an institution as well as the institution's external constituents

Greenleaf (1977) was careful to emphasize that the primary outcome of effective servant leadership is **not** organizational performance: "The best test and the most difficult to administer is: Do those served grow as persons? Do they, while being served, become healthier, wiser, freer, more autonomous, [and] more likely themselves to become servants?" (pp. 13–14).

The following section discusses key strategies that today's employers should adhere to in order to create and sustain a work environment in which the specific needs of millennials are considered primary.

RECRUITING, REWARDING, AND RETAINING MILLENNIALS

Human Resource departments exist to *find* the right people and to *keep* the right people once they are found. Among other objectives, this mission relates to three specific strategies: Recruiting, Rewarding and Retaining high-performing employees. All three strategies are integrated, and, in fact, there are significant overlaps among them (see Figure 8.1).

For example, as potential job candidates are being recruited, they will want to know about the kinds of rewards they can expect, and then decide whether those rewards will motivate and interest them enough to apply for the position. Retention may also be emphasized during the recruiting phase, as employees consider

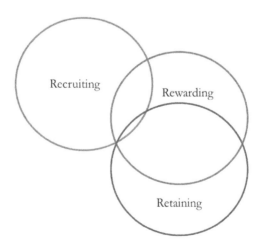

FIGURE 8.1. Recruiting, Rewarding, Retaining

joining Company XYZ for a career, and not just a job. Finally, there is significant overlap between Rewarding and Retaining, as many types of rewards are provided to employees to prevent them from leaving for greener pastures.

Importantly, as Schein (2010) offers, two of the most significant leadership behaviors which establish and maintain organizational culture relate to how rewards are allocated, and how leaders recruit, select, and promote employees. Considering these leadership behaviors, we will discuss Recruiting, Rewarding and Retaining in terms of the needs of millennials and the implications for servant leaders.

Recruiting

Finding the right employees begins with good recruiting practices. Recruiting must be performed strategically, just like any other function of the organization. Thus, if the organization is focused on hiring millennials, some strategies will be more effective than others.

For example, millennials are attracted to a psychologically healthy workplace as well as a workplace that supports corporate social responsibility (CSR). Thus, when recruiting millennials, it is important to communicate that the employer values CSR and psychological health. CSR refers to the extent to which the organization values protection of its environment, support of its community, and respect for its employees (Ferri-Reed, 2014). A psychologically healthy workplace is one which prioritizes work-life balance, professional growth and development, and recognition and involvement of all employees (Catano & Hines, 2016). All of these priorities are reflective of the characteristics of servant leadership.

In some instances, millennials were in favor of accepting lower wages if they felt the organization made a positive contribution to issues they felt strongly about (Cone Communications, 2015). Interestingly, CSR programs seem to be effective in attracting millennial candidates, regardless of whether the millennial is more strongly motivated by social concerns or making money (Catano & Hines, 2016).

Research has also demonstrated that millennials seek organizations in which the leadership provides regular feedback and is committed to open and transparent communication (Ferri-Reed, 2014). This transparency should begin with providing a realistic job preview for applicants, even as early as first contact. First contact with a potential applicant could occur in person at a job fair, on the organization's employment website, or through social media. Even early-career job applicants are savvy enough to know if they are being fed a company line instead of being given realistic expectations about the job (Tucker, 2012). A realistic job preview could mean providing employee testimonials or allowing the employee to experience the organization through an interactive simulation or "try-out day" (Sabel, 2018).

Millennials are also accustomed to communication via social media. They seek an organization that is able to promote social and technological integration (Ferri-Reed, 2014). A robust website and social media presence are requirements in the current recruiting market. These resources are of paramount importance to millennials who get much of their information from these sources. Posts to various social media platforms should be engaging and frequent, and websites should be easy to navigate and user-friendly.

Organizations that wish to attract millennials should also emphasize a healthy and responsible organizational culture in recruiting materials. Millennials generally prefer an organization that is willing to offer job security and a future within the company (Ferri-Reed, 2014). Best Companies to Work For, such as 3M, Google, St. Jude Research Hospital, and the Walt Disney Company, tend to promote this aspect of their culture (Thurman, 2016).

It is important for organizations to maintain focus on their purpose, and not just their products. Many firms complain that their work is not glamorous and, thus, will not appeal to millennials. For example, manufacturing and insurance are two critical industries that have historically been challenged to attract millennial job candidates (Duett et al., 2017; Putre, 2016). One solution is to focus the recruiting message not so much on what the company does, but on why the work is important and how it contributes to the community and society at large. Fully 60% of millennials said they chose their current employer to fulfill a sense of purpose above all (Islam, 2016). Millennials want to know that the work they do has significance and fulfills a need.

Finally, making it known that the organization values a culture of servant leadership is important for attracting millennials. This message should be a natural fit as servant leadership is congruent with many of the factors millennials value, including open, honest communication, CSR, a psychologically healthy workplace, and a focus on being purpose-driven (Marshall, 2018).

A culture of servant leadership is uniquely appealing to millennials because of their motivation to enact change that improves their organizations for the future; they want to make a difference and solve problems as soon as they begin a new job (Fox, 2015). Servant leaders who are willing to serve first and lead second are more likely to respond to the new organizational reality of volatility and complexity where millennials are the dominant employee population (Islam, 2016).

Rewarding

When considering Rewards, let's call the question: Which rewards can talent acquisition and human capital management professionals offer to attract and retain millennials? Perhaps a better question is whether there is one set of rewards that will appeal to every millennial. The likely answer is, no. The first rule of Total Rewards is an understanding that every employee is motivated differently; the key is to determine which incentives will be attractive to the majority of the workforce. For example, employers are realizing that compensation packages must be flexible to appeal to the largest number of employees with different needs and motivations. A recent compensation survey indicated that employees prioritize flexibility and choice in benefits offerings (Nyce & Gardner, 2017).

It is also important to note that there can be just as much diversity ***within*** a generation as there is ***between*** generations (Costanza, 2018). Certainly, some benefits appeal to some age groups more than others, but most employees—not just millennials—would prefer work that is flexible and offers some level of job security.

Typically, employers offer a combination of three types of rewards: Direct Financial Compensation, Indirect Financial Compensation and Non-financial Compensation. Direct Financial Compensation is easy to peg: here we're talking about wages, tips, commissions and bonuses, any tangible reward the employee earns that can be spent immediately. Indirect Financial Compensation is any tangible reward that has a measurable monetary value, but is spent on behalf of the employee, instead of being paid directly to the employee. These include employer subsidies of health care benefit premiums, administrative fees and matches for retirement plans, use of a company car, a housing allowance, or free meals. The employee doesn't receive the money for these benefits, but she does enjoy the reward that the employer is paying for on her behalf. Even paid time off can be considered Indirect Financial Compensation. While employees get paid directly when they call out for sick, personal or vacation time, the employer is potentially paying for someone else to cover the absent employees while they are out.

Direct Financial Compensation (a.k.a. pay) will always be a popular incentive for employees, and millennials are no exception. When asked about their priority for Rewards, at least 44% listed competitive wages as one of their most important priorities (Zimmerman, 2016). However, pay is not a generational motivator, but an early career motivator. Every past generation has hoped for a high-paying job after years spent perpetually pinching pennies and eating Ramen noodles while in school or training. This perspective can be particularly true when recent graduates are carrying historically high tuition and student loan debt (Zimmerman, 2016).

However, in a departure from previous generations, millennials don't necessarily only prioritize pay. Pay seems to run a close race with opportunities for advancement and professional development (Malcolm, 2016). Millennials rated "advancement potential" as their second highest priority in what made an industry desirable; their first priority was availability of jobs (Duett et al., 2017). Thirty percent of employees described "building a long term career" with their employer as a major career goal (Whitten, 2017). Consistent with advancement must come a focus on professional and personal development. Eighty-nine percent of millennials reported that they want to be constantly learning on the job (Islam, 2016). The organization must be intentional about offering their millennial employees formal and informal development opportunities (Fox, 2015). The dual motivations of pay and advancement underscore the importance of balancing a Total Rewards package with both Direct and Indirect Financial Compensation. Additional Indirect Financial incentives that are likely to be attractive to millennials include tuition reimbursement, which many organizations have been offering for decades. A few forward-thinking companies are even offering student loan debt repayment; this benefit is especially important to millennials, who graduated with an average of $37K in debt in 2016 (DiCamillo, 2017).

However, the jury is still out about which benefits millennials value most. Some surveys of rewards for millennials suggest that health care benefits are important (Zimmerman, 2017). This finding can be partially explained by rising health care costs throughout the U.S., and the challenge of starting a family while also recovering from student loan debt. Allowing more flexibility for employees to customize health care plans and benefits also appeals to millennials who are interested in optimizing the benefits they will use most (Gilmore, 2017). Cafeteria-style benefits plans, where employees can choose from a wide range of services that fit their needs, are most desirable. Other sources recommend early vesting periods for defined contribution plan matches, a budget allotment for technology tied to each employee, and time for outside projects and innovation (Kruman, 2016).

Ultimately, millennials are also concerned about fairness and equity. More than ever, employees are able to understand their comparable worth to employers through readily accessible commercial and government sources such as salary.com, glassdoor.com, the Bureau of Labor Statistics and the U.S. Department of Labor's Occupational Network Online (O*NET). Millennials seek pay transparency and information about how their compensation is determined (Dixon, 2016). Sharing this information with employees is simply a good business practice; if compensation is based on reasonable and fair standards, there's no reason those standards should not be shared.

Of course, some millennials would like to be rewarded with individualized perquisites. Perks like ping-pong tables, free snacks, nap pods and the opportunity to bring pets to work fit this category. These are only some of the high-end benefits that are trumpeted in popular press as evidence that millennials are *entitled*. Management may believe that these perks are a waste of time and resources. However, there are two major problems with this mentality. First, the price-tags of these perks to the employer are in reality not that high. As a matter of fact, the price can be considered low compared to the costs of health care premiums, higher salaries, and better matches toward deferred contribution plans that previous generations have come to expect. The second problem is that research continues to show that these perks actually work to lower employee stress, increase organizational loyalty, and improve contextual performance (Oden-Hall, 2017).

Many employers believe that they must throw money at employees (whether directly or indirectly) in order to attract millennials. While some attention must be given to Financial Compensation of both types, it is becoming clearer that supplementing rewards with Non-financial Compensation may be the most effective way to motivate employees, particularly millennials. Non-financial compensation includes those elements that are difficult (if not impossible) to put a price on. These include aspects of work that are often built into the organizational culture, such as a high degree of work-life balance, high quality of life at work, feeling valued, performing meaningful and challenging work, and having flexibility and autonomy. The good news is these benefits are low or no cost for the employer. The bad news is they can be difficult to effectively implement without significant attention to organizational development (Sommer, 2011).

Work-life balance is an important non-financial concept. Rather than representing one specific benefit, this concept refers to policies that allow employees to better attend to non-work responsibilities that in the past may have been impossible to address. Flexible hours, telecommuting or working from home, and a culture that values productivity over face-time are examples of perks that are essentially free to the employer, but can significantly improve employee performance, efficiency and even health (Gaskell, 2016). Establishing for job applicants that the organization encourages flexible scheduling can be a useful recruiting tool (Scalco, 2017).

Quality of life at work is an important consideration that can attract millennials. It is imperative for employees to feel valued by their organizations (Dixon, 2016; Malcolm, 2016). Respect from supervisors and management is one component of feeling valued. Millennials expect direct, straightforward communication and list respectful treatment as one of their top priorities (Gilmore, 2017). Millennials also appreciate regular constructive feedback that contributes to professional growth. Quality of life can also refer to how much control the employee has over his or her own work. Research shows that millennials who received regular feedback from their supervisors were significantly more engaged at work than their peers (Marshall, 2018). Millennials also prefer significant autonomy and the ability to self-manage their workload whenever possible (Islam, 2016). A physical example of how employers are emphasizing quality of life is the trend toward a less-traditional and more comfortable and collaborative work environment, eliminating cubicles and desks in favor of common areas and fewer walls (Islam, 2016).

Servant leadership, while not a reward on its own, is closely related to many of the elements of Non-financial Compensation. Servant leaders will strive for inclusion of employees in decision-making, emphasize empowerment and autonomy, and embrace opportunities to maximize quality of life at work (Barbuto & Gottfredson, 2016). Offering Financial Compensation can also be linked to servant leadership. For example, servant leaders empathize and put themselves in the place of their entry-level employees in order to appreciate which benefits would be most desirable and how to best motivate employees through fair and equitable rewards (Fox, 2015).

Any cultural change that will result in improved Non-financial Compensation must begin with support from leadership and an active effort to make the change work. Start small with achievable changes, such as allowing best performers to work from home on certain days of the week, or providing flex time to employees as a performance-related privilege. If these are successful and well-received, it will be easier to gradually make more significant cultural changes.

Retaining

Millennials have earned an undeserved reputation as *job hoppers*. It is thought that they leave jobs quickly, presumably for better opportunities. No matter the numbers or the reasons, losing a talented employee—of any generation—can be costly. As a matter of fact, the cost of replacing a fully trained professional employee, even at the early career stage, can be as high as $20,000 (Fries, 2017). Clearly, retaining employees should be a major concern of any organization.

Retention of high performing employees can be particularly difficult because these are the employees who have the most alternatives for better or different employment opportunities. This is especially true of millennials who are early in their working lives; thus, they are more open to changing jobs or even careers, particularly if they do not perceive opportunities for advancement or promotion. Organizations need to offer swift opportunities for advancement along with specific criteria for how to earn promotions and advancement. Entry-level jobs are often arduous, but they are always necessary. It is up to early-career leadership to help entry-level employees recognize the pathways between their current work and future opportunities (Fox, 2015). It should go without saying that a significant amount of recruiting and promotion should be focused internally to the organization. Here, Rewards must support Retention as leadership earmarks a significant budget for training and development. Millennials are also innovators. Creating opportunities for employees to work on specific problems, seek new business opportunities, or pitch new ideas can be rewarding for both the organization and the employee (Fries, 2017).

Open and efficient communication is also an imperative. For the most part, millennials have grown up with email, texting and instant messaging and may prefer more succinct, more frequent communications (Hackel, 2017). Transparency and directness in communicating what employees need to know will minimize the negativity of gossip and the office rumor-mill. Communication also means giving employees the opportunity to voice their opinions and contributions, regardless of their level in the organization (Malone, 2017). Communication even includes getting feedback when all else fails: the exit interview. Some employees will leave despite the company's best efforts; it is important for the organization to know why (Fries, 2017).

Servant leadership is important to Retention. Employees are more likely to remain with an organization where they are led by example, and when employees all the way to the C-Suite are expected to abide by the same rules, norms and values as everyone else (Malone, 2017). Contrary to the stereotypes about millennials' work ethics, they do not readily leave their organizations to seek more money or other rewards. The number one reason millennials leave their organizations is because they don't feel valued or respected by the people for whom they work (Reuteman, 2015). Displaying empathy and emphasizing a commitment to community and the growth and development of all people, servant leaders establish a culture in which employees feel heard, valued, and empowered to be their best selves.

YOU AND YOUR WHOLE GENERATION!

Millennials are pigeon-holed far too often. They are known as the "generation of entitlement," and "job-hoppers" who "cannot live" without their technology (Roepe, 2017). Based on the discussion in this research, it might be tempting to believe that millennials are seeking an awful lot of perquisites to which they may not be entitled. Yet, good strategies for recruiting, rewarding and retaining millennial' employees means understanding the resources they need to succeed. Providing a combination of motivating extrinsic and intrinsic rewards to employees is essentially what makes the employer/employee relationship work, regardless of the age or the career stage of the employee.

Generational labels, while convenient, can never be completely representative of every member of a generation. The rewards employees tend to seek are a combined product of their career stage and what is available in their time, not only their particular generation. Millennials seek many of the same perks that previous generations looked for when they were early in their careers. Additionally, not all millennials are seeking the same rewards. Shifts in the economy and the labor market do not conveniently happen every 20 years (Costanza, 2018). One researcher suggested that the millennial generation should be more accurately split into two groups: "Early Millennials" (born during the first half of the 1980s) and "Recessionists" (born between 1988 and the mid-1990s). These groups differ according to how much they are motivated by money and the degree of balance they desire between work and life (Roepe, 2017).

Further, while millennials may appear to take modern workplace perks for granted, they do so in the same way previous generations may have taken some elements of compensation for granted. For example, consider subsidized health care premiums, safety in the workplace, paid time off, or even a guaranteed minimum wage. Before these perks became standards, past generations would never have expected that most (or all) employers would offer them. When they first entered the workforce, most baby boomers and GenXers simply did not conceive that these rewards were even possible. After all, little emphasis was put on Non-financial compensation, and the importance of concepts such as corporate social responsibility and team-based incentives were less researched and even less understood.

CONCLUSION

Because they represent such a large and influential percentage of the labor force, attracting millennials is critically important for an organization's success and survival. Even as they appreciate the significance of this growing population, many organizations seem to be missing the mark in recruiting and retaining these employees. A review of the literature reveals that financial compensation may not be the only way, nor is it always the most effective way to engage millennials. Millennial workers seek opportunities to advance in their organizations, and they have a desire to innovate, create and contribute to their societies. They may also value flexible work schedules, autonomy at work, or the opportunity to telecommute even more than monetary incentives. These kinds of opportunities should not be viewed as isolated components on a list of benefits; rather, they are indicative of an organizational culture which acknowledges the significance of work life balance and is concerned about employees' quality of life at work. Establishing and maintaining such a culture requires leadership which values the needs and concerns of employees, prioritizes their personal and professional development, respects their ideas, encourages their creativity, and supports their quest to realize their potential. Servant Leadership is the answer. By leveraging Recruiting, Rewarding, and Retaining strategies that will attract, motivate, and keep millennials engaged, employees of every age are certain to be served.

REFERENCES

Abbot, L. (2013, December 4). *Business.Linkedin.com/talent-solutions/blog/2013/12/8-millennials-traits-you-should-know-about-before-you-hire-them.* Retrieved from https://business.linkedin.com/talent-solutions/blog/2013/12/8-millennials-traits-you-should-know-about-before-you-hire-them

Bass, B. M. (1985). *Leadership and performance beyond expectations.* New York, NY: Free Press.

Bass, B. M., & Avolio, B. J. (1993). Transformational leadership and organizational culture. *Public Administration Quarterly, 17*(1), 112–121.

Barbuto, J. E., & Gottfredson, R. (2016). Human capital, the millennials reign, and the need for servant leadership. *Journal of Leadership Studies, 16*(2), 53–64.

Blake, R. R., & Mouton, J. S. (1984). *The managerial grid III.* Houston,TX: Gulf Publishing.

Burns, J. M (1978) *Leadership.* New York, NY: Harper and Row.

Carter, D., & Baghurst, T. (2014). The influence of servant leadership on restaurant employee engagement. *Journal of Business Ethics, 124,* 453–464.

Catano V., & Hines, H. (2016). The influence of corporate social responsibility, psychologically healthy workplaces and individual values in attracting millennial job applicants. *Canadian Journal of Behavioral Science, 48,* 142–154.

Center on Leadership & Ethics. (March 2009). *Duke University executive leadership survey* (pp. 1–17). Retrieved from: https://centers.fuqua.duke.edu/cole/wp-content/uploads/sites/8/2015/07/Executive-Leadership-Survey-Report.pdf

Chaudhuri, M. R., Kettunen, J., & Naskar. P. (2015). Reflections on leadership styles from higher education in India. *Universal Journal of Management, 3*(10), 395–401.

Citigroup names new chairman. (November 5, 2007). *The Wall Street Journal,* A1.

Cone Communications (2015). *The 2015 Cone Communications millennial CSR study.* Retrieved from http://www.conecomm.com/2015-conecommunications-millennial-csr-study.

Costanza, D. (April 13, 2018). Can we please stop talking about generations as if they are a thing? *Slate.com.* Retrieved from: https://amp-slate-com.cdn.ampproject.org/c/amp.slate.com /technology/2018/04/the-evidence-behind-generations-is-lacking.html

Costanza, D. P., Badger, J. M., Fraser, R. L., Severt, J. B., & Gade, P. A. (2012). Generational differences in work-related attitudes: A meta-analysis. *Journal of Business and Psychology, 27*, 375–394.

Daft, R. L. (2010). *The leadership experience.* (5th ed.). Mason, OH: Thomson/South-Western.

DiCamillo, N. (2017, October). Can student debt repayment help credit unions retain millennial hires? *Credit Union Journal, 21*, 16.

Dixon, L. (August 31, 2016). 5 pay practices to attract, retain Gen Y talent. *Talent Economy.* Retrieved from: http://www.talenteconomy.io/2016/08/31/generation-ys-rise-as-the-most-populous-generation-in-the-economy-comes-with-a-nuanced-set-of-compensation-preferences/

DuBrin (2013). *Leadership: Research findings, practice, and skills.* (7th ed.). Mason, OH: South-Western.

Duett, E., Baggett, C., Pappanastos, E., & Hamby, W. (2017). Attracting millennials to the insurance industry: Will they fill the void? *International Journal of the Academic Business World, 11,* 39–45.

Eberly, M. B., Johnson, M. D., Hernandez, M., & Avolio, B. (2013). An integrative process model of leadership: Examining loci, mechanism, and event cycles. *American Psychologist, 68*(6), 427–443.

Ferri-Reed, J. (January 01, 2014). Millennializing the workplace. *Journal for Quality and Participation, 36*(4), 13–20.

Fox, T. (2015, March 5). Millennials make ideal public servants. *Washington Post.* Retrieved from: https://www.washingtonpost.com/news/on-leadership/wp/2015/03/05/millennials-make-ideal-public-servants/?noredirect=on&utm_term=.591f1288f66b

Fries, K. (January 18, 2018). 7 ways millennials are changing traditional leadership. *Forbes.com.* Retrieved from https://www.forbes.com/sites/kimberlyfries/2018/01/18/7-ways-millennials-are-changing-traditional-leadership/#39e672497dae

Fries, L. (May 30, 2017). Beyond recruiting: How to retain millennials. *The Business Journals.* Retrieved from: https://www.bizjournals.com/bizjournals/how-to/human-resources/2017/05/beyond-recruiting-how-to-retain-millennials.html

Fry, R. (May 11, 2015). *Millennials surpass Gen Xers as the largest generation in the US labor force.* Retrieved Nov. 1, 2017 from https:// www. Pew research org./fact-tank

Gaskell, A. (2016, January 15). Why a flexible worker is a happy and productive worker. *Forbes.com.* Retrieved from https://www.forbes.com/sites/adigaskell/2016/01/15/why-a-flexible-worker-is-a-happy-and-productive-worker/#7c98757714c4

Gilmore, M. (2017, September 25). What work benefits do Millennials really want? *Idealog.co.* Retrieved from https://idealog.co.nz/workplace/2017/09/what-work-benefits-do-millennials-really-want

Gordon, G., & DiTomaso, N. (1992). Predicting corporate performance from organizational culture. *Journal of Management Studies, 29*(6), 783–798.

Green, L., Heather, S., McKittrick, L., Naranjo, A., & Ward, C. (2005). *Understanding the multiple generations in the workplace.* Retrieved from http://www.saylor.org/site/wp-content/uploads/2013/02/BUS209-6.4-GenerationsintheWorkplace.pdf

Greenleaf, R. K. (1977). *Servant leadership: A journey into the nature of legitimate power and greatness*. Mahwah, NJ: Paulist Press.

Groves, K., & LaRocca, M. (2011). An empirical study of leader ethical values, transformational and transactional leadership, and follower attitudes toward corporate social responsibility. *Journal of Business Ethics, 103*(4), 511–528.

Hackel, E. (2017, November). Keys to recruiting and keeping millennial franchisees. *Franchising World, 49*(11), 15–16.

House, R. J., & Aditya, R. N. (1997). The social scientific study of leadership: Quo vadis? *Journal of Management, 23*(3), 409–473.

Islam, Z. (2016, March 10). Five trends that are shaping people experience. *Custerian. com.* Retrieved from http://www.custerian.com/5-trends-that-are-shaping-people-cxpcricncc/

Kahn, R., & Katz, D. (1960). Leadership practices in relation to productivity and morale. In D. Cartwright & A. Zander (Eds.), *Group dynamics: Research and theory*. Elmsford, NY: Pow, Patterson.

Kaiser, R. B., Hogan, R., & Craig, S. B. (February-March, 2008). Leadership and the fate of organizations, *American Psychologist, 63*(2), 96–110.

Keith, K. (2008). *The case for servant leadership*. Westfield, IN: Greenleaf Center for Servant Leadership.

Kirkpatrick, S. A., & Locke, E. A. (1981). Leadership: Do traits really matter? *Academy of Management Executive, 5*(2),48–60.

Kotter, J. P., & Heskett, J. L. (1992). *Corporate culture and performance*. New York, NY: The Free Press.

Kruman, Y. (2016, December 1). How to attract and retain Millennials and get them to do their life's best work for you. *Forbes.com.* Retrieved from https://www.forbes.com/sites/forbescoachescouncil/2016/12/01/how-to-attract-and-retain-millennials-and-get-them-to-do-their-lifes-best-work-for-you/2/#10d9376f60b8

Leader Network.org. (2007). *National leader of the month for September 2007.* Retrieved from http://www.leadernetwork.org/herb_kelleher_september_07.htm

Lewin, K., Lippitt, R., & White, R. K. (1939). Patterns of aggressive behavior in experimentally created "social climates." J*ournal of Social Psychology, 10,* 271–299.

Lowe, D., Levitt, K. J., & Wilson, T. (2008). Solutions for retaining Generation Y employees in the workplace. *Business Renaissance Quarterly, 3*(3), 43–57.

Mabrey, M. (February, 2015). Lead us! *US Naval Institute Proceedings, 14,* 344–349.

Malcolm, H. (2016, April 14). Millennials will take a happier workplace over pay. *USA Today.* Retrieved from https://www.usatoday.com/story/money/personal-finance/2016/04/14/millennials-workplace-happy-salary-pay/82943186/

Malone, R. (2017, July 20). Want to attract and retain 20-something employees? Don't treat them like Millennials. *CNBC.com.* Retrieved from https://www.cnbc.com/2017/07/20/want-to-attract-and-retain-20-something-employees-dont-treat-them-like-millennials.html

Marshall, D. (2018, March 9). *Confronting toxic company culture with servant leadership.* Oakland, CA: Berrett-Koehler Publishers. Retrieved from https://ideas.bkconnection.com/confronting-toxic-company-culture-with-servant-leadership

McCammon, R. (August, 2016). Want to understand millennials? It's simpler than you think. *Entrepreneur.com.* Retrieved from https://www.entrepreneur.com/article/278609, May 17, 2018

Nyce, S., & Gardner, J. (2017, November). *Global benefits attitudes survey. Research report: Willis Towers Watson.* Retrieved from https://www.willistowerswatson.com/-/media/WTW/PDF/Insights/2017/11/2017-global-benefits-attitudes-survey.pdf

Oden-Hall, K. (2017, February 9). Benefits of fun in the workplace. *Forbes.com.* Retrieved from https://www.forbes.com/sites/paycom/2017/02/09/benefits-of-fun-in-the-workplace/#73ae220178b1

Price Waterhouse Coopers (PWC). (2011). *Millennials at work. Reshaping the workplace.* Retrieved from https://www.pwc.com/gx/en/managing-tomorrows-people/future-of-work/assets/reshaping-the-workplace.pdf

Putre, L. (2016, November). Millennial recruiting magic. *Industry Week, 265*(6), 18–21.

Reuteman, R. (2015, March 1). "This is how Millennials want to be managed. *Entrepreneur, 1,* 6–12.

Roepe, L. (2017, April). Communications, culture and a clear career path matter to young workers. *HR Magazine, 62*(3)*,* 44–48.

Rost, J. C. (1993). *Leadership for the twenty-first century.* Westport, CT: Praeger.

Rubin, R., Munz, D., & Bommer, W. (2005). Leading from within; The effects of emotion recognition and personality on transformational leadership behavior. *Academy of Management Journal, 48*(5), 845–858.

Sabel, J-M. (2018, February 22). What is a realistic job preview? (And how to make them work for your organization). *Hire*Vue.* Retrieved from https://www.hirevue.com/blog/what-is-a-realistic-job-preview-and-how-to-make-them-work-for-you

Sendjaya, S., & Sarros, J. C. (2002). Servant leadership: It's origin, development, and application in organizations. *Journal of Leadership & Organizational Studies, 9*(2), 57–64.

Scalco, E. (2017, October). *6 reasons to empower employees with flexible schedules.* RecruitLoop.com. Retrieved from https://recruitloop.com/blog/6-reasons-empower-employees-flexible-schedules/

Schein, E. H. (1985). *Organizational culture and leadership.* San Francisco, CA: Jossey-Bass Publishers.

Schein, E. H. (2010). *Organizational culture and leadership.* (4th ed.). San Francisco, CA: Jossey-Bass Publishers.

Sommer, J. (2011, January 1). Non-financial rewards: Finding new ways to engage. *SHRM.org.* Retrieved from https://recruitloop.com/blog/6-reasons-empower-employees-flexible-schedules/

Southwest (2015). *Culture.* Retrieved from https://www.southwest.com/html/about-southwest/careers/culture.html

Spears, L. (1995). Servant leadership and the Greenleaf legacy. In Spears, L. C. (Ed.), *flections on leadership.* New York, NY: John Wiley & Sons, Inc.

Spears, L. (1996). Reflections on Robert K. Greenleaf and servant leadership. *Leadership and Organization Development Journal, 17*(7), 33–35.

Stogdill, R. M., & Coons, A. E. (1951). Leader behavior: Its description and measurement. *Research Monograph No. 88.* Columbus, OH: Ohio State University, Bureau of Business Research.

Stone, A. G., Russell, R. F., & Patterson, K. (August 2003). *Transformational versus servant leadership: A difference in leader focus.* Virginia Beach, VA: Servant Leadership Roundtable, Regent University.

Strauss, W., & Howe, N. (1991). *Generations: The history of America's future, 1584 to 2069*. New York, NY: William Morrow and Company, Inc.

Taylor, P., & Kester, S. (2010). *The millennials: Confident, connected, open to change* (p. 48). Washington, DC: Pew Research Council.

Thurman, S. (2016). *NSHSS scholar 2016 millennial career survey results*. Retrieved from https://www.nshss.org/media/29076/2016-nshss-millennial-career-survey.pdf.

Trice, H. M., & Beyer, J. M. (1993). *The cultures of work organizations.* Englewood Cliffs, NJ: Prentice Hall.

Tucker, M. (2012, January 1). Show and tell. *HR Magazine.* Retrieved from https://www.shrm.org/hr-today/news/hr-magazine/pages/0112tucker.aspx.

Twenge, J. M. (2010). A review of the empirical evidence on generational differences in work attitudes. *Journal of Business and Psychology*, 25(2), 201–210.

Yukl, G. (December 2008). How leaders influence organizational effectiveness. *The Leadership Quarterly, 19*(6), 708–722.

Yukl, G. (2013). *Leadership in organizations*. (8th ed.). Boston, MA: Pearson.

Whitten, K. (2017). How to hire Millennials now: National study offers insight on attracting Millennials into the banking workforce. *Connecticut Banking Magazine, Q4,* 10.

Zimmerman, K. (2016, November 20). Do top-dollar salaries really matter to Millennials? *Forbes.com.* Retrieved from https://www.forbes.com/sites/kaytiezimmerman/2016/11/20/do-top-dollar-salaries-really-matter-to-millennials/#3fb2ba20417c

Zimmerman, K. (2017, April 16). The surprising employer benefit Millennials really want. *Forbes.com*. Retrieved from https://www.forbes.com/sites/kaytiezimmerman/2017/04/16/the-surprising-employer-benefit-millennials-really-want/#342ab0d26376

CHAPTER 9

MILLENNIAL WORKERS AND THE EMPLOYEE ENGAGEMENT PHENOMENON

Has the Wave Crested?

Angela N. Spranger and Sierra Chen

INTRODUCTION

The concept of employee engagement has become ambiguous, a work-related psychological measure influenced by factors that scholars and researchers have focused on identifying. While the realm of research scholars seeks to identify it, the obvious effects of employee engagement, or, rather, disengagement are consistently observed in the workplace. A recent Gallup survey suggested that only 13% of employees around the globe are engaged on the job and disengaged workers outnumber engaged workers nearly two to one (Rana, Ardichvili, & Tkachenko, 2014). Research is trailing behind a phenomenon that is dominating the workplace.

By determining the factors that can predict levels of employee engagement, organizations can focus their efforts on active improvement. But, more importantly, by identifying employees' *expectations* of the factors of employee engagement, organizations can better understand the needs of their employees and tailor

Human Resources Management Issues, Challenges and Trends:
"Now and Around the Corner", pages 185–200.
Copyright © 2019 by Information Age Publishing
All rights of reproduction in any form reserved.

their organizational goals directly toward those needs. In a 1990 study, Kahn addressed the deeper components of engagement (meaningfulness, safety, and psychological availability) which form the basis of addressing what HR professionals and executives can do to help ensure their associates feel seen, safe, and valued (Spranger, 2015) in the workplace. These components of engagement create the foundation of the psychological expectations of employees and, as a result, their expectations of their managers and organizations.

In this chapter, we explore the employee engagement phenomenon to better understand the expectations of visibility (feelings or perceptions of being seen), safety, and value as related to engagement, particularly regarding the expectations of millennials entering the workforce. By studying the engagement phenomenon and the factors that impact it from the perspective of millennials and their expectations, HR professionals and executives can determine areas of change that might inject positive adaptation in their organizations. In this chapter, we seek to decrease the ambiguousness of the concept of employee engagement by determining millennials' *expectations* going into the workplace instead of focusing on their experiences in the workplace or after the fact. A primary research question then is, what are millennials' expectations of visibility, safety, and value in the workplace? Secondarily, if these expectations are not met, how does it impact their level of engagement?

LITERATURE REVIEW

Employee engagement is a phenomenon that is dominating the workforce and organizational culture. It is a concept substantiated by a rigorous academic conversation, which has caught up with the initial leadership of the consulting and practitioner community. As the significance of employee engagement becomes more firmly set in organizational culture, the generations are shifting, raising new questions about how an organization should best engage employees from different stages of life. Baby Boomers, one of the largest generations in history, are preparing to retire from the workforce while Millennials are flooding in with new expectations, demands, and work habits. Organizations must brace themselves for the changes that are about to occur, understanding how to engage millennials who will, by 2025, make up about 75% of the workforce (Deloitte, 2014; Donston-Miller, 2016). At its core, employee engagement manifests itself in the idea that an employee who feels seen, safe, and valued in the workplace will be more engaged. In this conceptual chapter, we emphasize the foundations of the term "employee engagement," and relate it to the current expectations of millennials as a young, technologically advanced generation that will bring new ideas, but also new expectations of visibility, safety, and value.

Defining Employee Engagement

Employee engagement is an ambiguous concept discussed by researchers, but difficult to define in clear, concrete terms. However, there are several foundations for the concept on which my research was built. The first foundation was Maslow's Hierarchy of Needs in 1970, a straightforward, conceptual framework for understanding the importance of fulfilling basic human needs (Kahn, 1990; Shuck, Rocco, & Albornoz, 2011). This theory of motivation relies on a model which arranges human needs in order of necessity, suggesting that higher-level needs cannot be met until lower-level needs have been met. The needs are arranged in a pyramid shape, demonstrating the most critical needs to survival as the lowest needs on the hierarchy according to foundational necessity.

The hierarchy's bottom level represents an individual's physiological needs; the theory suggests that these are the most potent of needs for human survival. This level includes needs such as food, water, and shelter (Shuck, Rocco, & Albornoz, 2011). The next level is safety, which is the feeling of personal protection and control over one's life. This need provides a fundamental concept of the idea of the importance of safety in the workplace. Humans have an inherent need to feel in control over their lives and personally protected. It also includes the need to feel a part of something bigger than oneself. Environments that do not foster this element of safety may be overly competitive and cold, which discourages relationship development and reduces productivity and innovation. In Kahn's employee engagement framework, safety promotes meaningfulness and psychological availability. According to Kahn, employees who do not feel safe become cognitively, emotionally, and physically "paralyzed" (Kahn, 1990).

The need for love and belonging is closely intertwined with the need for safety, as the need to develop relationships is especially prevalent in the workplace. Employees develop several relationships at work, all of which have the potential to influence employees' outcomes and experiences. Employees who interpret relationships with co-workers as positive are more likely to experience a positive workplace climate, which leads to higher employee engagement (Shuck, Owen, Manthos, Quirk & Rhoades, 2016). The importance of a mentor in the workplace also reflects this shared need for love and belonging, while underscoring the need to be seen and valued. Mentorship allows for more inexperienced employees to be recognized by a more experienced employee or manager which makes them feel included in the workplace.

Once the need to feel safe and experience love and belonging is satisfied, the need for esteem becomes very relevant as employees work to achieve career goals, manifesting the desire for respect and recognition. The need for self-actualization finishes the hierarchy with a need to realize potential and "become everything one is capable of becoming" (Maslow, 1970; Shuck, Rocco, & Albornoz, 2011). According to Kahn, self-actualization, the need to realize potential, parallels employee engagement (Kahn, 1990). If the most basic needs such as physiological needs, safety, love and belonging, and esteem needs are met, employees will be more equipped to realize their potential by sharing their knowledge and creating opportunities for other people.

Maslow's Hierarchy of Needs represent some of the most basic human needs that manifest themselves in humans and, therefore, organizations in which humans work and seek fulfillment. Employees within an organization are driven by an inherent need to be seen, safe, and valued. When such constructs are fulfilled, it enhances employee well-being and satisfaction in the workplace.

The second foundation for understanding employee engagement comes from Kahn's 1990 article which laid a psychological framework for employee engagement. Kahn emphasized the fact that meaningfulness, safety, and availability are all key factors in determining levels of engagement (Kahn, 1990; Shuck, Rocco, Albornoz, 2011). Kahn defined meaningfulness as the "positive sense of return on investments of self in role performance," safety as "the ability to show one's self without fear or negative consequences to self-image, status, or career," and availability as "the sense of possessing the physical, emotional, and psychological resources necessary for the competition of work" (Kahn, 1990). According to these three psychological constructs (meaningfulness, safety, and availability), Kahn asserted that when individuals are engaged, they bring all aspects of themselves (cognitive, emotional, and physical) to the performance of their work role. Thus, employee engagement represents the "simultaneous employment and expression of a person's preferred self in task behaviors that promote connections to work and to others, personal presence, and active, full role performance" (Kahn, 1990; Valentin, Valentin, & Nafukho, 2015). Utilizing this psychological foundation, we can also assign meaning to the difference between engagement and disengagement.

The concept of disengagement represents a clearly different phenomenon from simply low levels of engagement. Kahn defined disengagement as the "uncoupling of selves from work roles; people withdraw and defend themselves physically, cognitively, or emotionally during role performances" (Kahn, 2010; Saks & Gruman, 2014). Shuck, Zigarmi and Owen furthered this conversation by introducing a study that showed engagement as an experienced and complex psychological phenomenon that is experienced within the context of an employee's experience (2015). As it relates to this chapter, an employee who does not feel seen, safe, and valued in the workplace will not be engaged. Additionally, the level of that employee's disengagement will depend on the degree to which he or she perceives himself or herself as invisible, in danger, or of little value to the company. Human resource management and HR development professionals may engage employees by actively ensuring that they feel comfortable and appreciated in the workplace. This is not to suggest that Millennials, or any other employees, should be indulged or have policies and procedures relaxed to accommodate them in the workplace. Nor do we suggest that employees can, or ought to, be made to feel completely comfortable in the workplace at all times. Still, organizational development initiatives that intentionally address employees' needs to feel seen, safe, and valued in the workplace will yield significant impacts on the organization's culture, and the individual and organizational outcomes that are a proven result of high employee engagement.

Maslach, Schaufeli, and Leiter (2001) furthered the development of the concept of engagement by defining it as the opposite of burnout. By defining engagement as "an energetic state of involvement with personally fulfilling activities that enhance one's state of professional efficacy," the researchers characterized engagement by energy, involvement, and efficacy (Saks & Gruman, 2014). If this is true, we can add these components to our understanding of what engagement and disengagement are and how they affect the workplace and organizational outcomes. In their 2001 article, Maslach, Schaufeli and Leiter researched the idea that engagement is characterized by high levels of activation and pleasure, in that employees who are engaged in work are less susceptible to burnout because stress factors are reduced and replaced with satisfaction (Valentin, Valentin, & Nafukho, 2015).

Adding another dimension to the research on employee engagement, Macey and Schneider focused on the idea that employees may be predisposed to certain positive outlooks based on personality characteristics (Macey & Schneider, 2008; Shuck, Rocco, & Albornoz, 2011). These researchers have proposed that positive outlooks on the workplace may be based on innate personality characteristics and suggested that employees with a proactive personality may be more likely to be engaged in their work (Macey & Schneider, 2008; Shuck, Rocco & Albornoz, 2011). Instead of looking at employee engagement from an intrinsic, psychological perspective, they focused their research efforts on the external manifestation of internal employee satisfaction.

From this abbreviated summary of contemporary employee engagement research, and using Maslow's hierarchy of needs as a foundational concept, we move to considerations of the actual, practical significance of employee engagement. For this chapter, we define employee engagement as an employee's inclination to both internally and externally express satisfaction in the workplace according to an organization's efforts to make their employees feel seen, safe, and valued. We have taken Maslow's hierarchy of needs as a psychological foundation to address the factors that affect an employee's motivation in the workplace. From there, we incorporate the work of Kahn (1990) who explains employee engagement as an employee's perceptions of safety and meaningfulness combined with his or her psychological availability (or, the amount of cognitive energy he or she dedicates to the work). Finally, we acknowledge disengagement as a separate, important phenomenon as noted by Kahn (2010), Saks and Gruman (2014), and Maslach, Schaufeli and Leiter (2001).

THE SIGNIFICANCE OF EMPLOYEE ENGAGEMENT

There are several correlations and predictive relationships that can be observed from high and low levels of engagement in the workplace. These include enhanced employee well-being, improved productivity, positive financial business outcome, positive workplace climate, and reduced levels of burnout. Many organizations believe that employee engagement is a dominant source of competitive advantage on the basic premise that happy/engaged employees will perform better due to their connectedness to the organization (Saks & Gruman, 2014). Workers who feel supported, safe, and provided opportunities for learning are more likely to engage (Shuck, Rocco, & Albornoz, 2011).

In 2014, Kerns suggested that workforce engagement exerts an important influence on happiness and well-being in the workplace setting. Employees who find their relationships with co-workers to be positive and trusting are more likely to exhibit higher levels of performance (Shuck *et al.*, 2016). Forret and Love (2008) defined trust in coworkers as "holding confident positive expectations in situations involving risk with coworkers" (p. 249). This workplace concept, trust, has received significant attention in management research, leading to empirical determination of its relationship to increased organizational commitment, overall workplace trust, greater proactive behavior in the workplace, and lower intent to quit. The researchers investigated the relationship of perceptions of justice as independent variables (distributive, procedural, and interactional justice) to coworker trust and morale at the group level of analysis (Forret & Love, 2008). By analyzing survey data gathered from 264 employees at six small companies in the Midwestern U.S., Forret and Love controlled for gender, marital status, education, position and company tenure.

Organizational justice as a concept overall is based on fairness perceptions. Distributive justice is defined as perceived fairness of outcomes received, while procedural justice is defined as perceived fairness of company procedures used to determine those outcomes. Interactional justice is defined as the manner in which results are explained. It addresses the "quality of interpersonal processes and treatment of individuals (i.e., were they spoken to with sincerity and sensitivity) as well as the extent to which the reasons behind the outcome are explained" (Forret & Love, 2008, p. 249). The three subconstructs of organizational justice are interrelated but have been determined to be empirically distinct, accounting for "unique incremental variance" (Forret & Love, 2008, p. 249). Distributive justice predicts outcome satisfaction, withdrawal and OCB. It has also been associated with job and pay satisfaction, satisfaction with management, trust in organization and trust in manager. Procedural justice predicts of outcome satisfaction, job satisfaction, performance, organizational commitment, withdrawal and counterproductive work behaviors, cooperative conflict management, aggression towards management, and trust in management. Interactional justice related to evaluations of authority figures, job satisfaction, OCB, outcome satisfaction, commitment, withdrawal behavior and performance. Additionally, it predicts supervisor relationship quality, intent to quit, and intent to reduce work effort.

Forret and Love (2008) found support for all of the hypotheses in their cross-sectional field study, with positive associations and regression analyses showing that each variable predicted trust. Longitudinal research would show how justice perceptions influence coworker trust, but this cross-sectional self-report survey study left room for common method variance. Forret and Love (2008) made recommendations for increasing the subconstructs under organizational justice perceptions, in order to increase trust and other organizational outcomes. To improve perceptions of procedural justice, managers should ensure procedures are fair, involve employee input, and allow for formal appeals mechanisms. Human resource managers can improve perceptions of distributive justice by helping employees understand how organizational compensation works so that the employees understand reward allocation. Salary transparency, to the degree possible, helps with this—understanding how salaries are set, visibility on the company's effort to eliminate salary inequality, and other compensation-related initiatives will help improve distributive justice perceptions. Management should get a better understand of what their employees actually view as rewards, or as stated earlier in this chapter what motivates their employees, to make sure distribution is fair. To improve interactional justice, managers must treat employees with respect and dignity regardless of performance level, employing active listening without defensiveness when questioned.

Simons (2002) also discusses the potential gap between leaders' espoused and enacted values, stating that organizational norms emerge from the employees' experience of trust stemming from poor word / deed alignment in their leaders and colleagues. In a conceptual paper investigating trust as a highly complex construct which underpins the reciprocal commitments between employees and their employers, Simons enumerates multiple behavioral antecedents which create employee perceptions and combine with their interpretations of those behaviors, leading to specific consequences of a concept Simons describes as behavioral integrity. Those consequences include specific individual-level organizational outcomes, such as employee willingness to promote and implement change, intent to stay, organizational citizenship behaviors, and employee performance (Simons, 2002). Identifying the definitions and interrelationships between trust, credibility, psychological contracts, and hypocrisy, Simons suggests that behavioral integrity represents a perceived, ascribed trait that shows consistent alignment between a colleague or supervisor's words and deeds. In this chapter, we connect employees' perception of safety with the concept of trust in manager and trust in organization. Further, we suggest that a high degree of trust in the workplace manifests as high perceived value as well.

When employees are given opportunities to be seen and valued, such as training development opportunities, career development opportunities, resources and benefits given by the manager, or mentorship opportunities, they will also be more likely to engage (Rana, Ardichvili, & Tkachenko, 2014). These feelings of safety and value/recognition in the workplace demonstrate a positive predictive correlation between relationships and engagement. Kerns also suggested that engagement stirs employee optimism about positively impacting products, services, and quality, which increases the customer experience as well (Rana, Ardichvili, & Tkachenko, 2014).

Employee engagement also has a correlation with several factors that are reduced when employees are adequately engaged in the workplace. Both theory and practice support the clear predictive value of a culture of high engagement—not just high engagement scores. Practitioner research such as the Gallup meta-analysis of studies in 1997 popularized efforts to investigate the relationship of "employee engagement" as a workplace phenomenon with business and work unit profitability, productivity, employee retention, and customer satisfaction and loyalty across 1,135 business units (Harter et al., 2006). Later, the concept of "employee passion" emerged, briefly, in practitioner research. Zigarmi, Blanchard, Essary, and Houson (2017) suggests that employee passion encompasses such empirical constructs as intent to stay, organizational commitment, job commitment, discretionary effort, and employee endorsement. To have employee passion, certain organizational and job characteristics must exist: meaningful work, autonomy, career growth, recognition, collaboration, fairness, connection to leaders, and connection to colleagues. More recent scholarly research studies have shown that high engagement leads to a decrease in theft, turnover, burnout, and unhappiness (Kerns, 2014; Saks & Gruman, 2014). Researchers generally execute studies of employee engagement at the workgroup or business unit level of analysis, because at this level the data are aggregated and reported generally to maintain employees' anonymity and confidentiality. Measurable outcomes at the workgroup or business unit level of analysis include customer loyalty, profitability, productivity, employee turnover, and safety statistics.

When employees are engaged and satisfied in feeling seen, safe, and valued by their organization and employers, it promotes a sense of meaningfulness that allows employees to view their role in the organization as valuable and worthwhile. Employees need to have a sense of return on their cognitive and emotional investments before they are willing to fully engage with their work (Rana, Ardichvili, & Tkachenko, 2014). When employees' work and workplace give them satisfaction, it discourages them from leaving the organization. Employees who do not feel seen, safe, or valued in the workplace become cognitively and emotionally disengaged, which leads to low productivity in the organization (Kahn, 1990).

EMPLOYEE ENGAGEMENT AND MILLENNIALS

According to recent Gallup surveys, millennials are the least engaged generation in the workforce as organizations struggle to integrate different values and expectations in a workplace that has been shaped by Baby Boomers and Generation X (Adkins, n.d.; Rigoni & Adkins, n.d.). Around 86 million millennials will be in the workplace by 2020, making up about 35% of the total workforce (Asghar, 2014; Kurian, 2017). By 2025, the percentage will rise to millennials representing an estimated 75% of the workforce, as ten thousand Baby Boomers reach age 65 every day in the United States and begin to retire (Dannar, 2013). As the Baby Boomers retire, one of the largest generations in the United States will exit the workforce. This leaves room for the Millennials to integrate themselves into those openings, entering companies with expectations that differ dramatically from those of Baby Boomers (Asghar, 2014).

Surveys also show that 93% of millennials left their employer to change roles and 21% say that they have changed jobs within the past year, which is significantly more than the turnover rate of non-millennials (Adkins, n.d.; Rigoni & Adkins, n.d.). As mentioned previously, one of the reasons that employee engagement is significant to the effectiveness of a company is because productivity increases profitability. However, when employees are disengaged, which triggers high turnover, consultants estimate that it costs the U.S. economy $30.5 billion annually (Adkins, n.d.).

Gallup found that only 29% of millennials are engaged at work, meaning that only 29% are emotionally and behaviorally connected to their job and company. On the other hand, 16% of millennials are actively disengaged, meaning that they are actively working against the goals of the company and seeking to do damage to it. This leaves the remaining 55% disengaged workers who are interested in simply completing their tasks and leaving (Adkins, n.d.). Companies need to give these workers reasons to stay, attracting, retaining, and engaging their employees in the workplace so that they feel seen, safe, and valued. It is important to understand the millennials' levels of engagement now, before they make up the largest portion of the workforce. By understanding the expectations that Millennials bring to the workforce, companies can be more prepared and equipped to engage them and ensure that they feel seen, safe, and valued in the workplace.

Who are the Millennials?

In an increasingly diverse, multigenerational workforce, the challenges of navigating issues of communication and organizational commitment has garnered increasing attention from Human resources professionals and executives, as well as management scholars and researchers. Rodriguez (2006) stated that the biggest, most important factor driving executive level diversity and inclusion strategy would be the need to engage all employees' skills and creativity, and use those assets to add value to the customer experience. The term "diversity" in itself evokes the idea of differentiation in the workplace, and it is appropriate to identify Millennials in the context of varying qualities, experiences, work styles and values that make individuals unique. Diversity factors may be surface level, such as those which are visible and easily observed (age, race, gender, some disabilities) or it may be deep level, involving religion, some disabilities, sexual orientation and ethnicity. In the contemporary workforce the four dominant groups represent the Veterans, or Traditionalists (those born before 1946), Baby Boomers (born mid-1940s to mid-1960s), Generation Xers (mid-1960s to 1980), and Millennials (1980 to 2000). The latest generation, Gen Z, has reached working age (those born from 2000 forward) and will bring even more diversity and specific expectations into the workplace.

The Veteran workers in the United States workforce are the survivors of World War II and the Great Depression. They tend to hold great pride in and loyalty toward American values, and have significant respect for authority and chain of command. Baby Boomers, the children of the returning Veterans, value work but see it as a competition, as they had to prove themselves at every level of achievement they earned. Members of Generation X tend to desire feedback and flexibility, which require clear communication. However, Gen Xers resent close supervision and work to live, rather than operating under the need to prove their dedication through long hours and high visibility. The Millennials are the smartest, cleverest, healthiest, most wanted generation to have ever existed. They are quickly bored by routine, confident, assertive, and friendly with their parents (who may have adopted an overly-involved role in their lives, thus earning the term "helicopter parent") (Gurchiek, 2008).

There is an impending talent shortage, as the experienced individual contributors and managers of people from the Veteran and Baby Boomer generations exit the workforce. Additionally, and worse, traditionally there has been a limited transfer of knowledge between the groups. Gurchiek (2008) suggests that the generations rarely interact in the workplace, such that employee engagement, trust, and commitment are difficult to establish. Members of different generations on the same team may not recognize each other's skills and work ethics, or value one another's perspectives.

As mentioned earlier, Millennials are those individuals who were born between 1980 and 2000, between the ages of roughly 20 to early 30s. This generation will soon represent the largest portion of the American workforce (Asghar, 2014). Also known as Generation Y, the millennials have been described as globally aware, technologically sophisticated, ambitious, team-oriented, narcissistic, socially inept, and lacking in work ethic (Asghar, 2014; Dannar, 2013; Gibson, Greenwood, & Murphy, 2009). Millennials are curious, questioning and results oriented, a generation that accepts diversity and is comfortable with instant communication and social networking (Gibson et al., 2009). They have, however, been given names like the "Look at Me" generation to describe their overly self-confident, self-centered, disloyal, and unmotivated stereotypes (Myers & Sadaghiani, 2010).

A generation's values and behaviors are a manifestation of the relationship between parents, siblings, influential people, the media, and historical events that have a significant impact during formative years (Danner, 2013). Events such as 9/11, Columbine and other violent tragedies (such as school and theater mass shootings), and celebrity scandals have shaped millennials' culture and perspective, causing them to alter their expectations of companies for which they work (Gibson et al., 2009; Schweitzer & Lyons, 2010). Growing up in a true global economy, most members of the generation experienced instant gratification of microwave cooking, news and entertainment in small bites from music television videos, early exposure to personal computers and other digital tools. Millennials have experienced many influential events and now have an emphasis on an ethical business culture and an organization that lives out its values.

Technology is an integral part of the millennial identity as they are the first generation to be in continual communication with a network of friends and family. As a result, millennials view work and life as a balance that is equally achievable because of advanced technology. This can, perhaps, explain why millennials are perceived as lacking work ethics. Millennials have grown accustomed to easy access to information and are eager to eager to share their thoughts, opinions, and experiences on social networks (Dannar, 2013; Gibson et al., 2009). This generation was raised to believe, indeed to know, that their opinions mattered and were absolutely critical to people around the world. As a result, social media tools like Facebook, Twitter, Wikipedia, Snapchat and Instagram empower millennials and represent a significant part of millennials' lives, communication norms, and identities, even in the workplace.

Millennials are a unique generation because they are entering the workforce with superior knowledge of technology. They are also unique because they are a generation shaped by unique events that have drastically shifted their values and beliefs. Employers and companies should take what makes this generation unique and use it to their advantage, creating work environments that are more likely to engage and retain millennial employees.

Millennials' Expectations

Based on the values and beliefs that have come to define millennials, researchers seek to determine what they expect of their workplace. In determining these expectations, companies can be more prepared in learning how to engage them. For the millennial employee, the first three years of the employment life cycle are critical. Their loyalty, if any, is tenuous during that time period and they may be slow to trust institutions but may trust a manager instead. They may show no hesitation in expressing their perspective that if they are not engaged, do not like the job, the work, the workplace, or the management, they can quit and be well received at home or somewhere else. To avert these potentially negative trends, leaders and role models can help millennials design reasonable blueprints to get where they want to go professionally. HR and frontline managers can and should make it acceptable to deal with workplace problems, challenges, and conflicts in different ways. And, most importantly, encouraging congruence between the (organization's and the) managers' stated or espoused values and their enacted values, or walking the talk (Gurchiek, 2008).

IMPLICATIONS FOR PRACTICE

Popular literature suggests that millennials "want it all" and "want it now" (Ng, Schweitzer, & Lyons, 2010). They want work/life balance, good pay and benefits, rapid advancement, interesting and challenging work, and work that holds significance. Millennials place a heavy emphasis on work/life balance. Because of advancing technologies, millennials do not feel that they need to choose between work and life, regarding it as "symbiotic in nature" (Dannar, 2013). The events of September 11, 2001, when the United States experienced its most drastic loss of life due to foreign terrorist attacks, caused many millennials to re-evaluate their life priorities and choose work that allows them to adequately balance work and their personal lives. Millennials place their trust in organizations and have a strong preference for structured environments with clear rules (Schweitzer & Lyons, 2010). In this conceptual chapter we have laid the groundwork for a clearer understanding of millennial workers' needs to feel seen, safe, and valued in the workplace, set in the theoretical context of employee engagement.

Millennials want to be seen. They desire attention and feedback, regarding their leaders as mentors, and companionship and close relationships within the workplace that emphasize teamwork and collaboration (Dannar, 2013). Motivated by ambition, a desire to be respected, and the significance of the work, millennials seek rapid advancement in an organization. They are willing to leave the company if this does not happen fast enough (Danner, 2013). Millennials are exceptionally good at gathering and acquiring information and knowledge because of their technological expertise, but they expect their organizational leaders to provide guidance as to how that information should be interpreted (Dannar, 2013). They want to be mentored and provided with sufficient support for their advancement (Kurian, 2017). Mentoring allows organizational leaders to provide instruction and guidance, offer wisdom, guide skill development, and develop meaningful relationships with their employees (Dannar, 2013). Mentoring also serves as a compromise between organizational expectations and millennial expectations. A mentor can teach millennial employees the company's expectations in ways that makes sense to someone whose values have been shaped by different events and lifestyles (Asghar, 2014).

Millennials Want to Feel Safe in the Workplace

They want to enjoy the working experience and feel comfortable in the organizational culture. Close companionship is important for millennials, who prefer to collaborate rather than compete with co-workers (Dannar, 2013). Millennials want to collaborate with colleagues and managers that they respect and connect with colleagues inside and outside the office (Kurian, 2017; Asghar, 2014). Gurchiek (2008) suggested several specific actions that human resources and management professionals can integrate to improve intergenerational employee engagement:

1. Create training programs that address future senior leaders' preparation
2. Design a set of competencies to model desired behaviors, including knowledge transfer
3. Link compensation to goals of personal growth and career progression
4. Define the jobs or roles that are "mission-critical;" identify unique requirements, and target /develop the talent needed
5. Customize retention strategies to generational needs
6. Define expectations about performance and productivity and then stand by that

7. Use clear, straightforward language
8. Don't hint and don't assume
9. See the best.
10. Celebrate achievements.

To ensure that Millennials feel safe in the workplace, communicate expectations clearly and offer opportunities for achievement of personal and professional goals in a learning organizational culture, or an environment that does not punish mistakes or inquiries.

Millennials want to be valued. They have a constant need for gratification and appreciation for both small and big successes. A workplace that fosters open and honest communication is more likely to engage this generation because they want to feel like their ideas and opinions matter. They want to know that their insight has company-wide significance (Kurian, 2017; Ng, Schweitzer, & Lyons, 2010). Millennials value manager feedback and they view strong relationships with supervisors to be foundational to their long-term satisfaction in the organization (Myers & Sadaghiani, 2010). Because millennials are motivated by accomplishment, close companionship, and a desire to be respected, they want responsibility within the company, evidenced in the significance of the work, and want a chance for promotions (Dannar, 2013; Myers & Sadaghiani, 2010). By making work more exciting and relevant, managers can engage their millennials employees, showing them verifiable career opportunities (Gibson et al., 2009). According to Dannar (2013), a "delegation of employment-related duties should be utilized so millennials can experience high levels of responsibility, meaningfulness, and a sense of personal fulfillment" (p. 9).

Company leaders can foster a workplace environment that facilitates the best performance from all their employees, starting with making their employees feel seen, safe, and valued. These organizations may need to alter rules and policies, so they can fully utilize millennials' abilities (Myers & Sadaghiani, 2010). It is important for companies to understand the expectations that Millennials bring into the workplace so that they can better engage them. The impending influx of Millennials should excite employers, but it should also motivate them to prepare their workplace to ensure compatibility and compromise with millennial and organizational expectations.

IMPLICATIONS FOR RESEARCH

This initial conceptual foray into the dialogue around employee engagement has led to many practical ideas and considerations for HR managers and executives to consider. These considerations are particularly relevant with regard to improving employee engagement among the millennial generation as they enter the workforce *en masse* within the next two to seven years. Our initial research has indicated clear connections between established theoretical models and the idea that employees of all generations, but especially Millennials, need to feel seen, safe, and valued in the workplace. These connections link theories around employees' basic human needs with specific ways to address and validate those needs in the workplace. Additionally, we see opportunities for additional academic research into the dimensions of employee engagement and workplace motivation identified here. Specifically, we intend to identify validated scale items to capture employee perceptions of visibility, safety, and perceived value in their workplaces. Compiling such a scale from previously validated instruments, testing, and administering it, will provide a clear image of Millennials' expectations and actual perceptions of being seen, safe, and valued in their workplaces. We seek to compare these data points with responses to an abbreviated measurement of employee engagement such as the Utrecht Work Engagement Scale, or UWES or UWES-9 (Roof, 2015; Schaufeli, Bakker, & Salanova, 2006) to millennial employees with less than five years' workforce experience will provide a dataset from which we can identify the relationships between employee engagement and feelings of being seen, safe, and valued in the workplace, and what those factors indicate in terms of millennial employees' expectations.

One challenging limitation of the continued research motivated by this review of the literature is that while millennial employees may be willing to share their expectations and desires for their workplace experience, common method variance (CMV) is likely to pose a challenge, as with any self-report data gathering initiative. Additionally the challenge of social desirability bias may affect how participants respond to questions about whether they expected to feel seen, safe, and valued in the workplace prior to joining their current employer, and the degree to which they actually feel those things. Further examination of the employee engagement literature for validated scales that precisely capture employee engagement is required, as well.

CONCLUSION

This chapter established the linkages between individual motivation, employee engagement, and employee perceptions of visibility, safety, and value in the workplace. We have reviewed the literature on employee engagement and identified that among millennial workers there are specific demands which HR leaders and frontline managers and supervisors should acknowledge and address, to ensure higher engagement among the millennial workforce. We have also initiated analysis of the available scales and instruments with which we can measure and document employees' perceptions of engagement and identify correlations between engagement levels and feeling seen, safe, and valued in the workplace. As we add to the dialogue around millennial workers' expectations and existing perceptions of employee engagement, we do so with the desire to help consultants and practitioners in human resource development and HR management, as well as frontline managers and supervisors, to convert theoretical research results into practical steps that will positively affect productivity, performance, and employee commitment. In light of the constantly evolving body of knowledge around employee engagement and organizational commitment, trust, relative to the demands of the millennial workforce, we assert that the employee engagement "wave" has not crested, but that there is significant work yet to be done in this area.

REFERENCES

Adkins, A. (n.d.). Millennials: The job-hopping generation. *Gallup, Inc.* Retrieved from http://www.gallup.com/workplace/231587/millennials-job-hopping-generation. aspx

Asghar, R. (2014, January 14). What millennials want in the workplace (and why you should start giving it to them). *Forbes.com.* Retrieved from https://www.forbes. com/sites/robasghar/2014/01/13/what-millennials-want-in-the-workplace-and-why-you-should-start-giving-it-to-them/#1b27d8fa4c40

Dannar, P. R. (2013). Millennials: What they offer our organizations and how leaders can make sure they deliver. *The Journal of Values-Based Leadership, 6*(1/3). doi: http://scholar.valpo.edu/jvbl/vol6/iss1/3

Deloitte. (2014, January). *The Deloitte millennial survey.* Retrieved from Deloitte: https://www2.deloitte.com/content/dam/Deloitte/global/Documents/About-Deloitte/gx-dttl-2014-millennial-survey-report.pdf

Donston-Miller, D. (2016, May 5). *Workforce 2020: What you need to know now.* Retrieved from Forbes: https://www.forbes.com/sites/workday/2016/05/05/workforce-2020-what-you-need-to-know-now/#44b16e9b2d63

Forret, M., & Love, M. S. (2008). Employee justice perceptions and coworker relationships. *Leadership & Organizational Development Journal, 29*(3), 248–260.

Gibson, J., Greenwood, R., & Murphy, E. (2009). Generational differences in the workplace: Personal values, behaviors, and popular beliefs. *Journal of Diversity Management, 4*(3), 7.

Gurchiek, K. (2008, June 3). *Generational conflicts aggravate talent shortage.* Retrieved from Society for Human Resource Management: https://www.shrm.org/hr-today/news/hr-news/pages/generationalconflictstalentshortage.aspx

Harter, J. K., Schmidt, F. L., Killham, E. A., & Asplund, J. W. (2006). *Q12 meta-analysis.* Omaha, NE: The Gallup Organization.

Kahn, W. (1990). Psychological conditions of personal engagement and disengagement at work. *Academy of Management Journal, 33*(4), 692–724.

Kahn, W. A. (2010). The essence of engagement: Lessons from the field. In S. L. Albrecht (Ed.), *New horizons in management. Handbook of employee engagement: Perspectives, issues, research and practice* (pp. 20–30). Northampton, MA, US: Edward Elgar Publishing.

Kerns, C. D. (2014). Fostering and managing engagement: A framework for managerial leadership. *Journal of Leadership, Accountability and Ethics, 11*(1), 34–49.

Kurian, S. (2017). Meet the millennials. *Its her future* (pp. 1–22). KPMG. Retrieved from https://home.kpmg.com/content/dam/kpmg/uk/pdf/2017/04/Meet-the-Millennials-Secured.pdf

Macey, W. H., &Schneider, B. (2008). The meaning of employee engagement. *Industrial and Organizational Psychology, 21*(5), 376–387.

Maslach, C., Schaufeli, W. B, & Leiter, M.P. (2001). Job burnout. *Annual Review of Psychology, 52*, 397–422.

Maslow, A. (1970). *Motivation and personality* (2nd ed.). New York, NY: Harper and Row.

Myers, K. K., & Sadaghiani, K. (2010). Millennials in the workplace: A communication perspective on millennials' organizational relationships and performance. *Journal of Business and Psychology*, *25*(2), 225–238. http://doi.org/10.1007/s10869-010-9172-7

Ng, E. S. W., Schweitzer, L., & Lyons, S. T. (2010). New generation, great expectations: A field study of the millennial generation. *Journal of Business and Psychology, 25*, 281–292. http://dx.doi.org/10.1007/s10869-010-9159-4

Rana, S., Ardichvili, A., & Tkachenko, O. (2014). A theoretical model of the antecedents and outcomes of employee engagement. *Journal of Workplace Learning*, *26*(3/4), 249–266. doi:10.1108/jwl-09-2013-0063

Rigoni, B., & Adkins, A. (n.d.). Millennial job-hoppers: what they seek: *Gallup, Inc.* Retrieved from http://news.gallup.com/businessjournal/191585/millennial-job-hoppers-seek.aspx

Rodriguez, R. (2006, August 1). Diversity finds its place. *HR Magazine*. Retrieved from https://www.shrm.org/hr-today/news/hr-magazine/pages/0806rodriguez.aspx

Roof, R. (2015). The Association of Individual Spirituality on Employee Engagement: The spirit at work. *Journal of Business Ethics*, *130*(3), 585–599.

Saks, A., & Gruman, J. (2014). What do we really know about employee engagement? *Human Resource Development Quarterly*, *25*(2), 155–181. Doi: 10.1002/hrdq.21187

Schaufeli, W. B., Bakker, A. B., & Salanova, M. (2006) The measurement of work engagement with a short questionnaire a cross-national study. *Educational and Psychological Measurement, 66*(4), 701–716. Retrieved from https://www.wilmarschaufeli.nl/publications/Schaufeli/251.pdf

Shuck, B., Zigarmi, D., & Owen, J. (2015). Psychological needs, engagement, and work intentions: A Bayesian multi-measurement mediation approach and implications for HRD. *European Journal of Training and* Development, *39*(1), 2–21.

Shuck, B., Owen, J., Manthos, M., Quirk, K., & Rhoades, G. (2016). Co-workers with benefits: The influence of commitment uncertainty and status on employee engagement in romantic workplace relationships. *Journal of Management Development, 35*(3), 382–393. doi: 10.1108/JMD-02-2015-0014

Shuck, B., Rocco, T., & Albornoz, C. (2011). Exploring employee engagement from the employee perspective: Implications for HRD. *Journal of European Industrial Training, 35*(4), 300–325. Doi: 10.1108/03090591111128306

Simons, T. (2002). Behavioral integrity: The perceived alignment between managers' words and deeds as a research focus. *Organization Science*, *13*(1), 18–35.

Spranger, A. (2015). *StepOne Consulting*. Retrieved from StepOne Consulting, LLC: www.step1consulting.com

Valentin, M. A., Valentin, C., & Nafukho, F. (2015). The engagement continuum model using corporate social responsibility as an intervention for sustained employee engagement: Research leading practice. *European Journal of Training and Development, 39*, 182–202. 10.1108/EJTD-01-2014-0007.

Zigarmi, D., Blanchard, S., Essary, V., & Houson, D. (2017). *The leadership-profit chain. perspectives.* Escondido, CA: The Ken Blanchard Companies.

CHAPTER 10

THE UNCONSCIOUS BIAS

Impacting the Workplace

Ronda Mariani

INTRODUCTION

The concepts; diversity and inclusion are fundamental in today's workforce. Globalization and the reduction of borders have forced business not only to understand these concepts (e.g., diversity and inclusion) but to embrace the true meaning of what it entails to have a workplace that accurately has an understanding of its multicultural foundation. As of late, increasingly colleges have begun to infuse the importance of diversity and inclusion throughout its curriculum (Jackson, 2017, p. 22) in hopes of producing graduates that possess the sensitivity, understanding, and management skills to lead a global workforce. Once these students graduate they enter the industry and many times are left to their resources to further their understanding of what it is to work in a diverse organization. These same students who are now employed are exposed to individuals such as the Chief Diversity Officer or online training programs to now teach and instill values that should represent what a diverse and inclusive work environment should be. It seems that organizations go through the motions well, but are they addressing the idea of what it means to have a diverse work environment that promotes inclu-

Human Resources Management Issues, Challenges and Trends:
"Now and Around the Corner", pages 201–212.
Copyright © 2019 by Information Age Publishing

sion? Furthermore, how do those in charge of developing and maintaining the various organizational approaches, implement diversity and inclusion if these individuals do not have a deep understanding of their bias nature?

WHAT IS UNCONSCIOUS BIAS?

We have heard the term bias before, and the Merriam-Webster (2018) dictionary, in short, describes bias as an "instance of prejudice or unreasoned judgment" This judgment at a young age is instilled in us through experiences, which overtime impacts our views towards others and situations. Whether these situations are something we have witnessed, experienced, or have been introduced to through upbringing in our own culture; bias in many forms is a large portion of the societies that we live. Bias is a cognitive perception of how we perceive people and interpret situations. For several decades, "developments in cognitive sciences have demonstrated that automatic and unconscious cognitive processes shape human behavior, beliefs, and attitudes" (Teal, Gill, Green, & Crandall, 2012, p. 80).

Research findings indicate that most individuals are unaware of their own bias and furthermore a personal experience contributes enormously to the conditioning of bias (Banaji, 2001, Uhlmann & Nosek, 2012 as cited in Conaway & Bethune, 2015). Greenwald & Banaji (1995) also found that bias could develop with no experience at all and instead be influenced by "family history" known as "implicit social cognition"(ISC). A simple example of ISC could be applied to individuals of Mexican descent. Mexicans, like most Latin cultures, can display skin tone from light to dark. Many times light-skinned Mexican families are thought to be wealthier, having more possessions, and holding office jobs, whereas dark-skinned Mexicans are considered to be field workers, living in crowded situations, and lacking wealth. As we can see, even though these individuals may view themselves as both proud Mexicans, skin color creates an identifying factor of stereotyping among this group assuming that one group is better off than the other. Although this is an elementary example of bias, it is a real example of how the bias nature in an individual can effect and impact decision making about a group of people. Meaning, if an individual, whether of Mexican or other decent, held this described bias about Mexicans as the norm, this would impact their views towards this ethnic group.

The differences between bias and unconscious bias, also known as "implicit bias" are whether we are aware or not aware of our thoughts and actions. Unconcious bias is judgments we are unaware of, and in return, these thoughts influence our behavior towards others and situations. These influences many times demonstrate behavior that can be unkind and judgemental. Neither of these characteristics is appropriate in an organization and should not be present in a hiring manager or the processes. Clarifying the differences between bias and unconscious bias further can be applied to the context of an airplane. Airplanes can be flown by a human pilot or by a machine on autopilot. Both of these methods can fly a plane from point A to point B, but only one has organic human thinking ability when handling situations that arise. The other has a reaction ability based on situational programming. Meaning, bias, which would represent the human pilot whose reactions can be controlled because of the ability to have an awareness of thoughts and actions, whereas, unconscious bias is the autopilot whose reactions are based on programmed experiences.

Since the brain relies heavily on previous information in its decision making, it is not unlikely then that inappropriate decisions may take place because of the lack of conscious thought at any given moment. The human brain can take in millions of pieces of information each second of the day but only processes a small fragment of this information. Unfortunately, most of our decisions are derived only from these small pieces of information. Although the brain relies on this small amount of information to make decisions it still collects and categorizes all information it is receiving. The ability to do this creates efficiency and saves energy while providing faster response rates to situations. Therefore, decision making relies heavily on past experiences and information that has been collected and stored. However, this stored information is what provokes a reaction to situations. These reactions many times can be based on past information, which may or may not be accurate or appropriate for the desired situation causing incidences of unconscious bias.

STEREOTYPING

The word stereotype was introduced by Walter Lippman in 1922 referring to "pictures in our heads of social groups" (Bar-Tal, Graumann, Kruglan, & Stroebe, 1989). Now ask yourself; how does stereotyping impact unconscious bias and what is the difference between the two. "The difference between bias and stereotyping is that bias is a personal preference, like or dislike where a stereotype is a preconceived idea about certain characteristics, which are applied to all members of a group" (Reyes, 2016). Stereotyping can be such thoughts as Puerto Ricans only eat rice and beans, Asians cannot drive, and families always arrange marriages in Indian culture. These phrases or stereotypes are considered social norms by many individuals and unfortunately many times fail to represent the truth.

Stereotyping can be very dangerous because these implicit associations can cause discrimination "by influencing how individuals process and recall information about other individuals" (Lee, 2005). Stereotyping can originate from numerous instances and appear in many situations. Some of these instances can be in the form of comments, which are blurted out in situations that are public or among small groups of people? Furthermore, when these comments are made, it is to disparage the culture or to make fun. We can all relate one way or another to witnessing or being part of a situation regarding stereotyping. Many times these stereotypical judgments are applied by individuals with limited knowledge of that group. This application of false knowledge drives future bias towards individuals. Now apply this false knowledge to the workforce.

Exercise

For this exercise, pretend you are the human resource hiring manager. You receive three resumes from candidates that you feel have excellent qualifications to succeed at the position being advertised. Each candidate has a similar experience in the area of need and would be ideal if chosen. The first candidate (Mr. Highland) is a forty-eight-year-old white male, about 6'2," nice build, with twelve years of experience and a master degree from a state university. The second candidate (Mr. Levine) is a sixty-year-old white male with twenty-five years of experience, gray hair, fit in appearance, and received his bachelor's degree in 1979. The third candidate (Ms. Gonzalez) is a fifty-two-year-old Hispanic female, short in height, medium weight, who has just finished raising her family and has returned to the workforce about three years ago. She has a master degree from an online program that she obtained this past year.

Picture these three individuals in your mind and consider what stereotypes come to your attention. Locate a piece of paper and do the following: Make three columns, one for each candidate as seen below. List as many stereotypes that come to mind that correspond with that candidate. Remember this is an exercise.

First Candidate	Second Candidate	Third Candidate
List the stereotypes for this candidate.	List the stereotypes for this candidate.	List the stereotypes for this candidate.
1. XXX	1. XXX	1. XXX
2. XXX XXX	2. XXX XXX	2. XXX XXX
3. XXX	3. XXX	3. XXX

After you complete the table ask yourself the following questions. I recommend writing your thoughts on the same piece of paper.

1.   Which candidate would you hire? Why?
2.   What words triggered an association to a stereotype?
3.   What was the association and why?
4.   Can you recall in your life when this stereotype was learned? Where you young, with family, at work, among friends, etc.?
5.   Can you understand that some of these associations are a form of unconscious bias that have been shaped by some of your life experiences? Can you identify which ones?
6.   Ask yourself, how can I overcome these thoughts, associations, and bias to make myself a better hiring manager?
7.   Are there areas where I may be in denial? Which ones?

There is no right or wrong answer to this exercise. This exercise is not to make you feel immoral or cause anger but to let you know you are human just like the rest of us. With humanity comes unconscious bias. What is important is that you can admit that this bias exists within you and most likely everyone. The importance of this exercise is to aid you in recognizing what some of your biases are and that you are willing to understand and link the cause; this is the first step. The second step is to create and work on a mechanism within yourself that can help you understand your unconscious bias triggers and correct biases in situations. This new ability will create an improved individual while educating and retraining your brain to react more appropriately when confronted with situations.

DENIAL

Freud studied the human mind rather extensively. His analogy of the iceberg depicts the human mind as being quite vast under the surface. The iceberg analogy also represented the unconscious mind. He also knew that the unconscious nature of the human mind was compelling, much more potent than the conscious (See Figure 10.1). Looking back into the past, humans relied on instinct to make split-second decisions, such as warding off a wild animal or hostile tribe member (Ross, 2008). The fundamental way humans regard the world and their encounters are hard-wired based on a pattern of unconscious decision-making that is based on what feels safe and acceptable for our survival (Ross, 2008).

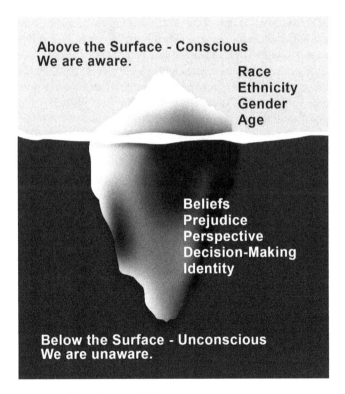

FIGURE 10.1. Freud's Iceberg Model

The human brain can filter out information very well. Many times information that is being filtered impacts our perception. This mechanism to filter information creates a "perceptual lens." This perceptual lens lets some information in depending upon how we interpret the information. However, much of this filtered information is based on our life experiences, which is in some form formulated based upon our bias perceptions (Ross, 2008). As a result "these pre-established filters create situations where individuals will see, hear, and interpret things differently than other people might or not even realize the circumstances at all" (Ross, 2008). These perceptions of reality will many times lead to denial of bias behavior. Denial of bias behavior may be attributed to individuals considering their bias reactions as the norm and what is acceptable to that individual's belief system.

Many times companies do not realize it is nurturing a culture of unconscious bias. Time and time again we will read headlines describing the unethical disputes with race, gender, disability, appearance, and age discrimination. These are just a few of the biases that can be present in an organization. Individuals in these organizations see themselves as being open-minded when in actuality they are not. Patti Watts, an assistant editor for *Management Review*, interviewed Dr. Bob Mezoff who trains managers and conducts workshops about cultural diversity. Dr. Mezoff stated, "one of the greatest obstacles to overcoming prejudice is denial" (Watts, 1987). Examples of denial can be something as simple as a person's last name and the prejudice that may arise when heard or read. Research has demonstrated that individuals with a caucasian last name were more likely to be hired than an individual with an ethnic last name (See Francis, 2018; Howard, 2015). Despondently, hiring managers many times are unaware of something as simple as name bias and because of this denial, these unconscious actions may be preventing the best candidate from being hired.

TITLE VII

Most of us are familiar with the legal regulation Title VII of the US Court Rights Act of 1964. Acts such as these were put in place to mitigate against actions of discrimination in our culture. These legal measures to prevent discrimination reside to promote equal opportunities. Companies are not only aware of this but seem to accept the challenge. Many companies have developed extensive diversity programs and make firm commitments to the inclusion of each member of its organizations. Title VII also implemented the Equal Employment Opportunity Commission (EEOC) to enforce Title VII laws, which has resulted in numerous lawsuits supporting equality within the workplace.

Probably one of the most famous lawsuits was *Wal-Mart Stores, Inc. v. Dukes*, where plaintiffs represented "a class of 1.5 million female Wal-Mart employees who alleged that Wal-Mart discriminated against women in violation of Title VII of the Civil Rights Act of 1964. Id. at 2547; see 42 U.S.C. Sec. 2000e-2(k)" (Amalfe, 2013). Plaintiffs alleged that Wal-Mart knowingly allowed managers to discriminate against female employees providing women with less pay and

promotion opportunities as compared to men. Plaintiffs argued that this unconscious bias be woven into Wal-Mart's corporate culture and placed women com-
panywide at a disadvantage. A social science expert testimony was obtained and
testified that unconscious bias is real and gender stereotyping does exist in today's
corporate world. Despite the testimony presented by the Plaintiffs to the District
Court, "the Supreme Court found that plaintiffs could not sufficiently allege a
single common reason for those employment decisions. Id. at 2552" (Amalfe,
2013). Therefore, the testimony was rejected, and the plaintiffs were unable to
present to the court with a single fact that could support unconscious bias in Wal-
Mart's management decision making. Wal-Mart continues to battle plaintiffs and
their accusations of discrimination. Until the courts can agree and accept what is
considered viable and tangible unconscious bias in the workplace, plaintiffs will
have a difficult time trying to prove unconscious bias.

Coca-Cola Company is another organization that has had its share of diversity
problems within its organization. There have been several lawsuits over the years.
Coca-Cola Company in 1999 was served with a lawsuit that accused the corporate
giant of discrimination against African American employees and in 2002 Coca-
Cola Company agreed to pay female employees 8.1 million dollars in back pay;
the reason wage disparity between male and female employees (Harvey & Allard,
2015). Today Coca-Cola Corporation considers itself an inclusive company. Its
motto "as inclusive as our brands" (Harvey & Allard, 2015) can be heard among
the company culture. Much of Coca-Cola Corporation corporate social responsibility efforts are geared at assisting multicultural consumers and supporting their
needs in leadership presence, community strategies, and commitment to education (Harvey & Allard, 2015, p. 105). Coca-Cola Corporation over the years has
taken all allegations seriously and has made diversity an integral part of its culture
today creating inclusive work environments for its employees.

Another famed company; Google has had its share of accusations about discrimination among its corporate culture. "Google, founded in 1998, released its
transparency report in 2014, this report indicated an overwhelmingly male, white,
and Asian work population. Google has been heavily criticized for confronting
the problem, diversity in their workforce as too little and too late" (Tiku, 2018).
Remedying situations such as these has not been successful for Google, instead,
Google has been accused of using and setting quotas as a method to create a
diverse organization in its hiring efforts. Google insists it does not use quotas or
identity as a method of hiring but instead hires based on individuals merit (Tiku,
2018). It does admit to setting goals to diversify its workplace population but
ensures it is not specifically targeting race to meet numbers. "Google has also
been training its employees how to recognize unconscious bias, but diversity is
not always perceived as part of Google's cultural values as written in Damore's
memo" (Tiku, 2018). Damore was fired after he released his memo challenging
Google's diversity efforts.

Although the face of discrimination has changed in the workplace; unconscious bias seems to be a very misunderstood form of discrimination. Unconcious
bias behavior is also complicated to prove as a tangible deed that can result in a
reprimand or disciplinary action. When you consider the question; how do managers discipline an employee that does not even know that they are unconsciously
doing something wrong; it is understandable that it would be difficult for a manager to choose an appropriate action for that employee.

Although governments, organizations, and HRM professionals have spearhead
these endeavors to improve diversity and inclusion while minimizing bias through
positive steps in developing laws and policies, little seems to have been achieved
to lessen the effects of unconscious bias in the workplace. Even when situations
arise such as employees that become victim to unconscious bias attacks, many
times these employees are are afraid to report what they have witnessed as bias
conduct towards them or others because of the fear of retaliation. We feel and see
unconscious bias happening, but at the same time, it is like chasing the phantom.
We know it is there, but we actually cannot see it. Title VII tries to capture this
phantom, but its success is far and too little in between each case.

ACADEMIC CONTRIBUTION

We can all safely agree that education provides the best tactic when combating
any problem in society. Education that is grounded in positive perspectives about
social norms can provide promising and impacting results. However, there are
vast differences between unconscious bias education and offerings such as diversity, cultural, or sensitivity training. In this instance, education and training are
dissimilar and provide different benefits although the outcome may seem comparable. "Unconscious bias education aims to increase awareness of how our minds
work, to help people and organizations adopt practices that improve decision-
making" (Bertschinger, 2017, p. 1).

As mentioned; increasingly colleges have begun to infuse the importance of
diversity and inclusion throughout its curriculum (Jackson, 2017). Although this
infusion of diversity into the curriculum is taking place, many times it is introduced only as a topic within an organizational behavior class. We probably could
all agree, introducing diversity in this manner, as a topic and not a class of its own,
would not provide enough time to create an atmosphere where deep conversations
and thought could take place. However, when offering diversity classes, both faculty and students may be apprehensive about the subject. When speaking of race,
cultural differences, and oppression, it has been noted and compared to walking
into a minefield (Williams, Dunlap, & McCandies, n.d.). Furthermore, this would
not be the same as educating individuals about unconscious behavior. If we are
to educate students about unconscious bias, this would mean curriculum that was
geared towards providing an understanding of how the human brain works and
reacts when presented with stereotypical situations. Educating about awareness is
difficult and can create triggers, issues, and reactions. Therefore it is the approach

to instruction that needs to change, and a more inclusive environment of learning needs to be incorporated simulating situations as well as correcting behavior.

Many schools offering majors in the medical field already understand the importance of student's awareness and the needed coping mechanisms to overcome unconscious bias behavior. Therefore, it is not uncommon to witness in the curriculum a class devoted to diversity, inclusion, and unconscious bias. More majors should think about following suit and include these critical classes in its curriculum.

CONTROLLING UNCONCIOUS BIAS IN HIRING

Developing a multi-cultural workforce that addresses the global needs of clients is imperative to the success of businesses. The development of a multi-cultural workforce is one way that companies can create a competitive advantage that speaks across borders. Although Human Resource Management (HRM) professionals accept the task of hiring and creating a competitive workforce, research and evaluation of industries have demonstrated according to Lee (2005) "the prevalence of unconscious bias has manifested itself in in hiring practices" (p. 485). Since unconscious bias is so deeply ingrained in who we are, it is challenging the appropriate judgments that should be made and affect decision making in organizations when it applies to hiring. As a result, organizations are becoming culturally the same. When organizational culture is the same, unconscious bias will go unnoticed and this in return will affect hiring. These individuals in charge of hiring will most likely hire like-minded candidates, this is known as affinity bias. Affinity bias occurs when a hiring manager is interviewing a candidate and begins to see a lot of their traits and behaviors in the candidate. These traits and behaviors may not necessarily be positive therefore perpetuating further the deep-rooted nature of unconscious bias.

TRAINING AND EDUCATION

Correcting unconscious bias in the workforce will be problematic. Afterall the human brain is hardwired to protect itself. A lifetime of experiences is now dictating our decision making. Organizations spend a great deal of time trying to make employees understand what diversity is, while not addressing the real problem, educating the human brain. HRM professoinal's implement annual diversity training but is this enough? Research demonstrates it is not. Training, especially short-term training does not correct or support the problem of unconscious bias. In fact, it does quite the opposite. Many times it is seen as an inconvenience or a manipulation of what one thinks or feels.

Changing the culture of an organization can be a challenge, there needs to be a process to the change. Educating is key to this process. Just like learning your time's tables in elementary school, it takes repetition. Unconcious bias education needs to repetitious. When situations arise, and discrimination takes place, HRM professionals need to evaluate the situation carefully and determine if this action was intent or unconscious. In many cases, individuals genuinely believe they may be doing good and may not realize their actions are wrong. Recognizing our human nature and that mistakes are part of the deal is very important. What counts is how we address these mistakes.

HRM professionals need to move away from the notion that we are protecting a class and focus more on the fact that fair treatment is what is essential to organizations. Surveying is an exceptional method when trying to obtain and collect information if individuals feel it is safe and will not compromise their job. Conducting quarterly surveys should be done as well as surveying individuals that leave the company. Many times companies become indignant to an individual giving their notice to leave instead of trying to learn why that employee wants to leave. Are there steps that could have been taken to stop them from leaving or reemploy them? Was it something they felt that made them leave, such as being underpaid because of their gender? Once results are obtained, education should be tailored to these results and implemented more than just once a year. Education can be conducted through outside educational groups, online learning, and community days that embrace culture and differences. Most importantly education should be geared not only to the employees but HRM professionals too.

Outside group support is also essential. Organizations will want to support groups that align with the culture of its company. Do not support a group because it is a minority group, instead support groups that will provide organizational interests to all individuals. Lastly, the importance of mentorship is critical. You are never too old to learn. One of the best ways to learn is through the intimacy of a mentor. Organizatons and HRM professionals can create diversity by having individuals work together and play together. An organizational audit is always a great way to conduct research about your company and learn where your companies deficiencies may be. The goal is to change behavior and create a competitive organization in the work environment.

CONCLUSION

Unconcious bias continues to grow within organizations and is a severe problem in our societies today. Organizations that are plagued with this component can incur costly outcomes, such as key employees leaving, reduced production, unwanted public exposure, and lawsuits. All of these weaken the establishment and its company's culture leading to poor human capital building and a weak competitive advantage. Unconcious bias also affects the lives of individuals. HRM professionals needs to develop active educational programs not only to educate and train the employees within their organization but also train the trainer and themselves.

REFERENCES

Amalfe, C. A. (2013). The limitations on implicit bias testimony post-Dukes. *Gibons Law*. Retrieved from https://www.americanbar.org/content/dam/aba/events/labor_law/2013/03/employment_rightsresponsibilitiescommitteemidwintermeeting/1_amalfe.authcheckdam.pdf

Banaji, M. R. (2001). Implicit attitudes can be measured. In H. L. Roedeger III, J. S. Nairne, I. Neath, & A. Surprenant (Eds.), *The nature of remembering: Essays in honor of Robert G. Crowder* (pp. 117–150). Washington, DC: American Psychological Association.

Bar-Tal, D., Graumann, C. F., Kruglan, A. W., & Stroebe, W. (1989). *Stereotyping and Prejudice: Changing Conceptions.* New York, NY: Springer Series in Social Psychology.

Bertschinger, E. (2017, March 16). Preparing for unconscious bias education. *ICEblog MIT* Retrieved from: http://iceoblog.mit.edu/preparing-for-unconscious-bias-education.

Conaway, W., & Bethune, S. (2015). Implicit bias and first name stereotypes: What are the implications for online instruction?. *Online Learning, 19*(3), 162–178.

Francis, D. R. (2018, December 15). *Employers' replies to racial names.* Retrieved on December 15, 2018, from The National Bureau of Economic Research: https://www.nber.org/digest/sep03/w9873.html

Greenwald, A. G., & Banaji, M. R. (1995). Implicit social cognition: Attitudes, self-esteem, and stereotypes. *Psychological Review, 102*(1), 4–27.

Harvey, C. P., & Allard, J. M. (2015). *Understanding and managing diversity.* Hoboken, NJ: Pearson Education.

Howard, J. (2015, October 8). New study confirms depressing truth about names and racial bias. Scientist has "never been so disgusted" by his own data. *Huffpost*. Retrieved December 15, 2018, from https://www.huffingtonpost.com/entry/black-sounding-names-study_us_561697a5e4b0dbb8000d687f

Jackson, S. S. (2017). Moving beyond a single diversity class requirement: colleges begin to infuse diversity and inclusion into more courses to better prepare students for the workplace. *Insight Into Diversity, 89*(4), 22–25.

Lee, A. J. (2005). Unconscious bias theory in employment discrimination litigation. *Harvard Civil Rights-Civil Liberties Law Review, 40*(2), 481–503.

Merriam-Webster. (2018, 15 December). *Bias (noun).* Retrieved from https://www.merriam-webster.com/dictionary/bias

Reyes, S. (2016). *Unconscious bias. American Association for Access, Equity and Diversity*. Retrieved from http://www.aaaed.org/images/aaaed/National_Conference/2016/Wednesday/Unconscious%20Bias%20-Sandy%20Reyes.pdf.

Ross, H. (2008). Exploring unconcious bias. *Proven Strategies for Addressing Unconcious Bias in the Workplace., 2*(5), 1–8.

Teal, C. R., Gill, A., Green, A. R., & Crandall, S. (2012). Helping medical learners recognise and manage unconscious bias toward certain patient groups. *Medical Education, 46*(1), 80–88.

Tiku, N. (2018, March 18). *New lawsuit exposes Goggle's desperation to improve diversity.* Retrieved from Wired: https://www.wired.com/story/new-lawsuit-exposes-googles-desperation-to-improve-diversity.

Watts, P. (1987). Bias busting: diversity training in the workplace. *Management Review*, 51–54.

Williams, M., Dunlap, M., & McCandies. (n.d.). Keeping it real: Three black women educators discuss how we deal with student resistance to multicultural inclusion in the curriculum. *Transformations: The New Jersey Project Journal for Curriculum Transformation and Scholarship., 10*(2), 11–22.

CHAPTER 11

SOLVING THE "QUARTERBACK PROBLEM"

Using Psychological Assessment to Improve Selection Decisions in Professional Sports

Kenneth Yusko, Juliet Aiken, Harold Goldstein,
Charles Scherbaum, and Elliott Larson

Assessing talent and accurately predicting long-term performance of athletes is one of the hardest tasks in professional sports. It is easy to understand why. The professional athlete's job is so extreme in terms of both physical and psychological demands that past performance at lower levels, such as college, may not translate as well to the pro level. Add in an order of magnitude increase in the stakes involved, an even more hyper-competitive setting, and an environment where every on-field and off-field move is scrutinized more intensely than in lower levels by both the team's management and the public- and trying to accurately predict performance may start to seem hopeless. And even if one is effective in identifying successful players in such a challenging setting, even the best performer's career can be derailed in an instant with a single injury.

The job context and requirements are so daunting that Malcom Gladwell (2008) observes that, for some high stakes jobs, like NFL quarterback, it is almost

Human Resources Management Issues, Challenges and Trends:
"Now and Around the Corner", pages 213–227.

impossible to predict how candidates will perform before they are hired. In fact, this phenomenon has come to be known as the "quarterback problem." Although Gladwell implies that little can be done to address the issue, this chapter will show how the "quarterback problem" can be solved and success rates in recruiting and hiring athletes can be improved by leveraging the latest developments in psychological assessment.

PRECURSOR TO PSYCHOLOGICAL ASSESSMENT: THE RISE OF DATA ANALYTICS IN SPORTS

The sports industry has been using historical data to try to predict future performance for a long time. Human capital decisions in professional sports historically relied predominantly on information regarding players' relevant past performance and measures of their physical capability. Over time, teams became more sophisticated in exploiting this data. In the early 2000s, the Oakland A's front office more deliberately, rigorously, and comprehensively leveraged data on historic player performance than ever seen before. The thesis was simple and powerful: use data to develop unique insights that yield a real competitive advantage. By using this approach, small market teams could compete by finding value that others overlooked, thus avoiding a bidding war with wealthier teams, and effectively paying less for under-appreciated talent. This approach, documented in the book *Moneyball,* by Michael Lewis (2003) revolutionized talent decisions in sports.

However, while the *Moneyball* approach changed the face of talent evaluation in sports, it tended to focus on passive, pre-existing data that was generally available to everyone (including competitors) rather than on measuring the athletes in ways that could yield proprietary data and resulting insights. So, although there was a time when even the basic use of analytics in sports was enough to provide teams with an edge, as analytics have become more widespread in their use to select and train talent in sports, tools that once were cutting-edge now only give teams table stakes (c.f., Davenport, 2014).

The low-hanging fruit is rapidly disappearing and Billy Beane, one of the pioneers of the *Moneyball* approach, laments that the game is so much smarter now. Data are largely available to everyone and the teams are using it better. So much so that a dollar of *Moneyball* yesterday may only be worth fifty cents today (Depodesta, 2016). In other words, basic analytical tools and techniques using external data sources have become so widespread that these tools no longer provide teams with a decisive edge over their competition (Davenport, 2014).

Success now depends on either getting data no one else has or using the data better than everyone else, including the use of advanced techniques such as video, locational/biometric data, and gathering and using proprietary data directly from players (Davenport, 2014). Data gleaned from well done psychological assessments precisely fit this need.

PSYCHOLOGICAL ASSESSMENT IN SPORTS

The data provided by psychological assessment instruments have great potential to yield significant competitive advantage to teams willing and able to leverage it. Done well, psychological assessment can be a game changer, helping to identify better talent, develop players in a more targeted way, enhance player-team culture fit, promote position fit, predict tenure and performance trends over time, and even be used to mitigate injuries.

Psychological data have long been used in both sports and non-sports contexts to select talent. For example, a meta-analysis on the predictive validity of integrity found that integrity is valid in predicting both job performance and counterproductive behaviors on the job such as theft (Ones, Viswesvaran, & Schmidt, 1993). Further, self-efficacy, self-esteem, locus of control, and emotional stability likewise show validity in predicting both job performance and job satisfaction across a number of different contexts (Judge & Bono, 2001). Similarly, conscientiousness has been found to reliably predict job performance across a number of contexts (Barrick & Mount, 1991). These examples are exactly that—the literature on psychological testing in selection is deep, with a number of traits and characteristics identified as valid predictors of performance across a number of common job contexts.

However, in order to provide any advantage, psychological characteristics have to be defined or specified in a precise way, be measured accurately, and ultimately integrated into a decision framework that unlocks their value. Just calling something psychological assessment does not make it useful to the organization. That is what the rest of this chapter is about- creating competitive advantage through better understanding and application of psychological characteristics in a sports context.

In this chapter, we first describe key current challenges in psychological assessment in sports. Then, we review the psychological attributes and characteristics that can and should be assessed in a professional sports context. Then, we discuss how these attributes and characteristics can be measured (e.g., standardized testing, interviews, player observations and scouting "intel," etc.). We will then review how these results may be leveraged for different purposes (e.g., selection, training). And finally, we discuss how some of the lessons learned in sports analytics can be generalized to better understand strategic human resources decision making more broadly.

CURRENT CHALLENGES IN
PSYCHOLOGICAL ASSESSMENT IN SPORTS

Psychological assessment in sports has traditionally suffered from a number of challenges. While there are calls in the literature to clarify criteria for success (Staminirovic & Hanrahan, 2010), psychological assessment efforts have tended to yield inconsistent findings, and have typically relied on less than ideal datasets. For example, many studies pull exclusively from data gathered from second-hand internet sources (e.g., Lyons, Hoffman, & Michel, 2009), gather data only from one team (e.g., Solomon, Haase, & Kuhn, 2013), or use dichotomies that do not generalize (comparing medalists versus non-medalists, e.g., Kishore, 2016). Many studies also rely on small sample sizes (e.g., twelve first division basketball players were studied by Alemdaroglu, 2012).

Some studies also focus on physical predictors of draft pick or performance, rather than including a range of possible predictors including psychological predictors. For example, Solomon et al. (2013) found that top draft picks for the NFL score higher on visual motor speed and reaction time relative to roster NFL athletes. Likewise, Dhar (2011) found that collegiate statistics (such as receiving yards, touchdowns, etc.) explain a higher proportion of variance in draft rankings than do NFL combine results. Further, Robbins (2010) found that a physical test battery exhibited little to no relationship with draft success into the NFL. And, Sierer, Battaglini, Mihalik, Shields, and Tomasini (2008) found that time in the 40-yard dash, vertical jump, pro-agility shuttle, and bench press predict who is drafted into the NFL. Lyons, Hoffman, Michel, and Williams (2011) found that collegiate performance has a stronger relationship with NFL performance than physical tests in the combine. Similarly, DeMoss, Hindenach, Vos, and Weaver (2015) assessed physical performance indicators of NFL running backs using collegiate performance statistics and NFL combine statistics. And, while Pitts and Evans (2017) did assess the impact of cognitive ability on quarterback performance, the majority of the predictors they employed in their study were physical or college performance-related (e.g., percentage wins in the final season at University, BMI, height, completion percentage final season, etc.).

A few studies have assessed whether intelligence predicts success in professional sports, particularly professional football, but these yield mixed results, as discussed in the next section of this chapter. However, measuring psychological constructs, such as personality, is graining traction (e.g., conscientiousness, integrity, emotional intelligence, mental toughness) in the world of professional sports. In the next part of this chapter, we discuss a number of attributes that can potentially be measured for selection, talent development, on on-field decision making in professional sports, including measures of cognitive ability and personality characteristics.

WHAT IS BEING MEASURED— PSYCHOLOGICAL ASSESSMENT COMPETENCIES

Cognitive Ability

One characteristic with potential to predict an athlete's performance in professional sports is cognitive ability. Cognitive ability does predict a number of outcomes across a wide range of professions (Schmidt & Hunter, 1998). Cognitive ability has likewise been employed as a predictor in professional sports contexts, particular in terms of selecting talent into the NFL. During the combine, in which potential NFL draftees are run through a battery of physical and psychological tests for decades players completed the Wonderlic, a cognitive ability test. The Wonderlic is a standardized multiple-choice cognitive ability test initially created in 1936 to measure general cognitive ability in math, vocabulary, and reasoning. However, in this context, the Wonderlic—which has historically been the most common measure of cognitive ability for the NFL—has not been consistently found to predict player performance.

For example, although Pitts and Evans (2017) found that Wonderlic scores predicted NFL performance, Lyons, Hoffman and Michel (2009), Mirabile (2005), Welter (2013), Kuzmits and Adams (2008), and Berri and Simmons (2011) did not.

There are a number of reasons why traditional cognitive tests such as the Wonderlic may not consistently predict performance in this context. First, the content of the tests themselves may not fit the specific task faced by professional sports athletes. For example, traditional cognitive tests may include components assessing knowledge of math such as algebra as well as reading comprehension, competencies that do not typically translate well to tasks required in professional sports. Instead, professional sports may require specific abilities such as dynamic, visual problem solving; cognitive tests tapping into this form of cognitive ability may yield more consistent predictive results. Faubert (2013) for example found that professional athletes rapidly learn complex, dynamic scenes more so than non-athletes and non-professional athletes. In other words, professional sports requires a different form of cognitive ability, one that is more dynamic and spatially oriented. Other key cognitive abilities for professional athletes may include the ability to learn, thinking quickly, making mental errors, direct thinking, complex problem solving, and the ability to visualize plays in advance. Again, this is because the context for professional athletes is one in which they must think on their feet during a game and adjust their decision making accordingly.

Of course, the type of dynamic thinking required for success may depend on the sport. In football, for example, plays may need to be precisely memorized and then run with small adjustments. Other sports, such as soccer or basketball, may not provide players with as much opportunity or control to call specific plays in advance (relatively to football, that is). Thus, for these sports, it may be imperative that players are able to evaluate, re-evaluate, and play around angles that are changing and unfolding as the game moves forward.

One key principle is that you can't measure what you don't understand and can't define. Thus, it is critical to describe each trait in very specific, behavioral terms. It also helps to build an integrated taxonomy, which may vary by sport or team, rather than trying to rely on a few general dimensions (such as general cognitive ability) for all-purpose use. Once one knows what dimensions drives success, then it is possible to focus on the very best way to measure these constructs.

An example of the above is a comprehensive project by the National Football League to match specific facets of cognitive ability to the exact type of cognitive performance behavior desired. In 2012, the NFL adopted a league-wide testing process that focused on measuring very specific aspects of cognitive ability that matched the type of behavior on the field (Yusko, Goldstein, and Scherbaum 2018). The assessment, called the NFL Player Assessment Test (PAT) relied on a custom job analysis approach involving a number of executives, GMs, and former players from across the league to identify specific cognitive ability dimensions that were particularly relevant to the game of football such as:

- Mental Speed
- Ability to Learn
- Mental Error Resistance
- Complex Reasoning
- Direct Thinking
- Visual Processing

Thus, instead of relying on a general test of cognitive ability to predict potentially widely divergent cognitive performance behaviors, the process identified specific cognitive abilities, including:

1.   The ability to learn to be able to quickly absorb new plays, improve one's understanding of the game, and, if necessary, master multiple positions quickly;
2.   Mental error resistance to minimize mental errors and breakdowns on the field, particularly when under pressure;
3.   Spatial visualization in order to better see the field and grasp the locations of players in relation to each other;
4.   The ability to make rapid decisions in order to make good decisions under speeded game conditions;
5.   Direct thinking in order to execute set plays as flawlessly as possible; and,
6.   Ambiguous thinking to better deal with breakdowns in plays and perform under conditions of uncertainty.

Several thousand prospective players were tested over the last six years using this process at the NFL combine in Indianapolis and teams from across the league provided detailed performance data on many of the players who were drafted. Assessing such specific cognitive abilities using the latest intelligence assessment technology resulted in the ability to predict a variety of criteria including coaches' performance ratings, on-field performance, and higher-level criteria such as pro-bowl selections.

Personality

In addition to cognitive ability, certain personality traits may also be useful for predicting performance in professional sports (c.f., Stanimirovic & Hanrahan,

2010). For example, Stanimirovic and Hanrahan (2010) theorize that emotional intelligence, integrity, and conscientiousness, among other characteristics, might predict success in a professional sports context. Additionally, mental toughness is likewise seen as key to success in professional sports (Connaughton, Hanton, Jones, & Wadey, 2008; Jones, Hanton, & Connaughton, 2002, 2007). Further, emotional intelligence, or the ability to understand and regulate ones' own as well as others' emotions, may likewise be critical to success in sports (Meyer & Fletcher, 2007; Perlini & Halverson, 2006; Zizzi, Deaner, & Hirschhorn, 2003). Further, Gee, Marshall, and King (2010) found that a composite score for competitiveness, need for achievement, independence potential, confidence, and coachability predicted goals, assists, and points scored by professional hockey players.

In addition to the personality traits that have been discussed above, several other key traits and characteristics may also drive success in a sports context. For example, an ability to focus on teamwork and on coordinating with others (such as on the offensive line in football) would likely lead to success in professional sports, where teamwork is essential for ensuring that plays are executed successfully. Additionally, due to the importance of consistency, dependability would be likely to contribute to success. Further, since professional sports create such a high pressure environment, the ability to handle stress is likely to differentiate successful professional players from less successful players.

Beyond personality, needs and motives may also play a role in predicting success in sports. Specifically, how do professional players approach each game? What motivates them? Motives may vary player to player. For example, some may play to satisfy a need to compete, whereas others may play to achieve, and others still just for the love of the game. Consistent with this expectation, Bois, Sarrazin, Southon, and Boiche (2009), for example, noted that high achieving professional male golfers had higher performance approach and lower performance avoidance goal motivations than lower achieving golfers.

Finally, a player's learning style may also affect his/her success. Professional sports players must learn dynamically and visually. Thus, how athletes learn best (e.g., learning strategies, style, preferred way through which to receive information, preferred learning context, and learning orientation) may therefore drive success in professional sports.

As with their approach to cognitive ability described above, the NFL's Player Assessment Test (PAT) used its custom job analysis approach to identify a comprehensive set of personality dimensions that could better predict the type of behaviors that teams valued on and off the field. Such personality dimensions included:

- Team Focus
- Dependability
- Mental Toughness
- Grit

- Stress Tolerance
- Decisions Under Stress
- Preparedness
- Leadership
- Self-Control
- Emotional Stability

In addition to personality variables, a set of needs/motives were measured, including:

- Need to Compete
- Need to Achieve
- Need to Play

Similar to the results described above regarding the use of specific cognitive abilities, a focus on carefully defined personality attributes measured with the latest assessment technology resulted in the ability to predict critical criteria including coaches' performance ratings, on-field performance, penalties, injuries, off-field behavior such as arrests, and pro-bowl selections.

WAYS TO CONDUCT PSYCHOLOGICAL ASSESSMENT

Once the critical psychological characteristics required for success are specified they can be measured using a variety of techniques. The most basic technique for measuring these traits is a standardized test, for example, a computerized multiple choice test that provides insight into how players typically think and react. Computer-based testing is efficient and offers a number of advantages, including a computer-adaptive testing (CAT) approach, dynamic or "deep" task items, multimedia stimuli, speeded options, integration of eye-tracking tasks (especially interesting for testing in sports), an immediate scoring option that can be instantly tied to development suggestions, and, of course, a standardized format.

However, there are a variety of other ways to gather information on psychological attributes including: interviews, player observations/scouting intel, and past performance data. Interviewing players provides potentially richer, narrative feedback on who players are than standardized tests do. Interviewing in a sports setting has historically relied on a clinical approach. With clinical interviews, questions tend not to be as standardized across athletes, as individual questions are typically customized to each player's experience. With this design, clinical interviews provide rich data on each individual athlete, but may not do so in a way that facilitates comparison across athletes as easily and often yield primarily narrative, rather than quantitative, results. So, while clinical interviews may be interesting, and may provide useful information, they can also be challenging to integrate into a system-wide selection process. Thus, they can be an excellent addition to the process but may not be as effective as a stand-alone, sole approach to psychological assessment.

Structured interviews may be employed to provide more rigor and consistent information about each player. Structured interviews typically both use the same set of questions across players, and have clear rules around how to evaluate, score, and quantify the quality of individual responses. Thus, structured interview responses are typically easier to quantify than clinical interview responses. However, structured interviews are not without disadvantages. Specifically, many players, particularly elite talent, may have some prior experience with structured interviews or someone to coach them through the process. Thus, they may be prepared to answer many typical structured interview questions. In other words, structured interviews may not yield unfiltered and unrehearsed responses from players simply because the questions can often be anticipated and are relatively straightforward to prepare for.

So, clinical interviews can be challenging to quantify and structured interviews can be easy to prepare for. One creative technique that might prove useful in capturing rich, honest, and measurable data on athletes, is a structured picture interview (Yusko, Goldstein, & Scherbaum, 2018). Specifically, players are presented with a series of pictures and asked to describe what each picture displays. The potential themes contained in each picture are laid out in advance and a series of probes are constructed for each. When the player looks at the picture and independently articulates a particular theme, the attendant probes are asked to flush out the emergent theme. Response guides should also be prepared in advance to cover any potential emergent themes/responses. The structured picture interview approach seems to be effective at getting past the player's defenses and encourages the athlete to provide a rich, thoughtful response instead of a thin canned reply. In addition to the structured question component, by piecing together multiple responses to the sets of pictures, trained psychologists can also derive deeper clinical insights into the candidate potentially making this approach both rich and standardized.

Player observations and other scouting "intel" can be a productive source of psychological data. Typically the domain of scouts, the evaluator may make inferences about psychological characteristics while watching athletes play or interact in a social setting such as the locker room or in a press conference. An obvious example is making a judgment on, say, self-control or emotional stability, when the athlete faces adversity on the field through a perceived bad call by the referee or a perceived provocation from the opposition. One concern with this approach is that typically scouts are former players or others close to the game and do not have any formal training on drawing psychological inferences. So, we may hear them talk about a "high character" player after only a brief, informal chat with the player's coach, family, or significant other. In addition, similar to the insights gleaned through clinical interviews, scouts often produce only narrative (vs. quantitative) data regarding psychological characteristics. Providing them training or partnering with scouts on both what psychological characteristics are important for his/her sport and team and how to make ratings that can be plugged into an overall rating system would go a long way to professionalizing the process and making the data more usable and valuable.

Drawing inferences on psychological attributes based on past performance data is a particularly fascinating possibility. Think of being able to accurately gauge how patient a player is from analyzing whether or not he/she swings given the pitch count and/or type of pitch. Currently, linking psychological insights to performance statistics is a largely untapped area. When it is done, the process tends to be dominated by "gut feel" and is not typically guided by formal research or a structured rating system. As the big data approach evolves and psychological measurement technology improves, the possibility of designing and validating a comprehensive statistics-based psychological measurement system is becoming a real possibility.

THE USES OF PSYCHOLOGICAL ASSESSMENT

As discussed above, psychological assessment can be useful in professional sports to identify the best talent and thus contribute meaningfully to the selection process. An additional benefit in terms of selection is the use of psychological assessment, particularly regarding personality, to help determine how well a player will fit a team's culture by matching the player's values and preferences to the values that define the culture. This is an important consideration beyond positional or on-field talent and is particularly valued by teams that have a well-defined "way" of doing things.

In addition to facilitating effective selection decisions, psychological assessment can also yield excellent insights into how to help players develop. For example, knowing how quickly players learn has great implications for how much information, say on new plays, one can provide in a given sitting. Watching some players attend a session installing a new set of plays can be akin to watching someone drink water out of a fire hose. So, players who need extra time to digest information may need to do some extra preparation or have things explained during or after the session.

Similarly, having an early warning signal that a player does not deal well with pressure or make good decisions under stress may allow the coaching staff to focus on extra drills on what to do when a play breaks down or using film to walk through the contingencies before they are encountered in a game situation. Simply put, knowing a player's psychological makeup allows for providing developmental opportunities in a more targeted, efficient way.

Understanding players' psychological characteristics can also improve a team's in-game coaching effectiveness, for example, regarding the use of situational analytics. Situational analytics is a process where, for example, the players know that when an opposing team lines up a certain way, 80% of the time they throw a pass in a particular direction. This allows the player to better anticipate where to go or to get a slight edge by leaning a certain way. Coaches constantly rue the inability of players to master this skill. Having a better, more accurate assessment of a player's cognitive ability to recognize formations, match them up to previous data, and make proper adjustments allows coaches to make decisions, such as deciding how much freedom to give players to "freelance," how much information to provide before a play, whether to call a timeout to discuss the play, whether to appoint a "captain" who can direct players around him, and whether to substitute certain players who grasp the situation better into or out of the game.

Other emerging uses of psychological data include improving a team's ability to predict a player's career performance trends. For example, players with great physical talent but limited capacity to learn and no motivation to improve may be able to play well initially but be "capped" in their ability to grow and develop over time. This has great implications, for example, whether or not to provide a second contract and/or how much the contract should be worth. Related to the above, a final emerging use of psychological data is forecasting "survivability." For example, will a talented player who has achieved his financial goals walk away from the game at the peak of his/her career? Will the love of the game keep a player contributing for as long as possible? These are questions into which a good psychological assessment can provide valuable insights.

IMPLICATIONS FOR HUMAN RESOURCES IN GENERAL

In many ways, sports-focused psychological assessment shares the same implications and processes with complex, high value jobs outside of sports in the public or private sector (e.g., executive, astronaut, teacher, etc.). For example, regardless of whether psychological assessment is being used in a sports or non-sports context, knowing how to speak the decision makers' language is essential for demonstrating value and influencing organizational (or team!) decisions. It is very common to hear a sports GM talk about how the psychologist or analytics specialist running the psychological assessment is the smartest person in the room, yet they have no impact because no one can understand them. It is imperative for anyone engaged in psychological assessment to avoid overly technical language and jargon and frame their insights using concepts and words that resonate with management. This will result in the information gleaned from psychological insights being translated into actual policies for selection, training, and decision making.

Psychological assessment in sports has a number of other implications for human resources. First, the need to focus on a rich variety of both predictors and criteria is essential in all human resource contexts. Performance is not just hours worked, or the quantity of output—within traditional organizations, tenure, patterns of performance over time (such as taking on progressively responsible roles), prosocial behavior, contributing to intellectual property, engaging in organizational citizenship behaviors, and enhancing the organization's brand may also be desirable outcomes to consider. Additionally, it is critical to think about performance on different levels. Not all outcomes operate on the individual employee/

player level. Some outcomes are at the team/organization level. For example, sports teams may care about winning more than individual player achievements, and teams in more traditional organizations may care about meeting project deadlines or delivering an excellent product or service more than the achievements of an individual employee.

In many ways, traditional HR typically employs a relatively limited set of possible selection criteria, with intelligence tests and personality being paramount in most selection contexts. Just as professionals in sports analytics are diversifying the criteria used to predict performance, traditional HR should likewise diversify their selection criteria. First, as opposed to targeting general cognitive ability, organizations should carefully think through and specify the types of cognitive ability most needed for success in their organization, and in a given role, and tailor cognitive ability tests to those specific needs. And, HR should go beyond assessing cognitive ability and personality and also consider the potential impact of drivers/motives, learning styles, and other characteristics that may enhance success in an organization.

As discussed early in this chapter, sports analytics historically focused on passive (i.e., publicly or widely available) data collection of existing information. Similarly, typical HR analytics tends to pull primarily from historic and passive data, such as information naturally collected in a Human Resources Information System. In the future, HR should take more of a proactive approach to data collection. Specifically, HR should think about how to gather information from employees using surveys, focus groups, and interviews. When doing so, however, organizations should be careful to ensure that they do not exhaust employees with constant requests for information. Repeated requests for input will eventually exhaust the employee base, making them less likely to want to engage. Organizations should therefore take a measured and strategic approach to collecting data on their employee base, using surveys and interviews to capture only the most essential information from employees as part of an integrated and forward-looking data collection plan.

Further, it is important for all organizations to think about criteria that not only narrowly relate to the job but also to greater success of the organization and criteria related to others' perceptions of the organization and the organization's involvement in the community. In professional sports, this may mean developing accurate predictors of enhanced uniform or athletic equipment sales, positive behavior such as service to the community, and/or negative behavior such as fights, arrests, suspensions, fines and other behavior with negative implications for the team and league branding. In more traditional organizations, this may mean developing predictors of activities such as developing new products or services, providing service to the community, helping to support the organization's culture, fostering diversity, supporting the organization's efforts around environmental sustainability, etc. In each case, organizations must think more broadly about what success looks like—individual job performance by itself is no longer sufficient.

Additionally, as we've discussed in this chapter, professional sports prediction by nature focuses on predicting top performers. Typical predictive work in organizations looks for linear relationships between criteria and outcomes. It may be helpful for organizations to take a page from the book of professional sports—how can they identify not only better and worse performers, but the absolute top performers? And then, how can these performers be tapped best and developed to attain peak performance? What makes an employee good may in fact be somewhat different from what makes an employee excellent. Taking an "elite performer" approach to analytics may shift how organizations view criteria as well as their analytical approaches. For example, it may even be helpful for organizations to develop profiles of top performers (using cluster analysis, for example), rather than considering each performance variable independent of one another.

Sports analytics focuses in part on predicting performance for different roles (e.g., quarterbacks, defensive linemen), as different roles are assumed to require different skills. To some extent traditional organizations typically customize selection to different jobs. However, HR can still improve in terms of determining how to predict performance in different roles on a team, even if those roles are being performed by people with the same general job description. At the same time, HR must be careful to ensure that selecting into different roles does not interfere with the fairness, appropriateness, or validity of any given test in order to ensure that the best candidates are hired through the selection process and protect against adverse impact.

Finally, psychological assessment specialists in any HR group need to think not only about measurement and analyses but also about partnering more strategically to accomplish the goals of the business. As strategic partners, analytics/ psychological assessment specialists need to be able to translate data into big-picture initiatives, to generate buy-in for ideas and add increasing value to their organizations.

REFERENCES

Alemdaroglu, U. (2012). The relationship between muscle strength, anaerobic performance, agility, sprint agility and vertical jump performance in professional basketball players. *Journal of Human Kinetics, 31*(1), 99–106.

Barrick, M. R., & Mount, M. K. (1991). The big five personality dimensions and job performance: A meta-analysis. *Personnel Psychology, 44*(1), 1–26.

Berri, D. J., & Simmons, R. (2011). Catching a draft: On the process of selecting quarterbacks in the National Football League amateur draft. *Journal of Productivity Analysis, 35*, 37–49.

Bois, J. E., Sarrazin, P. G., Southon, J., & Boiche, J. C. S. (2009). Psychological characteristics and their relation to performance in professional golfers. *Sport Psychologist, 23*, 252–270.

Connaughton, D., Hanton, S., Jones, G., & Wadley, R. (2008). Mental toughness research: Key issues in this area. *International Journal of Sports Psychology, 39*(3), 192–204.

Davenport, T. H. (2014). Analytics in sports: The new science of winning. *International Institute for Analytics.* Retrieved from https://www.sas.com/en_us/whitepapers/iia-analytics-in-sports-106993.html

DeMoss, A., Hindenach, K., Vos, Z., & Weaver, C. (2015). *What does it take? Deciphering performance indicators of NFL running backs through examination of collegiate performance and NFL combine results.* Retrieved from https://repository.usfca.edu/cgi/viewcontent.cgi?article=1058&context=artsci_stu

Depodesta, P. (2016). *Moneyball reunion.* Panel presentation at the 10th Annual MIT Sloan Sports Analytics Conference. Boston, MA.

Dhar, A. (2011). *Drafting NFL wide receivers: Hit or miss?* Retrieved from https://www.stat.berkeley.edu/~aldous/157/Old_Projects/Amrit_Dhar.pdf

Faubert, J. (2013). Professional athletes have extraordinary skills for rapidly learning complex and neutral dynamic visual scenes. *Scientific Reports, 3,* 1–3.

Gee, C. J., Marshall, J. C., & King, J. F. (2010). Should coaches use personality assessments in the talent identification process? A 15 year predictive study on professional hockey players. *International Journal of Coaching Science, 4*(1), 25–34.

Gladwell, M. (2008). Most likely to succeed: How do we hire when we can't tell who's right for the job? *New Yorker Magazine,* December 15 issue. Retrieved from https://www.newyorker.com/magazine/2008/12/15/most-likely-to-succeed-malcolm-gladwell

Jones, G., Hanton, S., & Connaughton, D. (2002). What is this thing called mental toughness? An investigation with elite performers. *Journal of Applied Sport Psychology, 14*(3), 211–224.

Jones, G., Hanton, S., & Connaughton, D. (2007). A framework of mental toughness in the world's best performers. *The Sport Psychologist, 21*(2), 243–264.

Judge, T. A., & Bono, J. E. (2001). Relationship of core self-evaluation traits—Self-esteem, generalized self-efficacy, locus of control, and emotional stability—With job satisfaction and job performance: A meta-analysis. *Journal of Applied Psychology, 86*(1), 80–92.

Kuzmits, F. E., & Adams, A. J. (2008). The NFL combine: Does it predict performance in the National Football League? *Journal of Strength and Conditioning Research, 22(6),* 1721–1727.

Lewis, M. (2003). *Moneyball: The art of winning an unfair game.* New York, NY: W.W. Norton & Company.

Lyons, B. D., Hoffman, B. J., & Michel, J. W. (2009). Not much more than g? An examination of the impact of intelligence on NFL performance. *Human Performance, 22,* 225–245.

Lyons, B. D., Hoffman, B. J., Michel, J. W., & Williams, K. J. (2011). On the predictive efficiency of past performance and physical ability: The case of the National Football League. *Human Performance, 24,* 158–172.

Meyer, B. B., & Fletcher, T. B. (2007). Emotional intelligence: A theoretical overview and implications for research and professional practice in sport psychology. *Journal of Applied Sport Psychology, 19*(1), 1–15.

Mirabile, M.P. (2005). Intelligence and football: Testing for differentials in collegiate quarterback passing performance and NFL compensation. *The Sport Journal.* Retrieved from https://thesportjournal.org/article/intelligence-and-football-testing-for-differentials-in-collegiate-quarterback-passing-performance-and-nfl-compensation/

Ones, D. S., Viswesvaran, C., & Schmidt, F. L. (1993). Comprehensive meta-analysis of integrity test validities: Findings and implications for personnel selection and theories of job performance. *Journal of Applied Psychology, 78*(4), 679–703.

Perlini, A. H., & Halverson, T. R. (2006). Emotional intelligence in the National Hockey League. *Canadian Journal of Behavioral Science, 38*(2), 109–119.

Pitts, J. D., & Evans, B. (2017). Evidence on the importance of cognitive ability tests for NFL quarterbacks: What are the relationships among Wonderlic scores, draft positions and NFL performance outcomes? *Applied Economics, 50*(27), 1–10.

Robbins, D. W. (2010). The National Football League (NFL) combine: Does normalized data better predict performance in the NFL draft? *Journal of Strength and Conditioning Research, 24,* 2888–2899.

Schmidt, F. L., & Hunter, J. E. (1998). The validity and utility of selection methods in personnel psychology: Practical and theoretical implications of 85 years of research findings. *Psychological Bulletin, 124*(2), 262–274.

Sierer, S. P., Battaglini, C. L., Mihalik, J. P., Shields, E. W., & Tomasini, N. T. (2008). The national football league combine: Performance differences between drafted and nondrafted players entering the 2004 and 2005 drafts. *Journal of Strength and Conditioning Research, 22*(1), 6–12.

Solomon, G. S., Haase, R. F., & Kuhn, A. (2013). The relationship among neurocognitive performances and biopsychosocial characteristics of elite National Football League draft picks: An exploratory investigation. *Archives of Clinical Neuropsychology, 28*(1), 9–20.

Stanimirovic, R., & Hanrahan, S. (2010). Psychological predictors of job performance and career success in professional sport. *Sport Science Review, 19*(1–2), 211–239.

Welter, J. C. (2013). *The wonderlic classic cognitive ability test as a measure of player selection and success for quarterbacks in the national football league.* Retrieved from https://pqdtopen.proquest.com/doc/1315240876.html?FMT=ABS

Yusko, K., Goldstein, H., & Scherbaum (2018). Moneyball plus. *Predicting player performance using psychological assessments: A comparison across the major sports.* Paper presented at the 12th Annual MIT Sloan Sports Analytics Conference. Boston, MA.

Zizzi, S., Deaner, H., & Hirschhorn, D. (2003). The relationship between emotional intelligence and performance among college basketball players. *Journal of Applied Sport Psychology, 15(3),* 262–269.

CHAPTER 12

HUMAN RESOURCES CERTIFICATION

Trends and Acceptance in Industry

Jonathan Shoemaker, Sheri Bias, Sean Gibbons,
Henry Adu, and Nicole Hawkins

INTRODUCTION

Certification lends credibility to an individual showing that there has been a mastery of a body of knowledge in a particular realm. This seems to be an important component of demonstrating professionalism in many industries, and many certifications have evolved that allow individuals to obtain a level demonstrated competence within a particular field. This research focuses on the various human resources certifications offered by credentialing bodies in the human resources industry, namely HRCI and SHRM. Across multiple industries and in order to produce a skilled and educated labor force, specific industry focused and recognized certifications and credentials have been developed.

Germaine to credentialing is to highlight the important relationship between learning the knowledge, skills and abilities necessary to successfully obtain and perform jobs within specific industries. The credentialing process also helps to

Human Resources Management Issues, Challenges and Trends:
"Now and Around the Corner", pages 229–243.
Copyright © 2019 by Information Age Publishing
229

provide a foundation for curriculum development within education and career institutions; that is, it establishes a career and educational pathway for those career focused disciplines from high school, two- and four-year higher education institutions. After all, formal education is thought to be a direct link to gainful employment. In order to fully explore this topic of relevance of credentialing, a brief history on HR certifications will lay the foundation for further understanding.

HISTORY OF HR CERTIFICATION

Certifying professionals on the body of knowledge is not new. In fact, the Human Resources Certification Institute (HRCI), previously called American Society of Personnel Administration (ASPA) was a predecessor to the current Society for Human Resource Management (SHRM) gave birth to the idea of credentialing in 1973. The first credentialing exam was administered in 1976 through the ASPA Accreditation Institute (AAI) which has subsequently evolved into a variety of credentialing exams now given by HRCI. HRCI has been known to be the leader in the industry for HR professional credentialing and touts having awarded certification to hundreds of thousands of HR professionals (HRCI History, 2018). The credentials that an individual can achieve through HRCI are:

- Associate Professional in Human Resources (aPHR)
- Associate Professional in Human Resources International (aPHRi)
- Professional in Human Resources (PHR)
- Professional in Human Resources California (PHRca)
- Professional in Human Resources International (PHRi)
- Senior Professional in Human Resources (SPHR)
- Senior Professional in Human Resources International (SPHRi)
- Global Professional in Human Resources (GPHR) (About HRCI, 2018)

However, in 2014, SHRM decided to undertake offering its own certifications. The reasons behind the split between HRCI and SHRM will be further discussed in the next section. SHRM offers two certifications: Certified Professional (SHRM-CP) and Senior Certified Professional (SHRM-SCP) (About SHRM Certification, 2018). One key difference between the exams offered by HRCI and those offered by SHRM are the situational judgment items (SJIs) tested on the SHRM exams. Beyond the rote memorization of knowledge items, the SHRM exam uses SJIs to "assess candidates' judgment and decision-making skills, which are not easily measured using tradition knowledge-based questions" (Description of Exams, 2018, p. 1). Essentially, this means that these types of exam questions have a best and then next best answer versus only having one right answer to the hypothetical questions asked.

In 2016, SHRM examinations met the standards for accreditation by the Buros Center for Testing. The Buros Center for Testing is known for certifying the testing protocols, processes, and policies for other examination such as licensure exams, educational achievement exams, and admissions testing for universities (Buros Center for Testing, 2018). Certification from Buros required extensive review of SHRM's testing infrastructure, methodology, and policy including site visits to various partners administering the examinations. HRCI examinations are accredited by the National Commission for Certifying Agencies (NCCA). The NCAA was one of the first to certify credentialing exams in the 1970s, and the standards for certification for an examination are applicable across the board to all professions and industries (NCCA Accreditation, 2018).

WHY THE SPLIT? HRCI V. SHRM

The bottom line on what some have called a rather bitter divorce between these entities is that SHRM wanted to embed a new competency model into the HRCI infrastructure of materials (SHRM Competency Model, 2018). This met with resistance from HRCI as the stance of HRCI was that the credentialing exam should be independent from SHRM. Based on this resistance from HRCI, SHRM decided to pursue certification examinations and providing credentials based on this new competency model outside of the relationship with HRCI; thereby, cutting ties with HRCI on certification efforts.

According to Berman-Gorvine (2014), the rationale provided by SHRM's CEO that for creating these new certifications was:

- To establish certifications that are highly relevant to employers and meets the needs of business;
- To grow certification in the HR profession, which has currently plateaued in the U.S. at round 12 percent; and
- To elevate the profession and create a universal standard for HR, (p. 1).

Essentially, the war between these two factions has created a lot of confusion in the marketplace regarding certifications. Those holding the HRCI certifications were afforded the opportunity to achieve the SHRM certifications by taking a web-training for the similar level of certification without having to actually take the SHRM exam to gain the credential. It has been noted that HRCI has experienced a slight decrease in the number of individuals recertifying for those exams (Prokopeak, 2015). Therefore, it is still to be determined the overall impact of this split between HRCI and SHRM on the marketplace for credentialing HR professionals as these organizations seemingly have no plans to work together in the future.

WHAT DO EMPLOYERS WANT IN
CREDENTIALS FROM CANDIDATES?

Based on personal experiences of the authors, as well as conversations with industry professionals, we sought to further understand if the marketplace preferred the HRCI certifications that had been in existence for many years, or the newly offering SHRM certifications when advertising to fill open positions in human resources. The information that follows details the hypotheses, research methodology, results, and discussion on the findings toward a point of inquiry on preferences for certifications.

Hypotheses

Hypothesis 1: Professional certification is an important qualification for many jobs and available human resource certifications are generally applicable nationwide (exception for California). Thus, a significant majority of human resource industry job postings will require or prefer some form of HR certification.

Hypothesis 2: While the professional certifications available through HRCI have been around longer, SHRM is more generally recognized in the HR industry as a source of human resource information and standards. Thus, when a job posting states that HR certification is required or preferred, equal consideration will be given to HRCI and SHRM certifications.

Hypothesis 3: Because of the distinct and substantial impact of employment laws and human resource regulations unique to in the State of California compared to the rest of the United States, significantly more job postings for positions in California labor markets will require or prefer some form of HR certification than other US markets.

Hypothesis 4: Advanced positions require more evidence of ability and higher qualifications. Thus, job postings that require or prefer a higher "years of experience" qualification will be more likely to require or prefer a professional certification in addition.

Methods

Investigators from Saint Leo University used LinkedIn.com's job search engine as the primary source of information. LinkedIn is a business-oriented social networking site (SNS) with over 400 million users as of 2015 (LinkedIn Blog, 2015). Members of LinkedIn can promote their skills, reach out to job recruiters by using the built-in instant messenger client, and search for job postings uploaded to the website by various organizations. LinkedIn's large user base and ease of use made it a good choice as the primary source of data for the research.

Initially, the geographic areas selected were concentrated on where Saint Leo University has satellite campuses. Saint Leo University offers on-ground courses in the Tampa-Saint Petersburg, FL market, Richmond, VA; Greater Atlanta and Norfolk, VA. The researchers also decided to include the Washington, D.C. metropolitan area (including Northern Virginia and Southern Maryland), reasoning that there would be significant awareness of these organizations in this labor market as this is the international headquarters of both the Society for Human Resource Management and the Human Resources Certification Institute. The researchers added Greater Los Angeles to address the fact that both certifying bodies offer a separate credential for HR professionals in the state of California because of the number of different state employment laws.

The researchers assume that all postings were legitimate and were listed by reputable companies, and that each job description was in full alignment with the requirements of the recruiter. Job postings in each market were searched using a combination of typing "human resources" in search box and checking "human resources" on the optional Job Function filter. This extra measure prevented jobs unrelated to human resources, but which mentioned the term (e.g., "for more information, contact **human resources**") from populating.

As expected, several of the locations searched had thousands of job postings. The most recent 100 job postings were used in each location. Two of the locations offered less than one hundred positions using this search criteria.

The following data were extracted from the job postings:

- Company
- Location
- Job title
- Years of experience required
- Years of experience preferred
- Degree(s) required
- Degree(s) preferred
- Certification(s) required
- Certification(s) preferred
- Level of position (coded as: Entry, Middle Management, or VP/Exec)

The data collected was coded into a Microsoft Excel spreadsheet. Each data point was entered exactly as it appeared in the LinkedIn description to minimize misinterpretation. Thus, three years of experience is coded as "3," but three-to-five years of experience is coded as "3 to 5." If a category was not applicable it was coded N/A. For example, if no certifications were required, Certification(s) Required was coded N/A. All LinkedIn postings were archived, and dates of coding were provided in case the posting was altered or deleted from LinkedIn. The researchers used Microsoft Excel's COUNTIF function to count the number of occurrences and created histograms based on the findings.

Results

A total of 483 job postings across the 6 markets were analyzed. The breakdown of postings per market are provided in table 12.1.

The Norfolk, VA and Richmond, VA markets included less than 100 cases as these markets are smaller and fewer cases were available that fit the research criteria at the time the data were collected.

Markets were analyzed overall and individually. It appears that none of the markets analyzed prioritized human resources certification, either as a required

TABLE 12.1. Job Postings Analyzed by Market

Market	Count of Job Postings
Norfolk, VA	32
Richmond, VA	51
Washington, DC	101
Greater Atlanta, GA	100
Tampa/St. Petersburg, FL	100
Los Angeles, CA	100

TABLE 12.2. Certification Required and Preferred by Market

Market	Certification Required	Certification Preferred
Norfolk, VA*	6 (19%)	0 (0%)
Richmond, VA	3 (6%)	14 (27%)
Tampa / St. Petersburg FL	0 (0%)	22 (22%)
Washington, DC	0 (0%)	37 (37%)
Greater Atlanta, GA	3 (3%)	23 (23%)
Los Angeles, CA	0 (0%)	23 (23%)
Overall	12 (2.5%)	119 (25%)

or preferred hiring criterion. Required certification was far from predominant in any market; in fact, in three of the six markets, 0 out of 100 or more job postings *required* job applicants to be certified. *Preference* for certification was relatively low and ranged from 0% to 37%, with the highest prevalence of preference for certification in the Washington, DC market (coincidentally the headquarters of both SHRM and HRCI). The number and percentage of required and preferred certification by market is presented in Table 12.2.

The Norfolk, VA market was an interesting outlier in that 19% of the job postings analyzed did require certification, while zero job postings stated that certification was preferred. The employers whose postings included required certification came from multiple industries including healthcare, administrative consulting, manufacturing, service, and others with no clear pattern as to why they might require certification. This finding may also be a result of the smaller sample size in the Norfolk, VA market.

Ultimately, none of the markets analyzed predominantly required or preferred certification. Thus, Hypothesis 1 that a majority of job postings would require or prefer human resources certification was ***not supported***.

The variety of certifications that were mentioned in job postings included certifications through SHRM, through HRCI, and several compensation- or benefits-related certifications from smaller certifying bodies including:

- ADP, Inc. Certified Payroll Specialist (CPS)
- American Payroll Association Fundamental Payroll Certification (FPC) and Certified Payroll Professional (CPP)
- International Foundation of Employee Benefits Plans Certified Employee Benefits Specialist (CEBS)
- WorldatWork Certified Benefits Professional (CBP) and Certified Compensation Professional (CCP)

While these certifications are respected in the human resources industry, they have a significantly smaller membership and were thus an unexpected artifact of the data collected. Figure 12.1 illustrates the frequency of each certification. A small number of the job postings did not mention a specific certification but instead mentioned one or both main human resource certifying organizations (SHRM or HRCI).

A chi-square test was performed to determine whether there were differences in likelihood to prefer or require certification from HRCI or SHRM. After consolidating the data, it is clear that (among the organizations that included mention of any certification in their job postings), requirement or preference for certifications from HRCI (including "HRCI," SPHR, and PHR) are significantly more prevalent

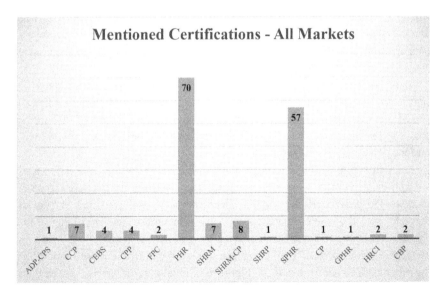

FIGURE 12.1. Frequency of Preferred or Required Certification

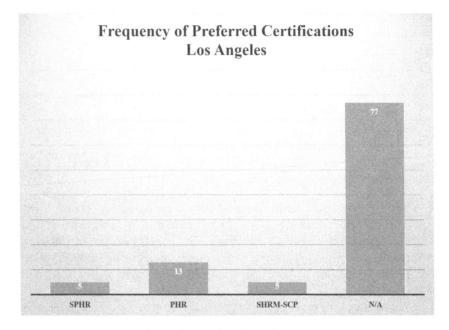

FIGURE 12.2. Los Angeles Market Preferred Certifications

than those from SHRM (including "SHRM," SHRM-CP, and "CP"), χ^2 (1, N=146) = 87.46, $p < .01$). Thus, Hypothesis 2, that both HRCI and SHRM certifications would be required or preferred with equal consideration was *not supported*. Note that the frequency of certifications is greater than the total number of employers who mentioned certification in their job postings as several employers mentioned more than one type of certification in the same posting.

The State of California has significantly more employment laws than other states and even the federal government (Letizia, 2018). Thus, both bodies (HRCI and SHRM) offer or will soon offer certifications that are specific to California. It stands to reason that job postings in California would more frequently require or prefer candidates with human resources certifications.

A chi-square test was performed to determine whether there were differences in likelihood to prefer or require certification in Los Angeles compared to other markets. The data did not support that conclusion; job postings in the Los Angeles market required or preferred certification at a rate almost identical to that of the Greater Atlanta and Tampa/St. Petersburg markets, χ^2 (2, N=300) = .038, *n.s.* In fact, the Washington, DC market rate for preferred certification was higher than the other markets (see Table 12.2). Figure 12.2 illustrates Preferred Certifications in Los Angeles (0 job postings requested Required Certification). Thus, Hypothesis 3 is *not supported*.

Finally, all markets were analyzed to determine whether job postings for more advanced positions were more likely to seek Preferred or Require Certification. An "advanced position" was operationalized to include conditions of either 1) more required or preferred "years of experience" qualification and/or 2) described in the job posting as being at the Mid-Career or the Executive/VP level, instead of an Entry Level position.

The first condition was analyzed by categorizing the Required Years of Experience variable into four groups; values ranged from "N/A" to "10–15." The categories and frequencies are provided below in Table 12.3. Preferred Years of Experience was not analyzed because of small nature of the sample (Only 27 cases listed Preferred Years of Experience out of the total N = 483 job postings).

A chi-square test was performed on the re-categorized data to determine whether there were differences in likelihood to prefer or require certification in each category. Table 12.4 provides the frequency distribution and relative frequencies for each category of required and preferred certification.

The results demonstrate that there is a significant difference between the categories in whether certification was preferred χ^2 (3, *N*=483) = 40.53, *p* < .01, but not whether certification was required χ^2 (3, *N*=483) = 4.52, *n.s.* Job postings for positions in the High and Medium categories of "Years of Experience" were much

TABLE 12.3. Categories for Required Years of Experience

Category	Examples	Count (Freq) N = 483
N/A	N/A (no requirement)	85 (18%)
Low (3 years and below)	0–1, 2–3, 3	115 (24%)
Med (3+ to 5 years)	3+, 3 to 5, 4	133 (28%)
High (5+ years and above)	4–6, 5+, 7–10, 10	150 (31%)

(Note: all categories are based on the highest required value given in the job postings. Frequencies may not equal 100% due to rounding)

TABLE 12.4. Frequency Distribution by Experience for Preferred & Required Certification

Years of Experience Category	Required				Preferred			
	Yes		No		Yes		No	
	N	%	N	%	N	%	N	%
High	7	5%	143	95%	57	38%	93	62%
Med	4	3%	129	97%	41	31%	92	69%
Low	0	0%	115	100%	8	7%	107	93%
N/A	1	1%	84	99%	13	15%	72	85%
Total	11	2%	472	98%	119	25%	364	75%

TABLE 12.3. Categories for Required Years of Experience

Category	Examples	Count (Freq) N = 483
N/A	N/A (no requirement)	85 (18%)
Low (3 years and below)	0–1, 2–3, 3	115 (24%)
Med (3+ to 5 years)	3+, 3 to 5, 4	133 (28%)
High (5+ years and above)	4–6, 5+, 7–10, 10	150 (31%)

Note: all categories are based on the highest required value given in the job postings.
Frequencies may not equal 100% due to rounding

TABLE 12.4: Frequency Distribution by Experience for Preferred & Required Certification

Years of Experience Category	Required				Preferred			
	Yes		No		Yes		No	
	N	%	N	%	N	%	N	%
High	7	5%	143	95%	57	38%	93	62%
Med	4	3%	129	97%	41	31%	92	69%
Low	0	0%	115	100%	8	7%	107	93%
N/A	1	1%	84	99%	13	15%	72	85%
Total	11	2%	472	98%	119	25%	364	75%

more likely to seek Preferred Certification than those in the Low category of years of experience (0–3 years) or postings with no mention of years of experience.

The second condition, Level of Position made it relatively easy to compare categories across Entry Level, Mid-Career and Executive/VP Level. In this analysis, the N/A cases were excluded as researchers could not determine what level of position was posted. The categories and frequencies are provided in Table 12.5.

A chi-square test was performed to determine whether there were differences in likelihood to prefer or require certification at each level. Table 12.6 provides the frequency distribution and relative frequencies at each level for required and preferred certification.

The results demonstrate that there is a significant difference between Levels on whether certification was preferred χ^2 (2, N=483) = 31.0, $p < .01$), but not whether certification was required χ^2 (2, N=483) = 1.17, $n.s.$). Mid-Career and Executive/VP level positions were much more likely to seek Preferred Certification. Thus Hypothesis 4, that advanced positions are more inclined toward professional certifications is *partially supported* under both definitions: Required Years of Experience and Level of Position, but only when certification is Preferred, not required.

TABLE 12.5.   Level of Position

Level of Position	Count (Freq) N = 483
Entry Level	159 (33%)
Middle Management	264 (55%)
Executive/VP	41 (8%)
N/A (excluded)	19 (4%)

Note: Frequencies may not equal 100%, due to rounding.

TABLE 12.6.   Frequency Distribution by Level for Preferred & Required Certification

Level of Position	Required				Preferred			
	Yes		No		Yes		No	
	N	%	N	%	N	%	N	%
Entry	3	2%	156	98%	16	10%	143	90%
Mid-Career	7	3%	257	97%	80	30%	184	70%
Executive/VP	2	5%	39	95%	18	44%	23	56%
Total	12	3%	452	97%	114	25%	350	75%

Note: N/A cases are excluded in this table. Frequencies may not equal 100%, due to rounding.

Discussion

The most important findings from this research are that Professional Certification is underappreciated and undervalued in the field of human resource management. In many professions, certification is an industry imperative. Certifications are of critical importance in the computing and information systems industries and in many health care job titles (Torpey, 2012). However, recent data from the Bureau of Labor Statistics reports only 3% of U.S. workers hold a professional certification without holding a license (Torpey, 2016). Possibly there is a stigma attached to certifications, which are generally required for job titles that require less education such as skilled labor occupations, not necessarily professional occupations. Thus, the SHRM and HRCI certifications which are specifically based on educational attainment and years of experience are atypical. In fact, despite recent relaxation of standards, both of these accrediting bodies still require candidates for certification to hold at minimum a Bachelor's degree.

Yet, other than degree or experience, a professional certification is one of three important ways to assure credentials. Particularly for entry level HR positions and early career job candidates, a certification can be the *best* method of assurance. Certification is one way to be certain that professionals with differing levels of experience and who may have a degree outside of field are knowledgeable about the core functions, responsibilities, capabilities and limitations of the industry. Thus, certificates hold a particular value for the field of human resources, where many professionals may not have a degree specifically in human resource management.

The message for human resources professionals who believe in the value of certification is that more work is needed. The responsibility to champion the importance of professional certification falls squarely on the shoulders of existing professionals, only 12% of which have any kind of HR certification (Greengard, 2016). The field of HR management should not be discouraged that too few hiring managers (and even too few recruiting/staffing professionals) ask for certification. It is up to the members of the field to educate business about the value of professional certification for HR practitioners. This may occur organically as more certified professionals obtain positions of higher responsibility within their companies, or even as more high-responsibility professionals understand the value of certification. It can also occur through better education regarding what human resources practitioners can provide to the organization. More data and research are also needed to demonstrate that certification is professionally meaningful to those in the field and—perhaps more importantly—financially meaningful to the organizations that employ them.

STUDY LIMITATIONS

This study focused on six metropolitan areas within the United States so there could be differences in credential preferences within other geographic areas or even international recognition. The researchers attempted to gain understanding of preferences using the selected geographic areas, and based on differences in laws and regulations by state, there could be areas that were not afforded the opportunity for consideration based on the selected geographic locations. Additionally, this particular research did not include an international component to ascertain what the preferences are by organizations operating in a global capacity.

Further, another limitation could be that while the certification was not specifically sought in the job vacancy announcement, it still could be something desired by the organization. This information could be discussed potentially during the interview with candidates having the credential who may be seen as preferred over those who do not. However, the question still remain is there one credential that is more preferred than the others?

Additionally, there can be a vast difference in titling of jobs such as can be noted through O*NET. Titles of various jobs within an organization would match the context of the organizational infrastructure but may not align with what other organizations are doing within the marketplace. Caution needs to be exercised to ensuring one is comparing apples to apples.

The nature of the study also limited how the researchers could interpret the data. One of the benefits of using LinkedIn is that the data were readily available without having to conduct lengthy surveys of HR recruiters at the companies. However, precision was sacrificed in only reviewing categorical data. Since the data were collected in a binary format (e.g., certification preferred or not, degree required or not, etc.) no information was available about the weight of each of these factors. Ideally, the numerous hiring criteria could be analyzed via multiple regression if the recruiters were contacted to rate which factor(s) the employer valued most. As stated earlier, it may be that some of the determining factors would be discussed during the interview stage of the hiring process, and would not necessarily be accurately represented in a job description.

Range restriction was also an issue. The researchers were surprised that few to none of the markets analyzed required certain hiring criteria that were central to the research, such as degree, years of experience and particularly certification. While a meaningful portion of the sample did *prefer* some sort of human resources certification, it was far from the majority throughout.

FUTURE RESEARCH

As referenced in our discussion on the limitations of our study, it would be beneficial to continue this research to ascertain how preferences are changing. While the certifying bodies that are HRCI and SHRM will continue to operate and provide certification opportunities, the importance for Human Resource (HR) professionals to maintain their certifications is essential to lifelong learning for the professional. Alonso (2018) posits that HR professionals often prioritize the professional management and development of the talent within an organization and often defer their own professional development. This action then may present as a gap of HR professional credentials within corporation C-Suites and beyond. What does this have to do with certification, per say? Herein, lies the issue.

With our previous findings do not indicate a strong preference for requiring certifications for HR professional position job postings from the junior to senior level, we believe this leaves an opportunity for growth and expansion for the profession. Alonso (2018) details the value of certification for HR professionals while painting a picture of the future of the HR profession. Alonso (2018) also posits that HR professions are expected to execute the dimensions of the HR core competencies as described by SHRM; yet, there is a skill gap in HR professionals regarding the competence and presence of the demonstrated HR body of knowledge. It seems that further development of HR professionals may actually be a lower priority within an organization in favor of prioritizing other identified needs first. Alonso (2018) also states that HR learning is not as detailed and planned as leaders in other organizational functional areas that benefit from coaching, mentoring and leadership development programs. HR learning "tends to be more static and one dimensional" (Alonso, 2018, p. 5), and these professionals are often not included in high potential executive development and training programs. The paradox lies in that often HR experts facilitate and development these very programs; thus, HR professionals can be compared to life savers who are giving oxygen to others without wearing an oxygen mask themselves. This rationale can help researchers and academicians evolve curriculum and build competencies within HR students and professionals in an attempt to better prepare them for operations in such workplace situations

Furthermore, such insight would benefit academicians in ensuring that they are building the appropriate competencies of students as well as organizations to have a common understanding of the value of these certifications and continue to position HR as a strategic business partner to add value to the organization. Focus could be on revisiting the same metropolitan areas to determine if any changes exist since the research was last conducted. Additionally, further insight can be gained from including additional metropolitan areas in the next research endeavor. Further, using the same methodology, and including international components may provide perspective on these US-based certifications, as well as if there are any others that may be preferred by international companies.

REFERENCES

About HRCI. (2018). Retrieved from https://www.hrci.org/about-hrci/overview/about-hrci

About SHRM Certification. (2018). Retrieved from: https://www.shrm.org/certification/about/AboutSHRMCertification/Pages/keybenefits.aspx

Alonso, A. (2018). *The value of certification/The future of HR: A journey to meaningful life long learning for HR professionals.* Society for Human Resource Management Atlanta Chapter 2018 Conference Materials.

Berman-Gervone, M. (2014). *SHRM debuts new HR credentials, drawing ire of HR. Certification Institute.* Retrieved from https://www.bna.com/shrm-debuts-new-n17179891674/

Buros Center for Testing. (2018). *Audits and accreditation.* Retrieved from http://buros.org/audits-and-accreditation

Description of Exams. (2018). Retrieved from: https://www.shrm.org/certification/about/ExamDevelopment/Pages/default.aspx

Greengard, S. (2016, June 13). HR credentials: Evaluating their value. *Workforce.* Retrieved from http://www.workforce.com/2016/06/13/hr-credentials-evaluating-their-value/.

History. (2018). *History: A brief history.* HRCI.org. Retrieved from https://www.hrci.org/about-hrci/overview/history

Letizia, M. (2018, March 8). The "California difference" in HR practice. *Society for Human Resource Management.* Retrieved from https://www.shrm.org/resourcesandtools/hr-topics/behavioral-competencies/pages/the-california-difference-in-hr-practice.aspx.

NCCA Accreditation. (2018). Retrieved from http://www.credentialingexcellence.org/ncca

Prokopeake, M. (2015). SHRM-HRCI split one year later: Less testy more testing. *Workforce.* Retrieved from http://www.workforce.com/2015/07/03/shrm-hrci-split-one-year-later-less-testy-more-testing/

Society for Human Resource Management HR Competency Model. (2018). Retrieved from SHRM.org

Torpey, E. (2016, September). Will I need a license or certification for my job? *Bureau of Labor Statistics (BLS.gov).* Retrieved from https://www.bls.gov/careeroutlook/2016/article/will-i-need-a-license-or-certification.htm.

Torpey, E. (2012, Winter). Certificates: A fast track to careers. *Occupation Outlook Quarterly,* a publication of the *Bureau of Labor Statistics (BLS.gov).* Retrieved from https://www.bls.gov/careeroutlook/2012/winter/art01.pdf.

ABOUT THE AUTHORS

Henry Adu recently graduated with an M.B.A. at Saint Leo University. He is currently working as a Risk Assurance specialist at PWC in downtown Tampa, Florida.

Juliet Aiken is the Program Director of the UMD IO MPS. She received her Ph.D. in Industrial Organizational Psychology and a Certificate in Statistics in Measurement at the University of Maryland, College Park. Prior to her work at UMD, Dr. Aiken served as an internal statistical and methodological consultant at Georgetown Law Center, where she conducted research on the legal profession and taught professional skills and how to critique research to JD, LLM, and SJD students. Juliet has also consulted for organizations and researchers on statistical analysis, networks, selection, leadership, mentoring, and adverse impact, among other topics. In addition to providing statistical training and conducting analyses, Juliet collaborates with her clients to design, launch, and evaluate workplace

Human Resources Management Issues, Challenges and Trends:
"Now and Around the Corner", pages 245–252.
Copyright © 2019 by Information Age Publishing

initiatives such as mentoring groups. Her work focuses on leveraging statistics to promote diversity in organizations, improve talent development, and enable organizational change.

Zhanna Bagdasarov is an Assistant Professor of Management at California State University, Fresno. She received her Ph.D. in Industrial/Organizational Psychology from the University of Oklahoma. Her research interests focus on ethical decision making in organizational contexts, trust repair between leaders and subordinates, and the influence of emotions in the workplace. She has published her work in such outlets as *Journal of Business Ethics, Journal of Management History, Ethics & Behavior, Science and Engineering Ethics,* and the *Journal of Empirical Research on Human Research Ethics.*

Sheri K. Bias, SPHR, SHRM-SCP, has over 30 years of experience in a variety of Human Resources capacities. She holds a PhD in Human and Organization Systems from The Fielding Graduate University as well as an MBA from William and Mary and an MA in Human Resource Development from George Washington University. She is currently an Assistant Professor at Saint Leo University where she leads several doctoral dissertation committees, as well as teaching undergraduate and graduate classes on human resources topics. She has also served as department chair and lead human resources faculty at other academic institutions. Dr. Bias previously led HR initiatives for organizations such as Anheuser Busch, Philip Morris, Pricewaterhouse Coopers, American Airlines, Pennzoil, and NASA Langley Research Center. Her research interests include generations in the workplace and risk management strategies. Dr. Bias has also been heavily involved in the Odyssey of the Mind Program having coached for multiple years and most recently serving in a judging capacity at World Finals.

James S. Bowman is professor of public administration at the Askew School of Public Administration and Policy, Florida State University. Noted for this work in ethics and human resource management, Dr. Bowman is author of over 125 journal articles and book chapters, as well as editor of six anthologies. Bowman is co-author of the prize-winning *Human Resource Management in Public Service: Paradoxes, Processes and Problems* (6th ed., Sage, forthcoming). He is also co-author of *Public Service Ethics: Individual and Institutional Responsibilities* (2nd Ed., Taylor & Francis, 2018). He served as the inaugural editor-in-chief of *Public Integrity* (1995–2014), an American Society for Public Administration journal co-sponsored by three other professional associations. A past National Association of Schools of Public Affairs and Administration Fellow, as well as a Kellogg Foundation Fellow, he has experience in the military, civil service, and business. He was elected to the National Academy of Public Administration in 2017.

M. Ronald Buckley earned his Ph. D. in Industrial/Organizational Psychology at Auburn University. He is currently the JC Penney Company Chair of Business Leadership in the Michael F. Price College of Business at the University of Oklahoma. He has published many articles on the topics of individual evaluation and fairness and continues to try and understand human resource management issues.

Sierra Chen is a rising junior in the Luter School of Business at Christopher Newport University. She is double majoring in management and marketing and has completed an internship in Training and Development. She is an intramural athlete, and a researcher in the areas of employee engagement and millennial employee perceptions of visibility, safety, and value.

James P. Eicher is the creator of Cognitive Management which applies research from the cognitive sciences to organization and leadership behavior. Mr. Eicher has held leadership positions at KPMG, Booz Allen Hamilton, Symantec and IBM, and has been interviewed by the *Wall Street Journal* and *Selling* magazine. Mr. Eicher is the author of the management communication text *Making the Message Clear* and many articles, assessments and book chapters. He is co-author, with the late John Jones and William Bearley, of the management assessments the *Matrix Manager Inventory: Leading in a Collaborative Environment*; the *Neurolinguistic Communication Profile; Rapport: Matching and Mirroring Communication* and *Post-Heroic Leadership: Managing the Virtual Organization.* Jim has also authored or co-authored many articles, assessments and book chapters including: *Cognitive Arbitrage: The Outsourcing of Intelligence;* the *Leader-Manager Profile; The Change Bully: When Demagoguery Masquerades as Organization Transformation; Making Strategy Happen; Post-Heroic Leadership; The Execution Gap: 7 Questions You Must Ask;* the *Strategic Action Profile;* and *Cognitive Management: Managing your Organization's Mind.*

Sean Gibbons graduated with honors with a B.A in Multimedia Management at Saint Leo University. Currently in Saint Leo University's M.B.A. program, Sean works as a Graduate Research Assistant to collect, analyze, and create reports for faculty members throughout the University.

Harold Goldstein is a professor of industrial-organizational psychology at Baruch College, The City University of New York. His primary areas of expertise are in personnel staffing and equal employment opportunity issues, leadership development and organizational culture. Dr. Goldstein is best known for his work on the design of tests of intelligence that produce reduced racial and gender-based subgroup differences. Harold regularly publishes in scholarly journals and books and is the lead editor of the recently published Wiley Blackwell Handbook of Recruitment, Selection, and Employee Retention. In addition, his work on designing intelligence tests earned him and his team the M. Scott Myers Award for Applied

Research from the Society of Industrial and Organizational Psychology and the International Personnel Assessment Council's Innovations Award.

Breanna Gonsalves is a December 2018 graduate as a management major from the Luter School of Business at Christopher Newport University. She is an intramural athlete, President's Leadership Program scholar and leadership minor. In addition to her student responsibilities she is also a part time University employee, working as a resident advisor and facilitating admissions office tours. Brenna's research inquiries center on gender equality and perceptions of leadership.

Nicole Hawkins is a two-time graduate of Ball State University where she completed Bachelor and dual Master's degrees in Communications and Organizational Development at the School of Communication, Information and Media. With a concentration in Human Resource Development and dissertation work in Leader Development, Dr. Hawkins earned a Doctor of Philosophy degree at the School of Business and Leadership at Regent University in 2015. Dr. Hawkins is also a 2017 Alumnus of the Harvard University Kennedy School where she completed the Executive Education Program in Adaptive Leadership Development. Dr. Hawkins brings her 20 plus years of professional expertise developing people and communities to serve as a full-time faculty member for Saint Leo University as an Assistant Professor of Human Resource Management in the Donald R. Tapia College of Business. In addition to service to the University, Dr. Hawkins' philanthropic and volunteer efforts include working with United Way of Greater Atlanta, Junior League of Atlanta and is a member of Alpha Kappa Alpha Sorority, Incorporated.

Shannon O. Jackson serves as a Professor of Management in the Tapia School of Business at Saint Leo University. Dr. Jackson teaches at the undergraduate, MBA and DBA levels. Prior to joining the faculty in 1998, Dr. Jackson taught at Hampton University and Ithaca College for a combined ten years. Prior to beginning her teaching career, Dr. Jackson worked in Public Relations for Ramada Inns Corporate offices in Phoenix, Argo Communications in New York City and Newport News Shipbuilding in Virginia. Dr. Jackson has focused her research on Leadership, Technology in the Classroom and Decision Making. She has presented at more than 30 state, national and international conferences and has published in distinguished journals like the Servant Leadership Journal (Gonzaga University) as well as having contributed chapters in several books. She is active in Virginia Region Center activities and making sure the faculty and students of the Centers in all locations are represented in University decisions. Dr Jackson is also active in her local community as a founding member of the Poquoson Educational Foundation.

Elliott Larson is a doctoral candidate in Industrial-Organizational Psychology at the Graduate Center and Baruch College, the City University of New York.

His research interests include personnel selection, training and development, and emotions in the workplace. Elliott has worked on several programs of research, including predicting performance in high-stakes testing and investigating the predictors of constructive and destructive reactions to envy in the workplace. His work has been published in Current Directions in Psychological Science, the Encyclopedia of Industrial and Organizational Psychology, and the Wiley Blackwell Handbook of the Psychology of Recruitment, Selection, and Retention. In addition, Elliott was one of the recipients of the International Personnel Assessment Council's Innovations Award for his work on cognitive abilities.

Pamela Chandler Lee is an Associate Professor, and the Associate Chair of the Department of Leadership and Management for Saint Leo University. A former officer in the U.S. Navy, she has also served as the Associate Dean of Students for two academic institutions. Dr. Lee has published and presented in the areas of women in leadership, the integration of faith in business, mentorship, and online learning and advising. She is a member of several leadership and management organizations, such as the International Leadership Association and the Southern Management Association. She is also a Board Member for the Selective Service System and the Treasurer and Board Member for Love and Hope Ministries, Inc. Dr. Lee primarily teaches MBA (Master of Business Administration) and DBA (Doctorate of Business Administration) courses at Saint Leo and chairs a number of doctoral dissertation committees. She is also an ordained minister and serves as Associate Minister of the Bethlehem Baptist Church in Chase City, Virginia, where her husband is pastor.

Alexandria MacDougall is an Assistant Professor of Management at Central Michigan University. She earned her Ph.D. in Industrial/Organizational Psychology from the University of Oklahoma. Her research focuses on a range of topics in human resources and organizational behavior including business ethics, training and development, leadership, and organizational citizenship behavior. She has published in various outlets including the *Journal of Business Ethics, Journal of Leadership and Organizational Studies, Research in Personnel and Human Resource Management, Journal of Organizational and Occupational Psychology,* and *Science and Engineering Ethics.*

Ronda Mariani is an Associate Professor and holds a Doctorate of Business Administration; Marketing, Master Science Education, Bachelor of Science Advertising, Associates Degree Applied Sciences, Advertising Art and Design, Graduate Certificate in Market Research and Social Media Analytics, Nanodegree Digital Marketing. She has several publications and research interests in digital advertising and marketing, social media, unconscious bias and communicating diversity in the workplace.

William (Billy) J. Mea, Ph.D. has been a program examiner in the U.S. Office of Management & Budget's (OMB) National Security Division at the White House for over a decade. He is on an extended assignment as the OMB Chair at National Defense University, where he teaches economics, business analytics, innovation, and leadership. Mea is also an adjunct professor at Georgetown University. His research interests cover diverse management topics. Dr. Mea received his doctoral degree in clinical and industrial/organizational psychology from Auburn University. Following graduate school, he was a clinical psychologist in the U.S. Navy. He retired after two decades of active and reserve service, including two deployments to Iraq. He was a manager at KPMG Peat Marwick, LLP specializing in Enterprise Resource Programs and a senior policy official in the President George W. Bush Administration.

Charles Scherbaum is a Professor of Psychology at Baruch College, the City University of New York. His research focuses on personnel selection, ability testing, and analytics. Publications of his research have appeared in journals such as Personnel Psychology, Organizational Research Methods, Journal of Business and Psychology, and Human Resource Management Review. Dr. Scherbaum was one of the winners of the 2011 M. Scott Myers Award from the Society for Industrial and Organizational Psychology as well as the 2011 and 2017 Innovations Award from the International Personnel Assessment Council for his research on cognitive ability tests. Charles received a PhD in industrial and organizational psychology from Ohio University.

Jonathan Shoemaker is an Industrial/Organizational Psychologist and a certified HR industry professional who started teaching full time in 2010. Dr. Shoemaker is an Associate Professor at Saint Leo University's Tampa Center and resides in Tampa, Florida.

Ronald R. Sims is the Floyd Dewey Gottwald Senior Professor in the Raymond A. Mason School of Business at the College of William and Mary where he teaches leadership and change management, human resources management (HRM), organizational behavior and business ethics. He received his Ph.D. in Organizational Behavior from Case Western Reserve University. His research focuses on a variety of topics to include leadership and change management, HRM, business ethics, employee training, and management and leadership development (i.e. Human Resource Development), learning styles, and experiential learning. Dr. Sims is the author or co-author of thirty-seven books, seventy-five chapters and more than ninety articles that have appeared in a wide variety of scholarly and practitioner journals. His most recent books published by Information Age Publishing, Inc. in 2017 are *"A Contemporary Look at Business"* and *"When a New Leader Takes Over: Toward Ethical Turnarounds."* Professor Sims has provided consultation and executive education in the areas of change management, business ethics/reputation management, human resource management (HRM) and employee and leadership development to organizations in the private, public, and not-for-profit sectors over the past thirty years. Professor Sims retired as a Lieutenant Colonel from the U.S. Army Reserves in 1997 after twenty-four years of active and reserve service.

Angela N. Spranger is a consultant and Gallup-trained Strengths coach, who also uses the MBTI and Emotional Intelligence tools to help clients identify and address issues that may hinder personal and professional development or team effectiveness. Dr. Spranger's instructional experience includes eight years of teaching adult non-traditional learners at Hampton University and Regent University in the business curricula, specializing in Marketing, Labor Management Relations, and Human Resources courses. As of 2012, she added instructional experience with traditional young adult learners at Christopher Newport University, facilitating courses in Leadership Theory and Research, Organizational Behavior, Human Resource Management, and Leadership in Business. Additionally, Dr. Spranger has provided professional development and motivational presentations to local churches, women's groups, military installations, and professional associations, and always seeks to offer a unique and inspirational way of approaching the theme topic. Dr. Spranger is a scholar-practitioner who worked for over 20 years in non-profit, state, and corporate management and HR positions while undertaking graduate studies.

Jonathan P. West is professor and chair of political science and director of the MPA program at the University of Miami. His research interests include human resource management, ethics, productivity, and local government. Professor West has published nine books and over 150 articles and book chapters. His most recent books are *Human Resource Management in Public Service* (5th ed., Sage, 2016) with Berman, Bowman and Van Wart; *Public Service Ethics: Individual and Institutional Responsibilities* (2nd ed., Routledge, 2018) with Bowman; and *American Politics and the Environment* (SUNY Press, 2016, 2nd edition) with Daynes and Sussman. Other books are co-edited with Bowman, *American Public Service: Radical Reform and the Merit System* (Taylor & Francis, 2007) and co-authored with Bowman and Beck, *Achieving Competencies in Public Service: The Professional Edge* (2nd ed., Routledge, 2014). He also co-edited *The Ethics Edge* (2nd ed., ICMA, 2006) with Berman. He was managing editor of *Public Integrity* for 16 years. He taught previously at the University of Houston and University of Arizona and served as a management analyst in the U.S. Surgeon General's Office, Department of the Army, Washington, D.C.

William J. Woska, JD, has been a faculty member at several colleges and universities including the University of California, Berkeley, Saint Mary's College, Moraga, Golden Gate University, San Francisco, and San Diego State University. He is presently on the faculty at Cabrillo College in Aptos, California. His research interests include employment and labor law, human resources management, local government, and ethics. He has more than 30 years of experience representing employers in employment and labor law matters. He is the author of 45 publications appearing in the Employment Law Forum, journal articles, book chapters, and book reviews. His publications address employment and labor law, workplace investigations, sexual harassment, human resources management, law enforcement, and local government issues. He is a member of the Labor and Employment Law Section of The State Bar of California.

Kenneth Yusko is Deputy Director of the Industrial/Organizational Psychology MPS program at the University of MD. He is an expert in the design of personnel selection, development, and performance management systems and has worked with Fortune 500 companies, small businesses, and government agencies, as well as professional sports teams and leagues. Some of Ken's current clients include the National Football League, the Sacramento Kings, the University of Nebraska, Merck, Morgan Stanley, and the Motion Picture Association of America. His research focuses primarily on improving the accuracy, and diversity outcomes, of employment testing systems. A current example of his work is the development and validation of league-wide psychological player assessments used by teams to improve their success rate in the NFL draft. Dr. Yusko regularly publishes in scholarly journals and books and he and his team were recently awarded the M. Scott Myers Award for Applied Research from the Society of Industrial Organizational Psychology and the International Personnel Assessment Council's Innovations Award for their work in developing and implementing the Siena Reasoning Test (SRT), a cognitive ability test that enhances both the diversity and quality of new hires.

CPSIA information can be obtained
at www.ICGtesting.com
Printed in the USA
BVHW042010290319
544120BV00005B/104/P